THE PRACTICE OF LANGUAGE RIGHTS IN CANADA

On what grounds should language rights be accorded in Canada, and to whom? This is the central question that is addressed in C. Michael Mac-Millan's book *The Practice of Language Rights in Canada.* The issue of language rights in Canada is one that is highly debated and discussed, partly because the basic underlying principles have been a neglected dimension in the debate.

MacMillan examines the normative basis of language rights in Canadian public policy and public opinion. He argues that language rights policy should be founded upon the theoretical literature of human rights. Drawing on the philosophy behind human rights, the arguments for recognizing a right to language are considered, as well as the matter of whether such rights possess the essential features of established rights. Another model that is examined is the idea that rights are a reflection of the established values, attitudes, and practices of society. This analysis reveals that there is a significant gap between what a political theory of language rights would endorse and what garners support in public opinion. MacMillan also scrutinizes the federal and provincial contexts in the development of a language rights framework.

From these explorations, a case is developed for a recognition of language rights that is consistent with the logic of human rights and that corresponds roughly with developing Canadian practice. *The Practice of Language Rights in Canada* is a unique contribution to the current literature not only because it conceives of language rights as a human right but also because it frames the whole debate about language rights in Canada as a question of values and entitlements.

C. MICHAEL MACMILLAN is Associate Professor of Political Studies at Mount Saint Vincent University.

C. MICHAEL MACMILLAN

The Practice of Language Rights in Canada

UNIVERSITY OF TORONTO PRESS
Toronto Buffalo London

© University of Toronto Press Incorporated 1998
Toronto Buffalo London
Printed in Canada

ISBN 0-8020-4279-1 (cloth)
ISBN 0-8020-8115-0 (paper)

Printed on acid-free paper

Canadian Cataloguing in Publication Data

MacMillan, C. Michael
The practice of language rights in Canada

Includes bibliographical references and index.
ISBN 0-8020-4279-1 (bound)   ISBN 0-8020-8115-0 (pbk.)

1. Language policy – Canada. I. Title.

P119.32.M32 1998   306.44'971   C98-930661-5

University of Toronto Press acknowledges the financial assistance to its
publishing program of the Canada Council for the Arts and the
Ontario Arts Council.

This book has been published with the help of a grant from the Humanities
and Social Sciences Federation of Canada, using funds provided by the
Social Sciences and Humanities Research Council of Canada.

In memory of my parents,
Roy and Marion

Contents

Acknowledgments

This book is the product of endeavours extending over a number of years. As is usually the case, its appearance has been materially assisted by several individuals and institutions along the way. The Institute of Commonwealth Studies of the University of London provided a convivial and stimulating environment in which I initially began exploring some of these themes while on sabbatical in the winter term of 1986. My university has extended financial support in the form of internal research grants to enable me to carry out different portions of the project for which I am very grateful. Robert Burge, of the Centre for the Study of Democracy at Queen's University, was most helpful in retabulating Decima data to accommodate my research needs. Marie-Lucie Tarpent, my colleague in our Modern Languages department, kindly read and offered supportive comments on my analysis of Aboriginal languages. Our library staff have been strikingly efficient and creative in responding to my various requests. Our department secretary, Sonia Verabioff, has capably solved various software puzzles for me and helped produce the bibliography. Chapters 1, 2, and 4 draw upon portions of material previously published in the *Canadian Journal of Political Science*, the *International Journal of Canadian Studies*, and *Queen's Quarterly*, and I appreciate their willingness to grant permission for their use in this manuscript. This book has been published with the help of a grant from the Humanities and Social Sciences Federation of Canada, using funds provided by the Social Sciences and Humanities Research Council of Canada. I am particularly grateful for the thoughtful analyses of the anonymous reviewers whose comments have materially contributed to its improvement. Virgil Duff, the Executive Editor, and Margaret Williams, the Assistant Editor, of the University of Toronto Press editorial staff, have shepherded my manuscript expeditiously through the process. I also wish to thank my copy editor, Kate Baltais, for her considerable efforts to render my often awkward prose more direct and clear.

As always, one's family become participants, willing or otherwise, in the writing process. I particularly want to thank my son, Andrew, for his stoic acceptance of my tiresome refrain that I could not engage in various recreational activities because I had to work on the book. My wife, Leslie, who shares in the special pleasures and tribulations of academic life, has offered both moral support and timely advice which have been extremely important in bringing this project to completion.

THE PRACTICE OF LANGUAGE RIGHTS IN CANADA

Introduction

In several ways, linguistic duality is both a blessing and a curse for Canada ... Managing this duality is Canada's greatest political challenge, however, and whether or not Canadians like it, the language issue will fuel the Canadian constitutional debate forever.[1]

With the passage of the federal Official Languages Act in 1969, Canada began to both formalize and broaden the understanding of linguistic duality in Canada. This duality has since dominated public policy, despite periodic challenges from one quarter or another to the practices that have evolved from it. Subsequent to the passage of federal act, several provinces have enacted legislation in the language area, either to curtail perceived privileges or to impose language requirements within their jurisdictions. This has resulted in a hodgepodge of competing principles regarding language policy at the federal and provincial levels. Recently, a number of books have appeared questioning both the underlying goals and the specific administrative applications of federal official language policy. Some have suggested that the existing policies are wrong-headed and counter-productive, while others have argued that the policies flagrantly violate any notion of justice – especially with regard to equality and fairness.

The renewed debate about the principles of language policy in Canada is part of the reason for this book. The theme of 'linguistic justice' is my central organizing principle. What has been conspicuously lacking in Canadian debates to date is any systematic attempt to articulate a set of political values to sustain an understanding of linguistic justice in Canada. The federal Commissioner of Official Languages, in his 1994 annual report, opined: 'The federal government should spend much more time explaining what it believes in and why'[2] – a further reminder of the ongoing absence of a statement of principles in the public debate on language policy. This lament has been reiterated in various studies of the language issue in Canada. The result of this void is that we have not come to terms with the application of principles of public policy to the variety of cases that present themselves, namely, the federal case of two large language groups in distinct regional concentrations; the Quebec case of a local majority language perceived to be perpetually threatened by the language of its minority; and, sporadically, cases demanding support for various other language groups. Each case requires different problems to be resolved, with different factors to be weighed.

Discernible and reasonable values have emerged and are being developed within Canadian debates and may become the basis of a societal consensus. Critical is the concept of 'language rights.' In the past decade, this notion has developed considerably from a 'mere' legal right to a substantive concept increasingly akin to conventional human rights. Yet, although language rights are invoked by virtually all participants in these public debates, their definition seems to vary with the speaker. Typical is a recent exchange between a Québécois nationalist and an anglophone Quebecker. The former asserted a virtually absolute right of francophones within Quebec to be served in French anywhere in the province, including in anglophone neighbourhoods. The anglophone Quebecker dismissed this language rights claim, and asserted the 'traditional language rights' of anglophones in Quebec. Neither party fully specified or justified the content of these rights, leaving each open to facile dismissal by the other. Both parties agreed that language rights are at issue, but disagreed as to the content, the justification, and the possessors of these rights.[3] Thus language rights continue to be an essentially contested concept.

Clearly, any future consensus must build upon an understanding of the foundations and scope of language rights. This requires moving beyond a discussion of the existing legal recognition of such rights, and the judicial interpretation thereof, to a discussion of the basic values leading us to conclude that there really are 'language rights.' Concomitantly, it is also necessary to consider the implications of alternative regimes of language rights for the broader policy goals – especially national unity – that were central to the original federal legislative commitment to language rights. A growing chorus of voices is recommending revision of Canadian language policy towards a 'territorial' approach. Such a change would make possession of language rights contingent upon geographic location – a development that could negate the very idea of language rights or possibly simply refine language rights in light of competing values of economy and equality of treatment. These issues must be addressed directly, lest any notion of language rights be lost entirely.

F.L. Morton, a Canadian political scientist and expert on judicial processes, expressed his objection to 'misty-eyed moralism about language rights.' He insisted that 'language rights in Canada are not about individual rights. They are about self-interest, the collective self-interest of the two founding peoples.'[4] This view is profoundly mistaken on a number of counts. First, it is a mistake to assume that rights are separate from self-interest. The case for any human right rests precisely on the ground that the right contributes to our essential well-being. On the other hand, the fact that something is in our interest does not create a right to it. However, interests are intrinsically linked to rights. The question then becomes, does our use of language affect our fundamental interests as human beings. Second, while it is true that recognition of language rights leads to a distribution of costs and benefits among language groups, the question of what is a fair policy is normative. To answer this normative question requires examination of the link between prevailing notions of language entitlements and the prevailing political values in our society. It also requires a comparison of the status and claims of various language groups in a multilingual society. Finally, precisely because the answer imposes recognizable costs and benefits on everyone is good reason to insist upon a hard-nosed, rather than misty-eyed, approach to developing a broadly acceptable notion of language rights.

The language claims of major language groups in Canadian society will be assessed in this analysis. The question is becoming more rather than less complicated. For example, as I write, some national magazines have just begun publication of Chinese-language editions for Vancouver and Toronto, a telling indication of the fast-growing Chinese language group in Canada.

In discussing language groups in Canada, it is necessary to explain the terminology. An unfortunate feature of language debates is that the terms in use are all to varying degrees misleading. Census reports in Canada have used three different measures of language group affiliation: ethnic origin, mother tongue (the first language learned and still understood), and home language (the language principally used in the home). Both ethnic origin and mother tongue may include people in a group who, in fact, do not speak the language attributed to them in their everyday life. On the other hand, someone may use a language as their home language without it being their mother tongue, as happens often in marriages across the two major language groups in Canada and routinely in immigrant groups over the course of several generations. The attempt to achieve more rigorous terminology can become quite complex.[5] Here 'language groups' are defined by their members' home language. Anglophones are people who use English as their home language. Similarly, francophones are people who use French as their home language. Aboriginal groups use Inuktitut or Native American languages. Finally, allophones are people whose home language is one other than English, French, or an Aboriginal language.

Taking home language to define language group membership is conservative, as generally it understates the number of those people who might wish to claim membership in a minority language group. This is particularly so with francophones outside Quebec, since this group experiences high rates of linguistic assimilation. However, home language has the important advantage of being a significant indicator of commitment to a language, reflected as it is in the effort to make the language part of the individual's everyday life. In this respect, home language dovetails with the conditions I suggest for the recognition of group claims to language rights.

In the first two chapters of this book, the case for language rights is explored in theoretical terms by applying two models of rights. First, the degree to which language rights meets the criteria for conventional human rights is assessed. Although there are important qualifications and conditions attached to the concept, language rights are broadly consistent with the prevailing understanding of human rights. Then the degree to which language rights are firmly established in Canadian society is determined. The analysis reveals, perhaps surprisingly, a wide acceptance of language rights in a limited set of services nationally. Moreover, Canadians endorse a broader array of language rights than are presently reflected in constitutional documents, an indication that there is some potential for a modest expansion of constitutionally entrenched language rights. This pattern is most pronounced in Quebec, where Québécois are notably more generous towards minority language rights than Quebec legislation itself would suggest.

The ensuing chapters apply the insights gained from this theoretical analysis to the language policies in Quebec, New Brunswick, and the federal government. Each of these offers a distinct approach to the recognition of language rights. The federal initiative has stressed the recognition of an individual's right to use French or English and a commitment to equal treatment of the two official languages. Federal experiences illustrate some of the inescapable conflicts that arise in the practice of language rights. On the other hand, Quebec policy embraces the opposite tack, by emphasizing language as a right of a community, and officially recognizing only one language in the community, while accommodating the other to some degree. This resolution by fiat has logical difficulties that have led to many disputes wherein individual rights are pitted against this imputed communal right. Somewhat paradoxically, Quebec language policy has grown significantly more tolerant and supportive of minority language rights than would seem to be appreciated by anglophone opinion, while remaining less generous than Québécois opinion would seem willing to endorse.

Although generally modelled after the federal approach, New Brunswick language policy is distinctive in that it has, if belatedly and rather tentatively, emphasized the equality of the two language communities. Equality of French and English figures more prominently in New Brunswick language policy discussions than elsewhere. This has not, however, significantly advanced our understanding of equality as it applies to language groups. If anything, New Brunswick's approach has shown just how limited any grounds for consensus here are.

Nevertheless, equality is an important dimension in considering the potential claims of Aboriginal and allophone groups to comparable treatment. This logic requires acknowledging that all language groups deserve consideration of their language rights claims. Furthermore, linguistic justice requires at a minimum that groups in comparable circumstances receive equal treatment. The merits of claims to recognition of Aboriginal and allophone languages are considered, and a set of criteria to apply in assessing these claims is identified. At present, however, those claims remain generally unpersuasive, though, for historical reasons. Aboriginal languages are entitled to some measure of support.

There is a definite risk that my discussion falls somewhere between political theory and public policy analysis. For the theoretically minded it may prove insufficiently theoretical, while being too theoretical and abstract for policy pragmatists. The material used for this project arise from language legislation, policy documents, and public debates. My focus is on the normative claims advanced therein, generally to the neglect of the conventional components of policy analysis (for example, the context out of which any particular legislation arises, the tactical calculations of the governments in framing their legislation, and the competing demands of interest groups, bureaucrats, and so forth). My reasons for this selective focus are twofold. Such analyses of language policy as do exist have tended to focus on the politics of the policy process and the political considerations shaping its content whereas the normative dimension has been relatively neglected, whether by participants in the policy process or by the political science literature.

Some may suggest that the normative dimension is merely intellectual 'window-dressing' for the otherwise naked exercise of political power and interest. To this I would reply that the normative dimension remains salient notwithstanding the motives inspiring the creation of language policy. First, language policy is inherently normative. To designate language entitlements as a right for some groups necessarily demands the articulation of an elaborate justificatory framework. Once articulated, the rationale tends to acquire a life of its own, serving both as a resource for new demands to broaden or enrich language rights and as a yardstick for evaluating new claims. A recent analysis of federal programs in support of linguistic minorities, among other groups, observed that they 'contributed to the peculiar emphasis on "identity" and "collective rights" in Canadian political discourse.'[6] These groups have merely elaborated a discourse already present in the constitutional dialogue. It is therefore important that the logic of this discourse be analysed and evaluated.

Although my focus is on the normative dimension of these policy debates, my discussion nonetheless tends to be grounded in the issues and arguments that arise within each setting. The modest goal of this endeavour is to suggest the broad outlines for possible consensus on a conception of language rights. I do recognize that this will hardly conclude the ongoing debate. Language issues have bedeviled Canadian politics throughout our history. They may not constitute Canada's greatest challenge at present, however, as the introductory quotation suggests, language issues will form a perpetual item on the Canadian political agenda. We can at best hope to move the debate beyond dispute over basic values towards one of 'fine tuning' the boundaries of their application.

Notes

1 Marcel Coté, 'Language and Public Policy,' in John Richards, François Vaillancourt, and William G. Watson, eds., *Survival: Official Language Rights in Canada* (Toronto: C.D. Howe Institute, 1992), 7–8.
2 Commissioner of Official Languages (Victor C. Goldbloom), *Annual Report 1994* (Hull: Minister of Supply and Services Canada, 1995), 3.

3 See the exchanges between François Vaillancourt and William Watson in John Richards et al., *Survival*, 63–133.

4 F.L. Morton, 'The Language Conflict Is about Power, not Poetry.' *Alberta Report* (15 May 1989), 16.

5 See R. Lachapelle and J. Henripin, *The Demolinguistic Situation in Canada: Past Trends and Future Prospects*, Dierdre A. Mark trans., (Montreal: Institute for Research on Public Policy, 1982), 3–4 for their distinctions in the use of terms.

6 Leslie A. Pal, *Interests of State: The Politics of Language, Multiculturalism, and Feminism in Canada* (Montreal: McGill-Queen's University Press, 1993), 15.

1

Justifying Language Rights

The politics of language policy, in Canada or elsewhere, is inseparable from the concept of language rights. Language rights, in turn, bear some necessary relation to various aspects of human rights and consequently to the general question of what regimes of promotion or protection may be lawfully imposed in the public interest.[1]

The constitutional recognition of 'language rights' in Canada has not been accompanied by the articulation of a philosophical rationale establishing their status as rights. This is in part because language rights have been perceived as obviously outside the realm of human rights. Two decades ago, K.D. McRae observed, 'It has seldom been argued that language rights are a universal human right, or a natural right of mankind' and, further, 'The question of linguistic rights should be kept conceptually distinct from "classical" human rights.'[2] McRae's reasons stemmed from a recognition of the special characteristics of language rights and the complexities of their implementation. The reality of these special features, which will be examined in due course, must be recognized, but they are nevertheless not decisive in removing language rights from comparison with the classical human rights. Moreover, as the introductory quote suggests, it is imperative that a comprehensive understanding of the moral dimensions of language rights be developed in order that we may define the contours of the legitimate expectations that accompany their recognition.

An important first step in the process of examining language rights, therefore, is to explore its foundations in the language of rights. It is important to define the key terms in this analysis. What are we referring to when we speak about 'language rights'? The question then arises, if there are such rights, what kind of rights are they? Are they among the universal human rights, on the same order, say, as the right to freedom of speech? Or are they simply a special set of rights, founded on political necessity, but lacking the status of human rights? As a prerequisite to further examination of the status of language rights, these are fundamental questions requiring some attention. Two lines of argument attempt to situate the concept of language rights in the established framework of human rights. These will be examined here and in the next chapter.

The Meaning of Language Rights

A language right is 'a right to use one's mother tongue or native language.' This is not a right to speak a language per se, but rather to speak the language because it is the language of one's heritage. The term is more appropriately used in the plural rather than in the singular form, because the specification of such a right necessarily involves enumeration of occasions where one is entitled to use it. The definition used by the Canadian Royal Commission on Bilingualism and Biculturalism captured the various components of language rights:

This term does not merely refer to the right of a citizen to communicate with his fellow citizens in his own language, whatever it may be ... The rights chiefly concerning us in this Report are those which a Francophone or Anglophone possesses, either by law or by well-established custom, to use his mother tongue in his dealings with public authorities. Strictly speaking, a linguistic 'right' is a specific legal protection for the use of a given language. It involves the use of language in the conduct of public affairs; in the parliamentary and legislative process; in the day-to-day administration of government; in the rendering of justice; and in the public school system. It may also involve private activities.[3]

Although this quote spoke in terms of legal, rather than human rights, it nevertheless identified the main areas of interest for the domain of language rights. Furthermore, it specifically limited itself to language rights for English- and French-speaking citizens, answering the implied question, 'Who is entitled to claim these rights?' – an issue that will be addressed later. In addition, the extent of the list of language rights may well vary depending on the circumstances and needs of different language groups.

A taxonomy of potential language rights appears in Table 1.1. These

TABLE 1.1
Linguistic rights: 'The right to use one's own language'[a]

Toleration Rights

1 Individual use
   a) The right to use the language at home
   b) The right to use the language 'in the street'
   c) The right to use the language for personal names (both first and family names)

2 Individual and collective uses
   a) The right to use the language in personal communications (e.g., letters, telephone conversations, telegrams)
   b) The right to use the language in activities designed to perpetuate its use in:
      1 Schools
      2 Newspapers, journals, magazines, books
      3 Radio and television broadcasting
      4 Movies
   c) The right to use the language in private economic activities such as:
      1 Business or manufacturing enterprise between workers
      2 Advertising (storefront, media)
      3 Record-keeping (order, invoices, inventories)
      4 Other communications (e.g., letterheads)
   d) The right to use the language in private associations in:
      1 Clubs of all types (social, sport, cultural)
      2 Churches and religious organizations

3 Individual and collective uses *vis-à-vis* the government
   a) In courts of law (with or without an interpreter supplied at government expense)

Weak Promotion

   b) The right to communicate with government and receive government services in one's maternal language
   c) In public notices (e.g., street signs, public information signs)
   d) In campaigning and running for public office
   e) In government reports, documents, hearings, transcripts, and other publications for public distribution
   f) In the federal legislature (e.g., debates), judiciary, and administrative agencies, bureaus, and departments
   g) The right to receive a publicly funded education in one's maternal language

Strong Promotion

4 Individual and collective uses *vis-à-vis* public and private institutions
   a) The right to work in one's maternal language
   b) The right to receive services from private business organizations in one's maternal language
   c) The right to be communicated with via public signs and advertisements in one's maternal language
   d) The *mandatory* right to an education in one's maternal language

---

[a] Adapted from Manfred W. Wenner, 'The Politics of Equality among European Linguistic Minorities,' in Richard Claude, ed., *Comparative Human Rights* (Baltimore: Johns Hopkins University Press, 1976), Table on 193.

rights may usefully be divided into three categories. The best known scheme for summarizing them was developed by Kloss, who distinguished between toleration-oriented and promotion-oriented language rights. Toleration-oriented rights are synonymous with liberty rights and refer to the right to be left alone. They are characterized by the absence of prohibitive legislation, or by legislation specifying that such languages are permissible in the private realms (at home, in social clubs, or both). These rights require governments to merely refrain from imposing restrictions on the use of a language in the private domain. Thus, a linguistic minority group is entitled to use its language at home, in voluntary associations, private schools, churches, newspapers, and so forth. Societal responsibilities in relation to such rights are fully met through legislation prohibiting discrimination on the basis of language (such as Article 2 of the International Covenant on Civil and Political Rights), coupled with a policy of 'benign neglect' *vis-à-vis* language.

Promotion-oriented rights express a commitment by the state to support a particular language. Primarily, this involves use of the language in public institutions, both political and administrative (including judicial), and in the public schools. These rights require actions and expenditures by public authorities on behalf of a particular language group.[4]

For purposes of analysing practices in the Canadian context, a further distinction needs to be drawn within this category between weak and strong promotion. Weak promotion refers to actions taken to ensure that a language can be sustained and in some measure encouraged. This requires policies similar to those embodied in the federal Official Languages Act (1969), which recognizes both English and French as languages of government legislation, administration, and service, as well as the complementary policy of publicly funding educational facilities and some mass media programming in the official minority language.

Strong promotion aims to ensure that individuals can live their lives in their own language. This entails broader ranging government policies requiring that a language be used throughout the public and private sectors. Strong promotion is best exemplified by the provisions of Quebec's Charter of the French Language.[5] Guarantees of private sector services and the right to work in one's own language are examples of such rights.

These three categories – toleration, weak promotion, and strong promotion – of language rights constitute an ascending scale of claims, each requiring different, and progressively more demanding rationales for recognition and justification. They differ as well in their compatibility with the essential features of human rights. To explore these complexities, I shall assess these three categories of language rights through an examination of the core features of human rights.

Language Rights as Human Rights

A voluminous literature has emerged on many aspects of human rights, with special emphasis on the epistemological grounding of human rights. I cannot hope to sort out the numerous questions raised of any general theory of rights, nor is that daunting enterprise especially germane to my task. The pursuit of a single theory to accommodate all human rights is akin to the quest for the Holy Grail – an inspiring pastime, the virtue of which consists largely in the activity itself rather than in the hope of its realization.[6]

Arguments for human rights, however, must still be couched within a framework of discourse about rights. Margaret MacDonald suggested a good model for such discourse in asserting that the justification of human rights is 'much more like the defence of his client by a good counsel.'[7] The defence of human rights involves a process of persuasion, of giving reasons why something ought to be treated as a human right. It does not mean, as the analogy might suggest, that one need be bound to the existing law on human rights as embodied in constitutions or case law. These usually represent at best the crystallization of previous consensus on what is right and just in these matters. Instead, these elements must be regarded as simply pieces of evidence among a variety of possible sources, in the development of a defence.

In what follows, two major approaches are outlined that will serve as the basis for the development of an argument that language rights, on the basis of their inherent criteria, ought to be considered as human rights. One line of argument will suggest that language rights correspond, with some important qualifications, to the established criteria of a human right; the other, that language rights are embedded in the established practices of Canadian society.

Rights as Claims

In the midst of an abstract discussion on the philosophical foundation of human rights, an unidentified law professor, exasperated by the esoteric character of the debate, countered with his own pragmatic theory of the basis of rights as follows: 'This is the way it is with rights. You want'em, so you say you got'em, and if nobody says you don't, then you do.'[8] This quote illustrates a number of important aspects of the character and politics of human rights. A human right is, in essence, a claim that is advanced against others (either individuals or institutions) for particular liberties, goods, or services. As explained by Wasserstrom, 'To claim or to acquire anything as a matter of right is crucially different from seeking or obtaining it as through the grant of a privilege, the receipt of a favor [*sic*], or the presence of a permission. To have a right to something is, typically, to be entitled to receive or possess or enjoy it now, and to do so without the consent of another.'[9] It is an especially legitimate demand since it is typically understood to be a demand for something to which the claimant is entitled. It therefore carries with it certain duties incumbent upon those to whom the claim is addressed.[10] For these reasons, Feinberg insisted, 'Legal rights are indispensably valuable possessions. A world without claim-rights, no matter how full of benevolence and devotion to duty, would suffer an immense moral impoverishment.'[11]

Rights are claims in the practical political sense in that they must be claimed and established in the political arena. This process necessarily begins with the claim that what one desires (e.g., language services, religious worship, adequate income) is or ought to be considered a human right. This invariably produces one of the most exasperating features of such a process, namely, the profusion of specious claims. One can readily share the exasperation of one critic upon being presented with the claim of a right to a sex break, and sunshine.[12] However, this represents simply part of the public dialogue on what is to be added to the recognized lists of human rights. It is useful to remember that, at one time, the notion of a right to freedom of religious worship was considered almost as outlandish as the currently proposed candidates appear to be. Two hundred years later, the idea of constraining religious freedom appears equally outlandish. Those easily offended by such frivolity might take some comfort in the thought that only candidates that appeal to a broad spectrum of the public will receive extensive consideration.

Three Tests for a Human Right

Human rights may best be conceived as a kind of claim. This does not mean, however, that they are to be defined as such. I shall follow Maurice Cranston's lead in defining a human right as 'a universal moral right, something which all men, everywhere, at all times, ought to have, something of which no one may be deprived without a grave affront to justice, something which is owing to every human simply because he is human.'[13] As is immediately apparent, the 'something' is left unspecified.

However, Cranston also presented three criteria for assessing the authenticity of a particular candidate for such status: practicability, paramount importance, and universality. Practicability refers to the actual possibility of acknowledging and providing a right. For example, there can be no right of anyone to fly like a bird, as it is physically impossible. This is an elaboration of the principle that for an action to be morally obligatory, it must at a minimum be possible to perform.

The second test, paramount importance, designates only things that are 'supremely sacred' to human life as human rights. The final test, the universality of a human right, is met in Cranston's view if and only if it is a right of 'all people at all times and in all situations.'[14] This excludes special types of rights such as status rights, whereby an individual has certain rights by virtue of the position he holds in the society. Thus, a guardian has certain decision-making rights over a child placed in her or his care that no one else has. A human right refers to rights held universally, that is, by everyone.

These tests aid in the determination of what specific entities may be accorded the status of human rights. They will be used when the discussion turns to the assessment of the claim of language rights to the status of a human right. Meanwhile, it is necessary to flesh out in a little more detail what it means for a right to be universal.

A right is universal when it is possessed by all human beings, and it must be possessed equally. In addition, a human right must be claimable against all relevant other people.[15] To put it another way, human rights impose corresponding duties upon every other person or institution to ensure the availability of the right to an individual. Thus, if I have a right to freedom of speech, a corresponding duty is imposed upon every other individual not to interfere with the exercise of my right.

This emphasis on the rights and duties of individuals raises a further issue: the question of the holder of human rights. Specifically, are human rights held, claimable, or exercisable only by individuals, or also by groups? We turn to that question at the end of this chapter. For the moment, it is sufficient to emphasize that Cranston's tests for the authenticity of a right are rigorous and therefore a useful starting point for a careful scrutiny of candidates for such status.

Language as a Human Right: Applying the Tests

Paramount Importance

The first test, paramount importance, examines the extent to which the candidate can be deemed essential to a fully human life. On this understanding, what can be said about one's native language? A constant theme in discussions of language is the integral relationship of language, culture, and community membership. Peter Berger explained the centrality of language when he observed, 'Every language is an immensely valuable depository of human experiences, of joys, sorrows, and uniquely irreplaceable perceptions of the world. Those whose lives have been shaped by a language have a basic right to its possession and, if necessary, its defence.'[16]

Language stands at the nexus of the individual, the cultural heritage, and the society. Edward Sapir suggested that this interrelationship is best understood through an emphasis on the symbolic impact of language on group life. He argued that 'the mere fact of a common speech serves as a peculiarly potent symbol of the social solidarity of those who speak the language.'[17]

Language has tremendous psychological significance for the individual member of the group. Language is an ever-present badge of membership, reinforced in the subtleties of linguistic styles. We would expect its significance to be all the stronger as the boundaries between languages become more obvious. Isaacs suggested that this process of using one's language to express group solidarity involves the evolution and maintenance of both group and individual identity. Thus, language is surrounded by an emotional intensity and an irreducible quality that signify its status as one of the 'primordial bonds' of group identity.[18] Language is critical in defining individual identity, culture, and community membership.

Kymlicka also developed an argument for the rights of cultural minorities, stemming from liberal egalitarian premises, when he asserted, 'Our language and history are the media through which we come to an awareness of the options available to us, and their significance; and this is a precondition of making intelligent judgements about how to lead our lives.'[19] Since cultural communities form the basis of the context of choice in the making of individual life plans, cultural membership must be viewed as a *primary good* in society, worthy of protection in culturally plural societies via minority rights, as required. Since language is often a central feature of minority cultural membership, language rights can be justified as part of a complex of protections for cultural minorities, to ensure that they enjoy the same equality of concern in society as enjoyed by members of the majority culture.

These observations provide compelling reasons to insist upon the importance of language. Are they sufficient to establish that one's traditional language is 'supremely sacred'? Put that strongly, the question invites qualification. Much depends on the circumstances of the case, particularly the role that the traditional language plays in one's daily life. The more central it is, as in a usual language of interaction at home or at work, the stronger the claim to paramount importance. Conversely, where it is not the usual language of discourse in a linguistic community, it is not arguably of paramount importance. This is particularly an issue where linguistic minority groups may be too small to sustain the use of their traditional language in the daily life of their community.

Many people choose to assimilate to a different language in certain societies, frequently for social and economic reasons, but sometimes through attraction to the particular culture. Yet, where the linguistic minority is able to sustain its language, there is some evidence that the prospects for personal development are far greater by virtue of the opportunity to express one's personality in all aspects of life and imbibe fully of the cultural life of the community. Jacques Brazeau, for instance, spoke of 'a disengagement of language from experience' among those who live separate portions of their lives in different languages (e.g., work life in English, home life in French) which apparently results in a constricted expression of one's personality.[20] If such is the case, then language rights are justified for the same reasons as traditional human rights – to permit the full development and expression of the individual. Moreover, in this respect, the strong promotion claim of language rights is more readily defensible than the weak, since it most fully responds to the intended purpose of these rights.

It is possible, for the reasons outlined above, to state that language rights pass the test of paramount importance, albeit with some qualification. Specifically, the 'paramount importance' of language rights is not simply to be presumed in each case (as with the right to free speech), but is to be assessed in light of the characteristics of the particular linguistic community itself.

Practicability

The test of practicability is equally complex, admitting no single answer. Depending on circumstances, language rights may require the same guarantees as the traditional political rights. At a minimum, this simply involves non-interference by the government. This would be the case where a language community is largely self-contained and self-sufficient.

The most interesting cases, however, are usually those involving positive action by government. An example would be the case where a language community is dispersed throughout a larger population of a different language, with no distinct territory or cohesion. In this instance, recognition of language rights places very great demands upon a society to secure these rights. The extent of the demands and the question of practicability depend initially upon which sense of language rights – their strong or weak form – is advanced.

Obviously, much less is involved in *preserving* a language than in ensuring that an individual can live her or his life in her or his native tongue. The former is usually feasible in the more affluent societies. The latter becomes less practicable as the size and concentration of the language community *decrease.*

In general, the stronger the claim entailed by language rights, and the more geographically dispersed the language group, the less practicable the claim becomes. It may or may not fail this test depending upon particular circumstances. Judgment about practicability, then, must be case-specific.

Beyond toleration-oriented practices, a government's impact can at best be to increase the prospects for minority languages, rather than to assure them. As a recent comparative study of the attempts to arrest language decline demonstrates, languages are affected by a variety of factors, many of which are far beyond the capacity of governments to control. The most important factors in the survival of languages are within the family, neighbourhood, and local community contexts.[21] Thus, in recognizing language rights, governments are at most able to contribute to the contemporary linguistic *security* of the language community, rather than ensuring its long-run *survival.*[22]

Certain additional difficulties of application based on features of language rights are better discussed under the criterion of universality.

Universality

A right is universal when it is held by all people at all times in all places. A classic example is the right to humane treatment, that is, not to be treated cruelly. It holds always and everywhere. Language rights do not quite attain that degree of universality. A wide array of circumstances are pertinent to the issue. The notorious American tourist might come to mind here. Has he been correct all along in insisting that natives of different cultures speak to him in English? A perhaps related case is that of an immigrant to a foreign culture, for instance, a Ukrainian in becoming a 'new' Canadian. What about the thriving subcultures that are adjuncts of larger communities? Visible examples are the Italian communities in many eastern Canadian cities which, despite losing use of their native language, continue to form identifiable networks of social interaction. Another example might be that of two Inuit families in northern Canada who move to a large metropolis in the southern part of the country where their language is not shared by anyone else. What about relatively separate linguistic communities that exist within a larger political community, but function independently as self-contained communities? The French-speaking communities of the provinces of Quebec and New Brunswick are typical examples of this class.

Each of these broad classes offer interesting problems for the claim of language rights to universal status. Reviewing the examples, it is clear that they represent a descending order of challenges to such a claim. The immigrant and the tourist are the most instructive challenges to the universality of language rights. The tourist would not usually be considered justified in insisting that his rights were being violated. If he were to do so, those to whom the complaints were addressed would point to the tourist's status as an *outsider* to the ongoing community, and perhaps note that the tourist *chose* to travel where English was not the dominant language. The native then would assert his priority as a member of the community where the transaction took place. The clear implication is that language rights are relinquished when the borders of one's own linguistic community are crossed.

Similar considerations pertain to the case of the immigrant. If the Ukrainian were to insist upon his Ukrainian language rights, these would almost certainly be denied. One counterargument would focus on the element of choice in his situation. The immigrant has opted (either voluntarily or involuntarily) to leave his native linguistic community for one where the language is different. Participation in that community requires interaction in the local language. Otherwise, the immigrant virtually constitutes a Robinson Crusoe–type figure, alone in the midst of a sea of unintelligible discourse. On a more pragmatic note, such an immigrant would find it pointless to maintain his language for lack of a person with whom to share it.

These two examples illustrate important features of a language right. In sharp contrast to the right of humane treatment, which all individuals hold in all times and all places, and whose denial implies a denial of one's humanity, a language right admits exceptions of both characteristics. One may refuse to speak to an individual in his or her native tongue, without apparently denying that individual's status as a human being.

In addition, language rights admit of situations where they do not hold for all individuals. The tourist and the immigrant cannot claim such rights. The explanation of this conclusion derives from the nature of language, particularly the fact that it is a *relational* concept. It is at once an individual property and a social property. It is individuals who speak language X or Y; yet languages require a social relationship, specifically a functioning cultural community. Speaking a language has no meaning outside the context of the language community. This represents an intrinsic limitation to the universality of a language right.

The groups of examples previously examined form a sliding scale of increasing communal and cultural life surrounding the individual. The final example, of a self-reliant and self-contained cultural community, fully meets the communal and cultural preconditions just mentioned. For that reason, the issue might normally be moot. Where it is not, it is usually the case that there are multiple cultural communities with distinctive languages, all perhaps having the same basis for a claim.

This represents a critical difficulty with the universality of language rights. There is an unavoidable internal conflict of rights and duties. If A has a right to a certain language does B have a duty to speak it to him? They could of course be bilingual, and each speak the other's language, but they would forego the strong sense of language rights. There is thus an irrevocable conflict of rights and duties between individuals if there is such a right.

Alternatively, the duties regarding such rights could fall upon the government or the society collectively, as it does with many of the social rights. However, the same difficulties are fully present in acting upon these responsibilities. Certain forms of societal action pose little difficulty. For example, a government may provide opportunities for participation in political and cultural life in one's own language. This would respond to the weak sense of language rights, serving to *sustain* it.

When a government seeks to acknowledge a strong claim to A's language rights, it necessarily involves a denial of B's claim. By legislating that all public speech must be in language A, it prevents language B from attaining the status of a *lived* language. The different claims to strong language rights are mutually exclusive. Thus, a government can only respond to its duties to some by violating its duties to others. These considerations lead to the conclusion that there cannot be a universal right to a language in the strong promotion sense. It can only be acknowledged in some version of the weak promotion form.

Governments may also have competing duties to the same individual or group. Where one's maternal language is not widely used in the economy, governments have a duty to ensure that each individual is equipped with the necessary skills to ensure equality of opportunity in the larger society. If fluency in English is necessary to get a job in Nova Scotia, then governments have an imperative duty to provide each schoolchild with an education to attain that fluency. Failure to do so would condemn francophone students to lives of limited economic opportunities and would constitute discriminatory treatment. This is despite the fact that, as many advocates of francophone language rights have insisted, English language education or even bilingual education undermines the viability of the French language. Here again, the language rights in question are dependent on judgments about the extent of community life available in the relevant language. Thus, the government's duty to provide an individual with equality of opportunity may override the duty to promote the individual's language community. Needless to say, this consideration speaks to the advisability of these language rights being treated as *option rights*, rights that individuals may choose whether or not to demand. Nevertheless, the manner in which these rights are contingent on situational factors is underlined.

These reflections lead to ambiguous conclusions. Although language rights are arguably of paramount importance to individuals and groups, this cannot always be presumed. Their importance depends on the place of a language in the daily life and the self-definition of the cultural community. Moreover, in their strong form, language rights fail to meet another definitive characteristic, universality. A persuasive case for language rights in the *strong promotion* sense, that is, of living one's life in a language, does not exist. If language is to stand as a right, it must be in the *weak promotion* form of a right to sustain the language. Only in this form is it possible to surmount the internal conflict of rights and duties that otherwise occurs in the strong form of the right. The weak form of language rights not only surmounts this fundamental problem, but also it is better able to meet the practicability criterion. Thus, one can conclude that the weak promotion form of language rights meets the criteria of a human right in the appropriate contexts. At the same time, these various qualifications suggest that language rights are not quite of the 'supremely sacred' stature of the traditional civil liberties. However, they meet most of the criteria applicable to human rights, and they can be invested with an importance for particular language communities that goes beyond the historical particularity of 'compromise rights.' Leslie Green has neatly captured the dual nature of language rights in his conclusion that language rights are 'compromise rights of a fundamental sort.'[23]

The Character of Language Rights

A recurrent issue in the discussion of language rights concerns the essential character of language rights. Are they best conceived as individual or group rights? Opinion remains sharply divided. Since divergent consequences for the substance of language rights flow from each approach, this is one of the basic conceptual issues in need of clarification. I shall approach the problem by examining the arguments for viewing language rights as individual, group, or collective rights in turn, assessing the problems and prospects of each.

Individual, Group, and Collective Rights

An individual right is a claim every person may make simply by virtue of being a person or, more restrictively, a citizen of a particular community or state. The right to freedom of speech is a classic example. Each individual may voice her or his opinions on public matters. If so, all other individuals have a duty not to interfere with the exercise of that right. Failure to observe that duty of non-interference generates a duty on the part of others to restrain such interference.

Group rights bear a problematical and multifaceted relationship to individual rights. It has been suggested that all group rights are reducible to individual rights, although others have held that group rights rest very uneasily on the individualistic foundation of human rights.[24] Van Dyke maintained that the locus of a right, in the individual or in the group, is more often than not a question of practicality. On his view, the rationale for a right might be individualistic, and, thus, group rights could in principle be reducible to individual rights.[25] In such cases, group rights are simply a shorthand expression for specific individual rights and the conceptual problem simply dissolves. Other group rights, however, are not so readily reducible. Accordingly, the relation of group to individual rights varies with the specific right under discussion.

The two categories are in fact overlapping in certain instances. Group rights are divisible into two categories of rights. The first category concerns non-discrimination rights: The group right is readily reducible to a corresponding individual right. For example, the right of black South Africans not to be subject to discriminatory laws is founded on the individual right to equality before the law. This type of right is theoretically contingent upon the continued practice of discrimination. When that practice disappears, so does the specific group right.

The other category consists of those group rights that require group membership for their existence and/or assertion, though they are actually claimed by individuals. In Canada, the members of certain groups (for example, Mennonites and Doukhobors) have a right to exemption from military service that stems from their membership in these groups. This is a group right that can be exercised by individual members of these groups. Is it reducible to the individual right of freedom of religion? Certainly, state respect for the core tenets of particular religious denominations is required. However, claims for exemption would require some evidence of ongoing participation in and commitment to such religious groups. In this sense, at least, it is not entirely reducible to the individual claim to religious freedom.

A further difficulty emerges in distinguishing group rights from collective rights. A collective right is a right belonging to a group characterized by internal cohesiveness, enduring ties, and a strong commitment to the survival of the group. In general, we have a better grasp of the structural features of collective rights than of their content.

Yoram Dinstein suggested two distinctive features of collective rights. First, a collective right requires that it be exercised jointly, rather than severally. Second, in evaluating deprivations of the right, it is the overall picture rather than individual deprivations that is important.[26] This is well illustrated in contemporary international law which recognizes three collective rights: the right to physical existence, to self-determination, and to natural resources.[27] These are rights of peoples, rather than nations. As such, they may be enjoyed by subnational groups such as the Innu people in Canada. They are rights that can only be exercised jointly rather than individually, and they frequently involve collective control over some goods, services, or governmental office.

The right to Roman Catholic denominational schools in Canada is an interesting illustration of these features. One analyst, M. James Penton, reported, 'In recent years Catholics in both Saskatchewan and Alberta have been forced to send their children to Catholic schools whether they wanted to or not. Curiously, the right of the parent to determine what sort of an education his children should have has been overridden by the courts in favour of the rights of the Catholic community.'[28] In this instance, the rights of the Catholic community as a whole are quite distinct from the rights of the individual members of the Catholic community. The right is not reducible to an individual right, as individual preferences regarding the exercise of the right are deemed irrelevant.

These are structural features of collective rights that are independent of their content. Two significant issues still to be addressed concern the content of collective rights and their justification. The right to self-determination may be categorized as among *political collective rights*. The example of Catholic denominational schools, however, falls under a group of *substantive collective rights* that relate to the preservation of the culture of a collectivity. Douglas Sanders maintained that substantive collective rights are cultural rights, which embrace rights to a variety of items pertinent to cultural survival, in particular, rights regarding language, religion, legal norms, and culturally important activities. He further suggested that the content is elastic, being governed by the degree of threat existing regarding the survival of the group.[29]

The latter suggestion indicates one of the distinctive difficulties attending these rights. Cultural rights differ from individual rights in that they are less amenable to general expression in universal norms, partly because '[they] assume the primacy of particularistic cultural variables over universal norms.'[30] This means that the specific circumstances of each group, and their understandings of the central elements of their respective cultures, determine the content of group rights. Dinstein, for example, in discussing the case of Soviet Jewry, placed much greater emphasis upon education about one's cultural heritage than on education in a specific language such as Hebrew.[31] Other ethnic groups might readily reverse these priorities. French Canadians, with their current emphasis on the centrality of language, provide a case in point. Furthermore, this same French-Canadian community, if consulted a century ago on a choice between rights to language or education, might well have chosen education in denominational schools as the priority. Accordingly, Gordon Means was quite right in stating, 'It is more appropriate for the thorny issue of group rights to be resolved in national or sub-national political arenas.'[32] In the international context, this means that one must be content to enunciate a set of guidelines or conditions for the recognition of such rights.

Van Dyke presented a set of criteria to apply in assessing any proposal for the recognition of collective rights. He maintained that a group has a stronger claim,

1 The more it is a self-conscious entity with a desire to preserve itself
2 The more evident it is that it has a reasonable chance to preserve itself
3 The clearer are the tests or criteria of membership
4 The more significant it is in the lives of its members and the more they identify themselves with it

5 The more important the rights it seeks are to the interests of its members, and the less costly or burdensome the grant of the right is to others
6 The more clearly and effectively it is organized to act and to assume
   responsibilities
7 The more firmly established is the tradition of treating it as a group
8 The more clearly the status and rights that it seeks can be granted com-
   patibly with the equality principle.[33]

The equality principle poses some vexing problems. In this context, it
operates as a limit on the diversities of status that are permissible. As Van
Dyke emphasized, 'If the grant of a certain status and a certain set of
rights to one group means that like groups cannot have a like status and a
like set of rights, then the requirement of the equality principle is not
met.'[34] This important criterion of acceptability is offset by the recognition that a degree of inequality is often necessary to rectify other inequalities, as occurs with affirmative action programs. Finally, programs aimed
at achieving equality for groups may conflict with individual equality.
Affirmative action policies allow the individual members of groups that
are their subjects to obtain some preferential treatment over non-group
members. On the other hand, individual members of a group may find
they experience less individual equality than non-group members
because they are required to participate in some group practice, whether
they want to or not, as in the denominational schools of Alberta and
Saskatchewan. Obviously, in making judgments on this criterion, the matter of equality must be examined in these various respects.

   These criteria, taken as a whole, are expressed in relative terms ('the
more ...'), without thresholds being identified, so that they require an
exercise of judgment in individual cases. Nevertheless, they offer a basis
for such assessments to occur.

   One issue that remains undeveloped in regard to collective rights concerns their content. Although it is initially informative to note that collective rights involve cultural rights, these rights need to be further specified
as to what they are a right *to*. Initially, this could be described as a right to
have one's cultural practices respected. This takes both positive and negative forms. The latter case occurs where a group is exempted from a standard requirement that falls on everyone else, such as the exemption from
military conscription that certain religious denominations enjoy. A positive form occurs where the cultural values of the collectivity are imposed
on the state or individuals in the community. One such example is the
case of a B.C. Roman Catholic schoolteacher fired by the Catholic school-

board because she married a divorced man, in violation of the teachings of Roman Catholic Church doctrine. The basis for her dismissal, which was upheld in court, was that she failed to provide a proper role model of Catholic moral teaching for her students.[35] Such cases indicate that respect for collective rights may violate individual liberty, in which case, the rationale for each must be examined to determine which should be sustained. Just as individual rights compete with each other in particular cases, so too can collective rights conflict with individual rights, other collective rights, or both.

These examples involving denominational schools suggest a conception of collective rights that is problematic. Both involve a *mandatory right* of participation in a community for its members, either through its institutions or its cultural norms. Second, in a context of a multicultural community, the exercise of these collective cultural rights must be several (individual) or else they must violate the equal treatment requirement for other cultural communities. One could not claim, for example, that because Roman Catholics were the most numerous religious denomination in Canada, that therefore all Canadians had a collective cultural right, a mandatory right, to participate in that denomination's religious services. If that is conceded, the distinction between group and collective rights, that is, the joint exercise of rights, is substantially eroded. Perhaps this illustration primarily serves to show that the substantive collective rights are not readily distinguishable from group rights at all.

This last example introduces a further qualification to the content of cultural rights herein discussed. Will Kymlicka offered the useful distinction between the norms, values, and institutions of a culture at any point in time versus the cultural structure as a *context of choice*, meaning 'its capacity of providing meaningful options for us, and aiding our ability to judge for ourselves the value of our life-plans.'[36] He argued that collective rights properly protect the latter rather than the former.[37] On this understanding, it would be an inappropriate assertion of cultural rights to punish an individual for failure to conform to a specific cultural norm. Thus, its legality notwithstanding, the dismissal of a teacher for violating the Catholic norm prohibiting remarriage after divorce, was arguably an illegitimate exercise of cultural rights. By the same token, participation in the denominational school system should be an *option* right for community members, when alternatives are available for their use.

Nevertheless, it is clear that cases can arise where the collective rights in question require restriction of individual rights. Kymlicka cited the case of Aboriginal groups being able to restrict individual rights of non-

Aboriginals (differential residency requirements for non-Aboriginals in the Northwest Territories, for instance) as a legitimate practice required to protect the cultural base of the Aboriginal communities.[38] In this case, the restrictions imposed on non-Aboriginals (belonging to a dominant culture that is not threatened) are relatively modest, while offering strong support to the survival of the Aboriginal community in their sole residential enclave.

Such conflicts invite consideration of the bases of these collective rights. Although they may not be reducible to individual rights, the rationales frequently attempt to ground them in the individual. Kymlicka, for example, argued that 'people are owed respect as individuals and as members of cultural communities.'[39] The latter may require differential treatment of minority cultures to ensure the broader goal that governments show equality of concern for the interests of the members of minority cultural communities. Thus, collective rights in his model are established upon the basis of equality of respect for individuals.[40] Similarly, one might seek to root collective rights for cultural communities as derivative rights stemming from a concern to protect the prerequisites for the integrity of the individual, one of which is the identity-conferring commitments arising from one's cultural heritage.[41] In both cases, a link is made to an ultimate grounding in the individual. Thus, although the conditions for exercising collective rights are significantly different from both individual and group rights, they nonetheless share a justificatory foundation in individual rights.

This review of the distinctions among these types of rights has been far from decisive. Individual rights shade into group rights and, in turn, group rights overlap considerably with collective rights. The main distinction arises with the contrast between collective rights viewed as a possession of the collectivity and individual rights exercised by individuals.

The boundaries of individual, group, and collective rights might not be so distinct as to permit tidy classification. Nonetheless, there is some question about where language rights fit within such a scheme. I shall examine the cases for treating them as both individual and group rights.

Language Rights as Individual Rights

Language rights are individual in the important sense that they are claimable and exercised by individuals. Most of the specific language rights claimed in Table 1.1, for example, are individual in this sense. What needs to be explored is the link between these and other rights. It has been suggested, for example, that language rights derive from, and are in turn limited by, specific individual rights. Alternatively, it has been suggested that language rights are a precondition to the equal exercise of a broad range of rights.[42]

William Conklin maintained that language rights are individual rights insofar as they are 'essential conditions for the effective exercise of those fundamental rights which are integrally entangled with "respect for persons."' Conklin further maintained that 'a constitutional obligation to respect the Francophone language in a variety of institutional settings better ensures that the exercise of fundamental rights are *equally* shared.'[43] The language rights under discussion concern francophone rights to communications with legislatures, courts, and government administrative bodies.

Conklin's approach offers an important but limited base for recognition of language rights. His examples illustrate how some language rights are simply consequences of particular individual rights. The right to an interpreter in a criminal trial, for instance, long predates recognition of 'language rights' as such, and flows from the realization that the right to a fair trial includes the right to understand and to be understood. Similarly, the right not to be discriminated against on the basis of language is a particular instance of the general right not to be discriminated against on the basis of one's social characteristics.

Experience in the United States, however, illustrates the possibilities and limitations of this approach. Although the American Constitution does not recognize language rights, the courts have favoured the establishment of services in a minority language where it is perceived as necessary to the exercise of fundamental rights or to the alleviation of indirect discrimination on the basis of national origin. The courts have required bilingual ballots in elections, for example, as voting is a fundamental right. They have not been so favourable, by contrast, to demands for bilingual education, or, more particularly, to bilingual government services.[44] This line may well correspond to the perceived limits of a purely individual basis for language rights. Incorporation of a richer framework of language rights requires a commitment to the second dimension of equal respect noted by Kymlicka, equality of respect for individuals as members of cultural communities.

The same point arises in regard to a particular challenge that might be raised of Conklin's argument. Conklin argued that francophone language rights are necessary for the equal exercise of standard political rights. One might ask, if French-speaking Canadians are able to exercise these fundamental rights substantially in English, then is Conklin's case for francophone language rights undermined? This is not a purely hypothetical question. In fact, a prominent advocate of French-language minority rights has acknowledged that 'all francophone minorities in English Canada are bilingual.'[45] That being the case, Conklin's grounds for language rights would appear seriously undermined. The argument might be rescued by emphasizing the commonplace observation that facility in a second language is usually subordinate to that of the mother tongue, in which case issues of *equal exercise* remain paramount. However, where individuals are functionally bilingual, the specific argument Conklin advanced loses some of its appeal. Once again, however, it can be significantly reinforced where the emphasis is not on the equal exercise of the standard political rights per se, so much as on the proper recognition of the members of the cultural communities themselves, as would be reflected in policies supportive of their language.

Language Rights as Group Rights

One argument for treating language rights as group rights stems from the manner of its embodiment in relevant constitutional texts, such as the Canadian Charter of Rights and Freedoms. The limitations on minority language services in government offices to places 'where numbers warrant,' effectively means, as Hanen emphasized, that 'not every individual, then, is in a position to claim these rights.'[46] They must be group rights in that they require the presence of a group to be available. This limitation, however, is one of practicality rather than principle. This is clearly illustrated in the Bilingualism and Biculturalism Report, where it stated: 'That although an Anglophone isolated among French speaking Canadians may possess all the theoretical rights imaginable, each is able to exercise these rights to a very limited extent. A milieu is not transformed for one individual; a university is not built for a single family.'[47] There must be sufficient demand for the service, then, to justify its provision. The issue turns on the minimum number necessary to warrant the service. The example does pose a serious challenge, however, to the claim that language rights are in some sense 'basic rights.' It is difficult to reconcile such a claim with the limitations just mentioned.

A more compelling point is that the special characteristics of groups are central to the identification of whether language rights exist. Put another way, the speakers of some languages have language rights in a given society: the speakers of others do not. The speakers of French and

English in Canada have language rights; the speakers of Ukrainian, Italian, and German do not. These differences are accounted for not by reference to individuals, but by the particular characteristics of their group as founding members, indigenous peoples, as functioning linguistic communities, and so on. Therefore, the character and status of the group determines the existence of the right.

Moreover, there is an ineradicable core of group rights in the idea of language rights, stemming from the fact that language itself presupposes community. Just as it may make little sense to provide government services in a minority language to a single person, it is unthinkable that one could have an entitlement to a language in the absence of a community of individuals with whom the language is shared. The existence of the language group is thus an essential precondition to the meaningful assertion of language rights.

Recognition of this fact led Laponce to argue that language rights in their most substantial, strong-promotion-oriented form are territorially rooted in the institutions and social networks of a particular geographic space.[48] Accordingly, recognition of language rights entails their recognition as rights of the group more so than those of the individual. On this basis, he criticized the language provisions of the Canadian Charter of Rights and Freedoms because, 'it seeks to obtain through individual rights what can only be obtained through group rights.' It fails to recognize that 'language rights are to be understood not only as the right to use one's preferred language, but also as the right to see preserved the language community within which that language is to be used.'[49] As an illustration of the correct approach, he cited favourably the Swiss policy of establishing fixed boundaries within particular cantons to determine the official language of all government services.

In effect, Laponce claimed that the group right to the survival of its language supersedes the individual right to use a language. He advanced a strong promotion model of language rights, designed to ensure that the group can live its life in its language. This stems in part from his conviction that 'a language is threatened a soon as it is no longer spoken universally at home, at work, at play, at market, with kin, with friends and fellow workers.'[50] For this reason, a language must be given an exclusive territorial domain in which to operate.

In fact, there is good reason to doubt that the English language constitutes a serious threat to the French language in Quebec. The census data, for instance, indicate extremely high rates of language retention among Québécois, to the extent that language loss is negligible.[51] Consequently, it is doubtful that the individual language rights for the anglophone minority in Quebec pose a threat to the vitality of the French language in Quebec. Accordingly, individual language rights for English-speaking Canadians in Quebec are compatible with group rights for the French-speaking majority.

If, for the sake of the argument, they did pose a threat, would this justify a denial of individual language rights? As Laponce indicated, the territorial language policy is fairly widespread in Europe and has been challenged by individuals insisting on the priority of individual choice or individual rights in these matters. The territorial system, however, does not represent such a predilection to respect group rights against individual rights as it appears at first glance. One of the best known cases occurred in Belgium in 1968. There, individuals appealed to the courts against the requirement that children be educated in the official language of the canton. In deciding against the appellants, the court assessed the education policy in relation to the principle of equality of treatment. It emphasized that this was a consistent policy that treated individuals equally because different national languages were enforced in different cantons. Consequently, in a national context, there was equality of treatment. The individual rights considered were those of a right to an education and to non-discrimination. The court maintained that neither right conferred a right to a particular language of instruction so long as it was in one of the national languages. Thus, the court endorsed neither an individual nor group rights model of language rights, but did insist that educational policy treat language groups equally.[52]

Equal treatment, of course, may in some instances require differences in treatment, where one language is threatened while the other is not. However, these differences in treatment must be proportionate to the differences in circumstances and not impose undue burdens on others. The territorial approach advocated by Laponce displays a certain measure of equality in that the no-rights of anglophones in Quebec are matched by the no-rights of francophones in every other province where they are a small percentage of the population. However, this is a perverse equality of deprivation for substantial numbers of people disproportionate to the requirements of the promotion of the respective majority languages. The language rights embodied in the Charter are far more supportive of both language groups without threatening either, and are to that extent more equitable.

Finally, the various link between language rights and the individual outlined previously render suspect any wholesale overriding of individual language rights on behalf of group language rights. At a minimum one would have to ensure that a system of group language rights was minimally intrusive upon individual language rights for cultural minorities, thereby fulfilling one of the important criteria for recognition of such group language rights.

These considerations offer good reasons for considering language rights as both individual and group rights. Language rights are partly individual in the sense that most of them are exercised by individuals, some of them derive from purely individual rights (for example, the right to an interpreter in a trial), and they are generally to be justified through the principle of equal respect for individuals both as citizens and as members of cultural communities. However, the full array of language rights require a foundation in a group, specifically the ongoing cultural community. For that reason, it is best to consider them as a *hybrid right*, in that they require some of the characteristics of each to be substantive rights. A group language right that was not claimable by individuals would be ineffective at best; an individual language right would be virtually meaningless in the absence of a language community sharing it. This is hardly a tidy answer to these questions. It does however have the virtue of acknowledging the standing constraints in formulating any regime of language rights.

Conclusion

The analysis has suggested that language rights are hybrid rights, partly individual and partly group rights, and they are justifiable as fundamental rights, albeit with some qualification. Insofar as a language is a vital component of a functioning language community, that community has a legitimate claim upon the larger community to make reasonable efforts to recognize and sustain that language. The next chapter explores the extent to which this understanding of language rights is reflected in the practices of Canadian society.

Notes

1 Max Yalden, Commissioner of Official Languages, quoted in Daniel Bonin, ed., *Towards Reconciliation? The Language Issue in Canada in the 1990s* (Kingston: Institute of Intergovernmental Relations, Queen's University, 1992), 21.

2 K.D. McRae, 'The Constitutional Protection of Linguistic Rights in Bilingual and Multilingual States,' in Allan Gotlieb, ed., *Human Rights, Federalism and*

Minorities (Toronto: Canadian Institute of International Affairs, 1970), 213, 214.

3 Royal Commission on Bilingualism and Biculturalism, *Report*, vol. 1 (Ottawa: Queen's Printer, 1968), 41.

4 Heinz Kloss, *The American Bilingual Tradition* (Rowley, Mass.: Newbury House, 1977), 21–5.

5 For an application of this distinction to Quebec's Bill 101, see my 'Language Rights, Human Rights and Bill 101,' *Queen's Quarterly* 90 (1983): 351–8.

6 See Arthur C. Danto, 'Constructing an Epistemology of Human Rights: A Pseudo Problem?' in Ellen Frankel Paul, Fred D. Miller, and Jeffrey Paul, eds., *Human Rights* (Oxford: Basil Blackwell, 1984), 25–34.

7 Margaret MacDonald, 'Natural Rights,' in A.I. Melden, ed., *Human Rights* (Belmont: Wadsworth, 1970), 58.

8 This is an unattributed quote in Danto, 'Epistemology of Human Rights,' 30.

9 Richard Wasserstrom,'Rights, Human Rights and Racial Discrimination,' in Melden, *Human Rights*, 98.

10 In addition to the claim model, there are also the alternative will and benefit models. For a discussion of their respective virtues, see Vinit Haksar, 'The Nature of Rights,' *Archiv fur Rechts – und Sozialphilosophie* 64 (2) (1978): 183–203. Haksar admitted that the claim model does not apply to the category of 'liberty rights,' but insisted that it is more broadly applicable than the alternative models.

11 Joel Feinberg, *Social Philosophy* (Englewood Cliffs, NJ: Prentice-Hall, 1973), 58.

12 See John Kleinig, 'Human Rights, Legal Rights and Social Change,' in Eugene Kamenka and Alice Erh-Soon Tay, eds., *Human Rights* (London: Edward Arnold, 1978), 40 n12.

13 Maurice Cranston, *What Are Human Rights?* (New York: Basic Books, 1962), 36. Cranston, of course, fully intended to include women as possessors of rights as well. The ensuing discussion draws extensively from my 'Language Rights ... Bill 101.'

14 Maurice Cranston, 'Human Rights, Real and Supposed,' in D.D. Raphael, ed., *Political Theory and the Rights of Man* (Bloomington: Indiana University Press, 1967), 49.

15 I have followed Wasserstrom's lead, somewhat selectively, in identifying these characteristics. Wasserstrom, 'Rights,' 100.

16 P. Berger, *Facing Up to Modernity* (Harmondsworth: Penguin, 1979), 161.

17 Edward Sapir, *Culture, Language and Personality*, ed. D. Mandelbaum (Berkeley: University of California Press, 1949), 16. Sapir was referring to small-group interaction here, but it appears appropriate to extend this application to larger scale groups.

18 Harold Isaacs, *Idols of the Tribe: Group Identity and Political Change* (New York: Harper and Row, 1977), 95ff.

19 Will Kymlicka, *Liberalism, Community and Culture* (Oxford: Oxford University Press, 1989), 165. Kymlicka developed his argument in relation to Aboriginal communities in Canada and the United States. My extension of it to the case of linguistic minorities is consistent with his line of reasoning.

20 See Jacques Brazeau, 'Language Differences and Occupational Experience,' *Canadian Journal of Economics and Political Science* 24 (1958): 532–40. See also Erwin Hargrove, 'Nationality, Values and Change,' *Comparative Politics* 2 (1970): 473–99.

21 Joshua A. Fishman, *Reversing Language Shift: Theoretical and Empirical Foundations of Assistance to Threatened Languages* (Clevedon: Multilingual Matters, 1991), 375.

22 This distinction is advanced as the basis of a general argument for language rights in Denise Réaume, 'The Constitutional Protection of Language: Survival or Security?' in D. Schneiderman, ed., *Language and the State: The Law and Politics of Identity* (Cowansville: Les Éditions Yvon Blais, 1991), 37–58.

23 Leslie Green, 'Are Language Rights Fundamental?' *Osgoode Hall Law Journal* 25 (4) (1987): 669.

24 The former position is espoused in Douglas Sanders, 'Collective Rights,' *Human Rights Quarterly* 13 (3) (1991): 369; the latter, in Vernon Van Dyke, 'Collective Entities and Moral Rights: Problems in Liberal-Democratic Thought,' *Journal of Politics* 44 (1) (1982): 37–40.

25 Van Dyke, 'Collective Entities,' 24.

26 Yoram Dinstein, 'Collective Human Rights of Peoples and Minorities,' *International and Comparative Law Quarterly* 25 (1976): 102.

27 Ibid., 105.

28 M. James Penton, 'Collective versus Individual Rights: The Canadian Tradition and the Charter of Rights and Freedoms,' in William R. McKercher, ed., *The U.S. Bill of Rights and the Canadian Charter of Rights and Freedoms* (Toronto: Ontario Economic Council, 1983), 175. A similar example is discussed in the Quebec context in Henry Milner, 'The Constitution and the Reform of Quebec Education Structure,' *Socialist Studies* 2 (1984): 242–54.

29 Sanders, 'Collective Rights,' 382.

30 Gordon Means, 'Human Rights and the Rights of Ethnic Groups – a Commentary,' *International Studies Notes* 1 (1974): 17.

31 Dinstein, 'Collective Human Rights,' 119.

32 Means, 'Rights of Ethnic Groups,' 17.

33 Van Dyke, 'Collective Entities,' 31–6.

34 Ibid., 34.

35 Cited in Sanders, 'Collective Rights,' 381.
36 Kymlicka, *Liberalism*, 166.
37 Ibid., 166–7.
38 Ibid., 150–1 and Chap. 9.
39 Ibid., 151.
40 Ibid., 151–2.
41 See Lesley A. Jacobs, 'Bridging the Gap Between Individual and Collective Rights with the Idea of Integrity,' *Canadian Journal of Law and Jurisprudence* 4 (2) (1991): 375–86.
42 William E. Conklin, *In Defence of Fundamental Rights* (Alphen aan den Rijn, Netherlands: Sitjhoff and Noordhoff, 1979), 235; Reynaldo F. Macías, 'Language Choice and Human Rights in the United States,' in James E. Alatis and G. Richard Tucker, eds., *Language in Public Life* (Washington, DC: Georgetown University Press, 1979), 89–94.
43 Conklin, *In Defence*, 226.
44 See Macías, 'Language Choice,' 89–94.
45 Joseph Eliot Magnet, 'The Charter's Official Languages Provisions: The Implications of Entrenched Bilingualism,' *Supreme Court Law Review* 4 (1982): 181.
46 Marsha Hanen, 'Taking Language Rights Seriously,' in Stanley G. French, ed., *Confederation: Philosophers Look at Canadian Confederation* (Montreal: Canadian Philosophical Association, 1979), 304.
47 Royal Commission, *Report*, vol. 1, xii–xiii.
48 Jean A. Laponce, *Languages and Their Territories*, Anthony Martin-Sperry trans. (Toronto: University of Toronto Press, 1987), 156.
49 Jean A. Laponce, 'Linguistic Minority Rights in Light of Neurophysical and Geographical Evidence: The Case for Partitions.' Paper presented at the Canadian Political Science Association Meetings, Ottawa, 1982, 20.
50 Ibid., 16.
51 See, e.g., Jacques Henripin, 'Two Solitudes in 2,001?,' *Language and Society* 4 (1981), 15–19. This issue is pursued more fully in Chap. 8.
52 European Court of Human Rights, 'Relating to Certain Aspects of the Laws on the Use of Languages in Education in Belgium' (merits) Series A. *Judgments and Decisions*, vol. 6 (1968) (Judgment of 23 July 1968).

2

The Practice of Language Rights: The Canadian Experience

An alternative theory of language rights can be approached through an examination of the practice in Canada. Richard Flathman emphasized that rights are grounded in the social practices of a community. Extending Flathman's model to language rights, and their implementation in Canada, reveals the makings of social practice in support of language rights.

The following is a sketch of the practice of language rights in Canada. National and regional public opinion polls have been used to determine regularities and conflicts about these rights. The public comments of participants in the public debates are also informative on the issues that these policy questions involve.

Rights as Practice

The analysis of rights as developed by Richard Flathman provides the framework here. The key terms are 'right' and 'practice.' According to Flathman, 'a right provides the agent who holds it with a warrant for taking or refusing to take an action or range of actions that he conceives to be in his interest or otherwise to advantage him. Once accorded or otherwise obtained, what we will call the administration of the right (and hence the acting) is in large measure at the discretion of the person who holds it.'[1] The possession of such 'warrants' imposes obligations on others to respect the "agent's" actions in relation to the warrants. These obligations arise in part because the said others agree on the meaning and implications of the warrants. It is at this point that the concept 'rights' makes contact with the idea 'practice.'

'Practice,' according to Flathman, refers to 'clusters, nodes, or foci of meaningful activity that form more or less distinct aspects of the life of a society or subsocietal social group.'[2] In particular practice is 'the acceptance, by participants in the practice, of rules according to which it is right, obligatory, proper, prudent, or simply expected that they act in certain ways and refrain from certain other actions.'[3]

Rules, in Flathman's perspective, are:

Conduct-guilding [*sic*] devices (1) that presuppose forms of action susceptible of choice and guidance; (2) that are thought to be important; (3) about which criteria of right and wrong, good and bad, wise or unwise have developed and been widely accepted. (4) These criteria have been accepted for reasons that can be stated and that can and do serve as guides to the interpretation and application of the rules to particular cases.[4]

Such rules are not, for the most part, captured in legal texts. They are the working understandings of the participants, their rationales and behaviour in responding to particular claims, and the kinds of criticisms they make of various justifications for various rights. The emphasis is on the *shared* understandings of the participants.

In Western liberal democracies there is a practice of rights expressed in these rules. For example, in order to claim a right to strike and picket, the claimant *A* must understand and invoke a series of rules: (1) the general rule regarding rights in the society, (2) the specific rule regarding the particular claimed right, (3) the rule regarding the application of the general and specific rights to the particular situation in which they are being claimed. As well, in the process, *A* advances the argument that there is such a right as the one claimed (to strike and to picket) and that *A*'s interests or objectives will be served by recognition of this right. These invocations and arguments are subject to dispute by others, and they will be disputed often. These disputes serve in turn to clarify the rules to the participants in the practice and to the observers.[5]

The analyst must elucidate the conventions and unwritten rules governing communication and action within a particular domain. The task, as understood by Flathman, is 'to identify and give a systematic account and assessment of the assumptions, beliefs, ideas, values, expectations, and modes of action that are prominent in the practice as its participants understand it and engage in it.'[6] This enterprise is more a process of clarification of that which is already known or believed, than one of creation or discovery.

To advance a claim for a language right, it would be necessary to show that the right is consistent with the rules governing rights in that society. Is that sufficient to establish the fact that it *is* a right? Apparently not. On Flathman's account, it only establishes the possibility that it *could* be a right, not that it should be or is one.[7]

Flathman's approach has the advantage of an observable referent to substantiate the claim that rights exist, that is, a set of practices, customs, and perhaps legal statutes in a particular society. Concomitantly, however, it succumbs to forms of social relativism that are not entirely consistent with the established concept of a human right. For example, it is entirely consistent with this 'social practice' model that right X (for example, the right to vote or freedom of speech) could be a right in one society and not in another. But this violates the widely accepted understanding of a human right as *universal*. If any one person has a human right, then all persons, in principle at least, have such a right.

In addition, Flathman's model proves unsatisfactory with regard to claims to as-yet-unrecognized rights. To say that a right is not a legitimate right because it is not already recognized as such, is not very useful. Flathman's model does seek some criteria by which to analyse rights, and thus potential candidates for rights, but the drawback is not overcome, because of Flathman's insistence that what makes something a right is its presence in a recognized network of social practices viewed as rights.

This application of Flathman's approach is definitely of the 'garden variety' sort. It eschews, for the most part, the language-games focus that is the basis of its inspiration (deriving from Wittgenstein). Instead, it emphasizes the values, beliefs, and understandings of the participants in the practice of language rights. The topic itself necessitates that this analysis must be preliminary and exploratory, in no small measure because the associated practices are themselves relatively undeveloped and only now in the process of rule formation. Moreover, the same might be said of the general rules regarding rights in Canadian society, which have become a focus of attention only in the past two decades. This is to some extent advantageous, in that the practice is itself the object of substantial dispute, and therefore displays quite explicitly the values and beliefs that are the focus of contention.

Public Opinion on Language Rights

Interest in public attitudes regarding language rights in Canada first emerged with the investigations of the Royal Commission on Bilingualism and Biculturalism in the 1960s (B and B Commission). Since then, attention to public opinion has waxed and waned in conjunction with the outbreak of linguistic controversies at the federal or provincial levels. Analysis of public opinion has focused on responses to these particular events, with the unfortunate result that the findings are only selectively comparable over time. The most important manifestation of this variability has been the absence of any systematic analysis of public perceptions regarding language rights as such. These caveats aside, however, the patterns of opinion are sufficiently consistent to suggest the presence of a continuing practice, or perhaps practices, of language rights in Canada.

One of the studies for the B and B Commission examined English and French Canadian attitudes towards language rights. This material was analysed to determine the reasons for the distributions of opinion, focusing particularly on the attitudes of English and French monolinguals, the people thought most likely to be threatened by policies of official bilingualism and therefore most likely to challenge them. Jonathan Pool found substantial variations in support for official bilingualism depending on the social and political context.[8] Specifically, Pool found that 81 per cent of English monolinguals supported making the federal government accessible to people in both official languages. The level of support dropped to 53 per cent for official bilingualism in all provincial governments. Among French monolinguals, support for these policies was extremely high, remaining at over 97 per cent in both cases.[9]

As these principles are extended into personal and social domains, support plummets dramatically, the closer its application comes to the respondent. A bare majority (51 per cent) of English-speaking monolinguals agreed that individuals working in a company primarily composed of French speakers should themselves learn to speak French, though 64 per cent would accept this principle if it were limited in application to the province of Quebec. Still fewer, 26 per cent, agreed that English speakers should speak French in the province of Quebec, and only 16 per cent supported the notion that private sector services should be available in French. In contrast, French monolinguals extended strong support for the reverse side of these principles, ranging from 72 to 88 per cent agreement.[10]

In attempting to explain the variation in support for bilingual policies, especially among anglophones, Pool ventured the suggestion that 'those who live amidst members of the other language group are more likely to agree with policies benefitting that group than are those living in comparatively segregated environments, since those surrounded by members of the other language group are more likely to have high competence in the other language.'[11] Although such an explanation is highly probable, its invocation here is rather curious given that the variation Pool wished to explain was among English-speaking *monolinguals*. More compelling and potentially significant was his report that *'monolinguals were in general more likely to approve of concessions, the smaller the proportion of the local population that their ethnic group constituted'* (emphasis in original).[12] This suggests that the *size* of the French group in the immediate experience of English-speaking individuals is important to their disposition to recognize the appropriateness of official and informal recognition of the French language and the personal and political obligations thereto. There is a sharp distinction between federal versus provincial level of recognition of bilingualism, and an even more pointed distinction between the public and private sectors.

A 1977 study of public attitudes regarding Canadian national unity reinforced and somewhat extended this analysis. It reported high levels of agreement with the language principles that 'all Canadians should have the right to receive services from their federal government in either English or French' and that 'the provinces should provide opportunities and facilities wherever practicable for education in either the French or English language for those who want it.' The study concluded that this indicates 'a strong commitment of all Canadians to minority language education, and strong support for one of the cornerstones of the federal bilingualism policy, the right of the individual to deal with his government in his own language, be it French or English.'[13] Such support, however, derived from a variety of beliefs and perceptions. The most common was that the policy of official bilingualism was primarily a concession to Quebec in the interests of national unity rather than an expression of fundamental rights.[14]

In addition, the study indicated ambivalence about some of the possible implications of the policy. There was strong agreement that 'English should be the more important or privileged language,' and relatively strong agreement that 'everybody living in Canada should be able to speak English.' On the other hand, there also appeared to be moderate agreement with the proposition that 'everybody living in Quebec should be able to speak French,' though nationwide individual bilingualism was strongly rejected.[15]

These patterns of opinion appeared again in a more recent national poll of attitudes towards language policy. A Canadian Facts survey in the fall of 1985 discovered that 74 per cent of Canadians support federal services in both English and French, 57 per cent support provincial bilingual services, and 53 per cent are in favour of having business services in both English and French. Once again, francophones were significantly more supportive of these policies than were anglophones. Support levels among the former ranged from 72 to 88 per cent; among the latter, 44 to 68 per cent.[16] Within English Canada itself there was substantial regional variation in the responses. In Atlantic Canada, provincial bilingualism was endorsed by 74 per cent of the respondents, while in British Columbia only 36 per cent endorsed the policy.

More strikingly, the 1985 survey revealed a distinction between attitudes regarding support for bilingualism in general versus support for specific applications of it. For example, 57 per cent of B.C. respondents supported minority language schools and 55 per cent hospital services in the minority language.[17] This suggests a respect for meeting the vital needs of minority language members in their own language, while nevertheless rejecting the general principle of official bilingualism for that province. Given the extremely small French-speaking group in British Columbia, this is readily understandable. Nevertheless, the important point remains that specific language services continue to enjoy significant support even in these circumstances.

In explaining the regional variation in attitudes, the Canadian Facts survey pointed to the frequency with which individuals hear the other language spoken as part of their daily life in their own communities, and to the individual's degree of familiarity with the other official language. Only 29 per cent of anglophones outside Quebec who never have contact with the French language approve of department store services in the French language, while 81 per cent of those who have daily contact support them.[18] As with the earlier study for the B and B Commission, this strongly suggests that the perceived legitimacy of minority language demands depends upon the extent to which the minority language is a normal part of everyday life.

A July 1990 national poll reported that 57 per cent of English-speaking people in Canada supported the continuation of bilingual government services at the federal level. Two-thirds supported this policy in a comparison with the alternative of a French unilingual Quebec and English unilingual policy elsewhere. A narrow majority (52 per cent) disapproved of resolutions passed by several municipal governments in Ontario declaring themselves to have English only as their official language.[19] This study demonstrates a consistent pattern of opinion in support of official bilingualism among anglophones in Canada.

Francophone opinion in this study continued to demonstrate a pattern of consistently high levels of support for official bilingualism at the national level, at 88 per cent support, and, like the anglophone group, two-thirds opted for bilingualism in preference to a policy of French unilingualism in Quebec and English unilingualism elsewhere. Within the province of Quebec, francophone opinion was somewhat ambivalent, though still generally supportive of English minority language rights. Francophones were overwhelmingly convinced that the French language needs special protection in Quebec to ensure its survival (94 per cent agreement). Nevertheless, 60 per cent agreed that English should be permitted with French on outdoor signs in Quebec. Moreover, a large majority of francophones were opposed to passage of 'French only' laws for their communities comparable to the 'English only' laws passed in Ontario municipalities.[20] This consistently strong support for bilingual policy in Quebec is remarkable in the context of the political turmoil over language in the past decade.

Canadian Practice(s) of Language Rights

We might query the extent to which these findings represent a body of rules within which a practice of language rights might be at work. The questions posed in these surveys do not generally use the terminology of rights, thus placing significant limits on the interpretation of practice. They do, however, refer to the substance of the rights claims and to some extent the operating rules, and therefore they provide relevant information regarding their initial persuasiveness.

In exploring the extent of shared understandings through survey data, the question immediately arises as to what level of uniformity constitutes substantial agreement. Obviously, anything less than unanimity involves a certain measure of arbitrariness. However, in an area that is highly controversial, such as rights in general, much less language rights, extremely high levels of agreement are virtually impossible. Recognizing this, a working figure of 66 per cent has been adopted as the indicator of substantial agreement. My rationale is simply that a proportion that is accepted as decisive for such important decisions as constitutional revisions in democratic organizations – two-thirds – fits nicely with established political practice.

If this working definition is accepted, the result is a fairly consistent, if limited understanding of the practice of language rights in Canada. Taking the country as a whole, it would appear that there is a shared understanding regarding three particular areas of language rights:

1   Access to *federal* government services in both official languages
2   Entitlement to minority language education for the residents of a province
3   Entitlement to hospital services in the minority language for residents of a province[21]

Each of these elements receives the required two-thirds support nationally and majority support in all regions of the country. The underlying principles elicited in these examples reveal only that they relate to governments rather than to individuals or organizations and, second, that they concern areas of vital interest to the individual. Where the vital interests of the individual are involved, the public appears to recognize the propriety of serving them in a manner that permits the individual to judge the extent of protection to those interests.

This does not translate into a general obligation on all governments to respond to individuals in their own language, as the responses regarding provincial government services attest (57 per cent support). Only two regions, Quebec and Atlantic Canada, demonstrate sufficiently high levels of support for provincial government services to meet the requirement for recognition as language rights. This is somewhat surprising since it is generally conceded that the provincial governments have greater visibility and importance in the daily lives of people. But these are the only two regions where the respective linguistic minority communities are strongly concentrated and sufficiently vibrant to form self-sustaining language communities.

The answer to this puzzle is partly to be found in the noticeably strong regional variation in the extent of agreement to these propositions. The Canadian Facts survey reported its results in the same five regions of Canada – Quebec, Atlantic Canada, Ontario, the Prairies, and British Columbia, as seen in Table 2.1. In relation to the three aspects of language rights, none received the required level of support in all five regions. All three were substantially accepted in Quebec, Ontario, and the Atlantic region. A majority accepted each of them in British Columbia, but none receive the required two-thirds support. In the Prairies, there was substantial agreement solely with respect to minority language schools. Only Quebec and Atlantic Canada indicated substantial agreement that similar entitlements should extend to provincial government services and to services from business.[22]

TABLE 2.1
Regional support for bilingual services[a]

Those Naming English & French for:	Region (%)					
Service	Atlantic Canada	Ontario	Prairies	B.C.	Quebec	CANADA
Federal services	82	71	62	59	88	74
Provincial services	74	55	45	36	72	57
Business services	70	46	37	30	76	53
Minority language education	76	68	72	57	88	74
Hospitals	78	69	56	55	89	71
Post offices	73	54	53	49	85	63
Department stores	62	41	36	29	82	52

[a]Data from Canadian Facts survey reported in *Language and Society* (19 April 1987).

These results indicate that there are several practices of language rights in Canada, corresponding to the different regions. They are virtually non-existent in British Columbia, and quite extensive in Quebec and, to a lesser extent, Atlantic Canada. They obtain their broadest support in Central and Atlantic Canada. This helps explain the apparent discrepancy in responses for the federal and provincial government language services. Only three regions of Canada widely accepted the notion of federal bilingualism, and although they also supported provincial services, it was to a lesser degree and therefore insufficient to create a substantial majority. Regions of the country with substantial numbers and/or percentages of their populations as members of an official language minority supported these language claims. In these areas minority languages form part of the everyday life of the immediately relevant political communities.

On the basis of this fairly demanding standard for defining a practice of rights, there is in Canada, broadly speaking, an accepted practice of a very limited array of language rights. This practice is accepted fully in only some regions of the country but nonetheless, is accepted by a majority in all regions. Moreover, various studies, in emphasizing the relationship between age and attitudes regarding language, routinely emphasize that the supporting group can only grow.[23] Over time, therefore, we might reasonably expect the practice of language rights to be more generally embraced across the country.

An important component of a practice of a right is the kinds of duties and obligations that the members of a community assume in relation to the holders of the right. Despite widespread acceptance of language rights, there is virtually universal rejection of the associated duties that would be attached to individuals and organizations in recognizing these rights. The lowest levels of support for bilingual services in Table 2.1 related to department stores (52 per cent) and business services (53 per cent). These practices would entail extending the duties for provision of such services far more pervasively throughout Canadian society than is the case at present and impinge on many individuals. The prevailing attitude is that the linguistic minority may receive bilingual services so long as these services do not constitute an imposition on the majority community. This attitude is conveyed repeatedly in various surveys and involves a rejection of any individual obligations to accommodate other language groups. This is not the devastating restriction on language rights, that it might seem. As with social rights more generally, the duties attendant to language rights more properly rest with institutions than with individuals. The surveys do, however, provide fresh evidence of the ease with which support for the language rights can disappear if they are viewed as at all burdensome to the supporters.

Public Comment

The survey responses present one picture of public attitudes on questions of language rights. But they tend to be structured in ways that may not reflect the nuances and qualifications accompanying support for these general principles. Thus, it is also of value to look at what people have said in the context of particular disputes, where they themselves were participants. Often these results can be strikingly different. The point was neatly captured by D'Iberville Fortier, commissioner of official languages, who, noting the majority support for the principle of official bilingualism in Canada, tartly observed that 'the base of support for specific manifestations of linguistic equality is about as reliable as ice in springtime.'[24]

In Kapuskasing, Ontario, bitter dispute arose over a municipal bylaw declaring the town to be officially bilingual. One anglophone town councillor who opposed the bylaw argued, 'In the future we see, there will be nobody but a French person who will be hired in any of the jobs, and we don't feel that's right in an English-speaking province.'[25] The comment is all the more intriguing when it is noted that the population of Kapuskasing is 65 per cent francophone – a striking contradiction of the pattern earlier observed between the relative size of the linguistic community and acceptance of bilingual policies for government services. The councillor's comment makes it obvious that access to jobs is a major concern when evaluating the impact that proposals to make a community officially bilingual might have. There was no apparent recognition that the immediate recipients of municipal services, in fact *the majority*, have an entitlement to service in their preferred language. That there is an English-speaking majority in the province of Ontario overall was seen to have substantial bearing on what was perceived to be fair.

Taking a broad look at language rights, the *Globe and Mail* attempted to specify their appropriate domain:

A French-speaking resident in a largely English-speaking community cannot expect by right to be served in the stores in French or to be guaranteed a job where English is not required. But he should be able to expect, in Ontario, to be served in French by the province and in the courts; to be able to have his children educated in French, in a school limited to those who speak French and run by trustees who speak French; and to obtain health care and social services in French.[26]

This editorial did not refer to such services as rights. Nevertheless, it strongly suggested as much when it observed that 'to make French-speaking Canadians fight in other provinces for rights which English-speaking Canadians have long enjoyed in Quebec is to tell them that they are using their language on the sufferance of the government of the day.'[27]

This delimitation referred only to the provincial, and not municipal levels of government. Beyond that, the basis for the distinction between public and private services was not readily apparent. More importantly, the grounds on which that reasonable expectation is founded were only implied, rather than asserted. They rest partly on the implied statement that the use of one's mother tongue is not simply a matter of governmental toleration, but of active support. They may also be based on notions of reciprocity concerning the treatment of the English-speaking minority of Quebec.

It does appear that if language rights are to be considered as rights, they are not fundamental rights. In the series of public hearings sponsored by the Task Force on Canadian Unity, in the 1970s, the public offered diverse views on the appropriate status of language rights in Canada. Francophone minority groups argued for a more expansive understanding of language rights than that included in Section 133 of the Constitution, encompassing education rights and social services, and applying to both levels of government. As one franco-Ontarian maintained, 'We don't want merely to be served in our language; we want to be able to live all aspects of our lives in it.'[28] While the task force found broad acceptance for constitutional entrenchment of some language rights, these were distinguished in the public's mind from 'fundamental' rights.

Apparently, the view of the Human Rights Commission of Prince Edward Island was widely shared:

Language and language-of-education rights should be protected, not because they are 'basic or fundamental human rights' but because they have acquired a 'special and powerful status' in the life of the country, and because they 'may be integral to the existence or survival of a culture, which some citizens may regard as tied to their own identity.' In that context, they would be 'constitutional rights' only.[29]

This quotation is intriguing. The significance of language for culture and identity is recognized, but only as having intermediate significance – important enough to be afforded constitutional protection, though not fundamental. It is recognized that language rights have acquired a powerful status in this country and therefore they deserve public support.

Similar judgments have been voiced elsewhere. In response to a statement by an Ontario MPP that heritage language classes are a 'fundamental right' for non-official language minorities, the Globe and Mail replied, 'Fundamental rights are the sort of thing you find in the Canadian Charter of Rights and Freedoms, and they generally deal with such things as rights of mobility, religious freedom, equality, democratic rights and rights before the law. The rights to language education speak only of English and French.'[30] Accordingly, rights to official (French and English) language minority education are properly designated as fundamental because they are so designated in the Charter. The precise status of the other languages remains unclear. The position taken by the Globe closely resembles that revealed both in the public opinion polls and in other public comments.

In summarizing the results of such public comments, what stands out are the tensions between qualified acceptance of some principles associated with language rights and rejection of their implementation. It is hard to envisage how governments can meet an obligation to provide minority language services without hiring bilingual personnel or even unilingual individuals from both language groups. Yet strong reservations have been expressed about doing so. It would appear that language rights attach to the individual primarily in the role of citizen–consumer of government services and not as worker or neighbour. These limitations suggest sharply delimited parameters to the prevailing practice of language rights in Canada.

More systematic examination of the bases of support for language rights is necessary. Although some observations have emerged from the public opinion polls examined to this point, they are selective and insufficiently developed. One study, however, has addressed support of language rights in considerable detail, and, examined the basis of support for language rights *as rights*.

The Charter Project Study: Explaining Support for Language Rights

The Charter Project was conceived as an analysis of Canadian public opinion on the rights of individuals and communities entrenched in the Canadian Charter of Rights and Freedoms.[31] It presented the rather ambivalent message that although language rights are broadly accepted in Canadian society, support is nevertheless highly volatile and inherently fragile. The study concluded that bilingualism has become a legitimate value throughout the Canadian public, in general, and more so among Canadian political and administrative elites. The francophone public was more supportive of the principle of maintaining two official languages than was the anglophone public. Of francophones 96 per cent considered it very or somewhat important compared with 73 per cent of anglophones. Also noteworthy were the significant differences in assessing its importance; 80 per cent of francophones consider it very important to maintain two official languages, but only 37 per cent of anglophones share this view.[32]

Apparently there was consensus among Canada's elite in support of two official languages at the federal level. Political, legal, and administrative elites all strongly supported the policy. Levels in favour exceeded 80 per cent for all groups except the Progressive Conservative elite at 74 per cent. Even the Parti Québécois elite were strongly supportive (88 per cent) of the federal policy, even though their own party policy diverges significantly from it. The study concluded that the strong support among administrative and legal elites was especially important because, as these are the groups responsible for the interpretation and implementation of policy, it indicates that support for languages rights at the federal level is an established component of official political culture.[33] It is not, however, so strongly endorsed as to constitute a social norm, that is, something that everyone feels obliged to endorse. The high rates of 'somewhat important' responses, even among these administrative (30 per cent) and legal elites (32 per cent), suggest that support, particularly among anglophones, is significantly qualified.

In relation to the specific Charter language rights, the study found majority support in both language communities. Francophones overwhelmingly supported the right to federal government services in their own language for francophones outside Quebec (95 per cent) and anglophones inside Quebec (91 per cent). Anglophones were even more supportive of the right of anglophones in Quebec to federal government services (97 per cent), but significantly less so for francophones outside Quebec (64 per cent).[34] The same pattern emerged, at somewhat lower levels of support, for minority language education rights. Of anglophones 90 per cent supported the right of anglophones to English language instruction in Quebec, but only 53 per cent supported the same right for francophones moving from Quebec to another province. In contrast, 76 per cent of francophones supported the right of anglophones to English language education in Quebec, and 79 per cent supported French language education for francophones outside Quebec.[35] While both groups are more favourable to the rights of their own group, the important points are that in both instances majorities endorse these rights for both groups and substantial majorities of each group claim these rights for themselves. This supports the contention that the Canadian public tends to view these language entitlements *as rights.*

The Charter Project study emphasized two additional features of this support – that it was influenced by the appearance of symmetry across groups in the recognition of language rights and that it was significantly pliable. This pliability is characteristic of both support for and opposition to language rights.

Pliability of political opinion on language rights was examined by exploring how susceptible the respondents expressed views were to counterarguments. The results were instructive. Support for rights to a French language education outside Quebec was reduced by half among anglophones and by one-third among francophones should it involve higher taxes. Support for English language education in Quebec was reduced by half (52 per cent) among francophones and 16 per cent among anglophones should it threaten the majority position of the French language in Quebec.

The same pattern, though less pronounced, appeared regarding opposition to minority language education rights. One-fifth to one-quarter of anglophones and francophones could be talked out of their opposition to minority language rights by offering them indications of the consequences, such as the minority feeling less at home or losing choice of language instruction.[36] Accordingly, support for minority language rights could be increased as well as decreased, depending on specific circumstances and the kinds of values invoked in a particular debate.

One such important circumstance is the reciprocity of respect for language rights. 'A group right ... distinctively blends strategic and normative considerations,' it was suggested, 'We are more willing to grant them a right that we ourselves want and believe we are entitled to exercise, and still more willing if our exercising it is contingent on their possessing an equivalent right.'[37] Support for the language rights of other groups is influenced by their perceived support for your language rights.

Although confirming the continued existence of majority support for the notion of language rights, these findings raise important questions about the bases of languages rights and the strength of public commitment to them. They illustrate the important caveat that such support is neither absolute nor insensitive to other political considerations. It should be emphasized that this hardly distinguishes language rights from other civil or human rights, as is well illustrated by a finding from another dimension of the Charter Project study, namely, support for anti-hate legislation. Initially, three-quarters of the public sample supported laws prohibiting speech or publications that promote hatred against groups; but one-half of this group said they would change their minds if such laws to limited freedom of speech on important public issues. Similarly, over 40 per cent of those opposed to such laws would change their minds if such speech or literature were to increase racial prejudice in our society.[38]

Clearly, support for rights in general is variable. It is simply one of a number of values and priorities individuals apply in making judgments about particular situations. This variability of public support is an important factor to consider in identifying the boundaries of an acceptable practice of language rights. There are some qualifications regarding this analysis of the bases of language rights.

Bases of Language Rights

As a by-product of a larger project, the explicit purpose of which was to examine Charter rights, the Charter Project study focused on two important language rights, the right to *federal* government services and the right to minority language education. This is unfortunate, as these constitute a limited subset of the range of entitlements that some Canadians (to varying degrees) believe *are* language rights – such as the right to health services, to business services, and to provincial government services. Identifying the content of language rights for Canadians and the extent of their support for them is a necessary prerequisite to the explanation of Canadians" attitudes on language rights. Also, the particular rights examined in the Charter study are the *least* controversial of the language rights recognized in Canada, being the ones that are the most widely accepted.[39] Analysis of other language rights would produce greater diversity of responses and perhaps offer more scope for explaining attitude patterns. The study did, however, address two of the three elements central to a practice of language rights in Canada. Moreover, any evidence of ambivalent support for even these language rights is very telling in regard to the whole domain of language rights.

The study asked respondents whether they believed people had a 'basic right' to federal government services and education in the official languages. Respondents were not asked *why* they thought these were basic rights. Thus, the basis of public support for these language rights is unclear – were they accepted as legal rights simply because they are in the Charter, or were they viewed as fundamental rights that therefore *ought* to be entrenched? If viewed as fundamental, why are they so perceived? The study chose instead to investigate the relationship between attitudes towards language rights and attitudes towards civil liberties and egalitarianism.

Only weak relationships were found between support for selected traditional civil liberties (for example, freedom of expression, freedom of association, and the right to avoid self-incrimination) and support for the language rights in question. This implies that language rights have only a tangential relation to conventional notions of rights. However, the Charter Project study reported a stronger relationship with egalitarian values, and this suggests that the right to equality is a more important value base for language rights than is the right to traditional civil liberties. Two factors were identified as being central to understanding patterns of support for language rights in Canada: strategic calculation of interests and core political values (specifically egalitarianism) and support for civil liberties (in general).

The weak relationship between language rights and traditional civil liberties deserves some comment. Support for rights appears to vary significantly between different pairings of rights. The Charter Project found the relationship between support for silence and freedom of expression and association to be dramatically weaker than that between expression and association. Evidently, the right to silence invokes a somewhat different complex of competing values than do the rights to freedom of expression and association. The language rights investigated are quite different, again, from these classic civil liberties and the right to silence, because they are *positive* rights to government services, as opposed to *negative* rights of non-interference by governments. Thus, it is perhaps not surprising that there should be a very weak relationship between support for these civil liberties and acceptance of these language rights.

One curious finding from the Charter Project study is the marginally stronger positive relationship found between language rights and support for silence than between language rights and expression and association.[40] This suggests that language rights involve a different complex of values relevant to rights from those captured by traditional civil liberties. Moreover, it is entirely possible that different rationales might be invoked by Canadians to justify recognition of specific language rights; for example, the rationale for minority education rights may well differ from that for government services in one's own language. In short, the structures of thought that Canadians employ in approaching language rights require more direct examination.

Reciprocity and Strategic Calculation

The concepts of reciprocity and strategic calculation are key in accounting for the Charter Project's findings. It was hypothesized that support for rights for majority and minority groups should vary according to individual calculations of group benefits and losses: 'There is ... a built-in asymmetry to reciprocity in rights. A political minority has a stronger interest in acknowledging that the majority is entitled to a right that it wants itself to exercise than the majority has in acknowledging that a minority is entitled to a right that *it* wants to exercise.'[41] Accordingly, majority and minority groups will differ in their recognition of group rights. The majority group will be more supportive of rights for itself than for the minority, because it has the political power to enforce such a double standard. A minority will tend to support rights for both majority and minority more equally, because that is the only condition under which the minority has any prospect of enjoying the right itself. The hypothesis is simply relational. It specifies a difference in group responses without suggesting any predictions about degree of support in either group. However, the logic of the argument suggests that majority group support for minority rights should be low, and minority group support for majority rights should be high.

This line of argument is open to the criticism that it makes unwarranted assumptions about majority and minority behaviour. It neglects the possibility that the majority may be quite supportive of minority languages, perhaps more so than the minority. Such appears to be the case in Switzerland, for example, where the German-speaking majority is more likely to have a facility in French than the French-speaking minority is to have a facility in German, and cross-language contacts are more likely to be in French. Both these Swiss patterns are the opposite of what occurs in Canada, and they strongly suggest that attitude patterns on linguistic issues are influenced by a wider array of factors than simply relative group size.[42] This is not to say that the behaviour of the German-speaking Swiss is not based on strategic calculation – such might be the case. It does indicate, however, that the conclusions of such strategic calculations can vary for both majority and minority groups.

Because it has featured prominently in the justification for the entrenchment of language rights, strategic calculation is an appropriate choice as an explanatory factor in the Canadian context. Pierre Trudeau, as Prime Minister, justified the policy of official bilingualism primarily on the grounds that Quebec was crucial to Canada's continued existence. Trudeau's appeal, it should be emphasized, invites a strategic calculation along a different dimension (the consequences for national survival) than the dimension emphasized by the Charter Project study (that is, a group's ability to control the decision-making process). These two dimensions point to different conclusions from the strategic calculation.

Acceptance of Trudeau's argument would presumably *increase* majority support for minority language rights, thus reducing the incidence of double standards. But other factors might also be brought to bear in the calculus. For all its obvious centrality, there has been no direct attempt to explore the existence or content of strategic calculation in Canadian attitudes concerning language rights. Instead, the existence of strategic calculation has simply been inferred from the patterns of support for language rights themselves.

The study's evidence was broadly consistent with the hypothesis it presented. Francophones demonstrated much more consistent support for recognition of language rights for both majority and minority groups than did anglophones. However, it is also possible to view these findings as offering challenges to the hypothesis. For instance, if strategic calculation was at work, why was anglophone support so high (greater than 50 per cent in both cases), given that anglophones are the political majority? Such high levels of anglophone support constitute *prima facie* evidence against the kind of strategic calculation that might be expected. The evidence is, however, consistent with a Trudeau-inspired calculation. This observation reinforces the need for direct analysis of the factors in the calculus.

The need for direct analysis becomes even more apparent in the interpretation of francophone attitudes on language rights. In explaining francophone support for language rights, the Charter Project study followed a rather convoluted path to demonstrate that francophones were in fact acting on the basis of strategic calculation. To support this conclusion evidence was cited that francophones are more negative towards immigrants and Jews than are anglophones, and they are more inclined to practise a double standard on mobility rights.[43] In addition, it was emphasized that both anglophones and francophones were inclined to withdraw their support for minority language rights where it conflicts with other values. For anglophones, the threat of a significant increase in taxes was sufficient to reduce support by approximately half. Francophone support for anglophone minority language rights was reduced by half where such rights were perceived to threaten the dominance of the French language in Quebec. Thus, it was concluded that both groups practise a double standard in their support for language rights.[44]

The evidence is open to several criticisms. The evidence for francophone 'double standards' is open to the charge that it is an unfair comparison. In Quebec, immigration and mobility rights are particularly sensitive issues, being related to the problem of protecting the viability of the French language. Accordingly, the perceived costs for francophones in these issues are dramatically higher than they are for anglophones. A balanced comparison of strategic calculation across groups must attempt to control the scope of the costs and benefits in any assessment of similarities and differences.

The design of the sample and the questions of the Charter Project study appear to have precluded the most direct comparison of the two groups. Since francophones represent a majority within Quebec, it would be very interesting to ask them about the right of anglophones to *provincial* government services and compare that with anglophone responses in other provinces. This would produce a more symmetrical relation of the response groups regarding the role of strategic calculation. Decima poll results (reported earlier) concerning support for French-only laws for their communities contradicted the thrust of this argument, as the French majority rejected policies that would presumably benefit them and that they would be able to enforce to their own advantage in that context. Obviously, the content of their calculation is imputed rather than known, but it challenges the strategic calculation hypothesis. In addition, such a strategy raises the question of group identification. With which groups do anglophones and francophones identify – provincial or national? The answers to this question are significant factors in strategic calculation.

The same general criticisms apply to analysis of reciprocity as a core element of support for language rights. Reciprocity, observed the Charter Project Study, 'tends to be a central, if implicit, consideration in judgments about group rights.'[45] Certainly, the proposition has considerable intuitive appeal. However, the key word is 'implicit.' To demonstrate the significance of reciprocity, one would have to show how the observed degrees of support for group rights are related to perceptions of adherence to reciprocal rights by the other group. No such evidence was presented. The strongest evidence in support of their analysis is related to the question of normative consistency as applied to both groups. For example, with regard to mobility rights (the right of individuals to live and work anywhere in Canada) both francophones and anglophones tended to support the use by other groups of principles that they would apply to themselves. When asked if individuals in their own province should have preferential access to jobs within the province, approximately the same percentage of anglophones (52 per cent) endorsed the proposal as endorsed the corollary that residents of other provinces should receive preferential access to jobs in their provinces. On the same comparison, francophones displayed some variation in support (74 per cent for the former versus 63 per cent for the latter), but significant majorities in both cases endorsed both propositions.[46]

Both groups appear to maintain normative consistency – they accept the principle of preferential treatment for local residents both when they themselves are the beneficiaries of and when they are disadvantaged by such preferential treatment. Similarly, majorities of both anglophones and francophones endorse the principle that they should be able to compete for jobs in other provinces on an equal footing with local residents, and vice versa – people from other provinces should be able to do the same in their province. The support levels for the former proposition are higher than for the latter for both groups (93 per cent versus 81 per cent for anglophones; 94 per cent versus 65 per cent for francophones), but in both cases significant majorities were even-handed in applying the principle. This evidence indicates that people were consistent in applying principles to themselves and others, which although presumably an important precondition for reciprocity, does not demonstrate that reciprocity was actually a factor in this process.[47]

The same may be said of the illustrations of the lack of reciprocity. The evidence for the 'built-in asymmetry to reciprocity in rights' is the greater francophone support for language rights in the Charter and, in the Quebec context, 'the propensity of French Canadians to declare that they are entitled to benefits and rights in Quebec that English Canadians in Quebec are not'[48] The study referred to the gap, which appeared in two surveys, in anglophone and francophone opinion over the use of English in advertising in Quebec. When asked whether English should be prohibited in advertising in certain parts of the country, 94 per cent of anglophones, but only 57 per cent of francophones disagreed with such a proposal. This gap expanded in a subsequent survey (which followed the December 1988 Supreme Court decision striking down Quebec's sign laws), wherein 94 per cent of anglophones, but only 30 per cent of francophones agreed that businesses in Quebec should have the right to use whatever languages they wish on signs outside their buildings.[49]

These findings are consistent with the hypothesis that support for rights for majority and minority groups should vary according to individual calculations of group benefits and losses. They do not address the logic at work in francophone opinion. It is, for example, possible that reciprocity is the basis for francophone responses. Francophones may well reason that Quebec is entitled to be as French in its commercial signs as Ontario is English in its signs. If that were the case, then francophones would be maintaining a commitment to symmetry in language practice. Alternatively, francophones might well doubt that advertising falls within the range of language rights and therefore is not something about which one need be reciprocal. More specifically, the option selected by most francophones, that is, that 'a business in Quebec should ... accept that Quebec is basically French and put only French on signs outside its buildings,' is one that does not necessarily involve a rejection of the idea that businesses have a right to post signs in other languages. This would be consistent with the astute observation that 'claims may be made not only as to what French Canadians may do, but also as to what English Canadians may not do; and French Canadians as a whole are ordinarily more likely to rally around the first type than the second.'[50] In short, the illustrations in the Charter Project study are not at all decisive instances of the tendency to asymmetry in the recognition of group language rights.

Finally, the authors of the Charter Project study have presented an intuitively plausible hypothesis to explain support for language rights in Canada. They have not, however, explored their key explanatory variables in sufficient detail to sustain their case. In the process, nevertheless, they have outlined some important avenues for the further examination of these critically important issues. In particular, the conclusions that the readiness to respect language rights is a variable, not a constant; that there is an ongoing asymmetry in respect for group rights; and that political compacts to recognize group rights are necessarily fragile, deserve further examination and constitute an important reminder that the foundations of language rights in Canada remain largely an uncharted terrain.[51]

Conclusion

The primary question addressed here has concerned the existence of a practice of language rights. The answer that emerges is a qualified affirmative, with the attached caveat that a careful distinction must be drawn between the federal and provincial domains. At the national level, there is a reasonably high level of agreement regarding a limited set of entitlements regarding the official languages (English and French). This set includes services from the *federal* government, minority language education, and hospital services. Provincially, substantial regional variation, with Quebec and Atlantic Canada accepting a somewhat more expanded list, and British Columbia accepting none, leads to the conclusion that there are at best highly selective regional *practices* in this context. In fact, the Manitoba–Ontario border constitutes a dividing line between the acceptance of a practice of language rights and its rejection. However, Western Canada extends either plurality or majority support for the various elements of the practice accepted in the rest of the country. Nevertheless, it becomes clear why discussions of language rights invariably produce sharp regional differences in opinion, usually pitting the East against the West. Although the West comes reasonably close to endorsing the currently accepted list of language rights, it is far from supporting an extension of such a list.

In the previous chapter, I outlined a philosophical argument for language rights, and distinguished two broad types of such rights, the right to sustain a language and the right to live one's life in a language. The evidence from the practice of language rights strongly indicates that, for English Canada at least, it extends no further than a right to sustain one's language. Quebec, on the other hand, tends to embrace the latter concept, *for both English and French minorities,* in its support of business services being available in the language of the minority residents of a province. There are obvious qualifications and limitations to this support, as it is significantly at odds with some important provisions of Quebec's Bill 101, which will be examined in detail in a later chapter.

Viewed in terms of a national practice, however, there is a significant disjunction between what a philosophical theory of language rights would support versus that which garners significant support in public opinion. A theory that treats language rights as a fundamental human right is inherently expansive, extending progressively through the various domains of individual life. It invites extension into such areas as the language of work, opportunities for cultural expression, and availability of private sector services in one's language. The existing practice embraces a limited set of language rights, covering government services, hospital services, and minority language education. Even in these areas, support is qualified by the requirement that such services not impinge on the job prospects or economic well-being of the English-speaking majority to any significant degree. The practice of rights is therefore largely immune to expansion, for the practical reason that any expansion would offend the operant qualification.

There is then an ongoing tension between what a theory of language rights as human rights would propose and what the prevailing practice of rights will tolerate. This tension will be explored in the ensuing chapters, as its resolution in the federal, New Brunswick, and Quebec contexts is examined.

Notes

1 Richard Flathman, *The Practice of Rights* (London: Cambridge University Press, 1976), 1.
2 Ibid., 17.
3 Ibid., 14.
4 Ibid., 107.
5 Ibid., 24–5.
6 Ibid., 17.
7 Ibid., 83.
8 Jonathan Pool, 'Mass Opinion on Language Policy: The Case of Canada,' in Joshua A. Fishman, ed., *Advances in Language Planning* (The Hague: Mouton, 1974), 481–92. The B and B Commission study was conducted in 1965, involving a national adult sample with 4,071 completed interview schedules. Unless

otherwise specified, 'official bilingualism' always refers to the English and French languages. My review of these studies, it should be noted, is not exhaustive, though it does include those that have been the focus of academic discussion of these matters.

 9 Ibid., 484–6.

10 Ibid., 484–5.

11 Ibid., 490.

12 Ibid., 491. See Pool's Table 1 for the comparison of responses from English-speaking monolinguals in polling districts where French names represented less than 25 per cent of the electoral lists, compared with responses in districts with greater than 25 per cent French names. Given the high rates of linguistic assimilation outside Quebec, such a measure is of course rather suspect. As well, the small number of responses from those in the second category inspires interpretive restraint.

13 Goldfarb Consultants Ltd., *The Searching Nation* (Toronto: Southam Press, 1977), 89. The document consists of the findings and analysis of a study commissioned by Southam Press.

14 Goldfarb, 78.

15 Ibid., 89–90, S7T23–S7T28. The latter entries are to be deciphered as Section 7, Tables 23–8. They are not paginated. No figures are presented here because the study used an Index of Agreement in its analysis, rather than reporting the percentages of respondents accepting a proposition.

16 Stacy Churchill and Anthony H. Smith, 'The Time Has Come,' *Language and Society* 19 (April 1987): 4–8. The entire issue is devoted to responses to this survey. The major summary tables are presented at the end of the issue. The study itself consisted of a sample of 4,000 Canadians, completed by Canadian Facts for the Commissioner of Official Languages. The francophone category here means Quebec responses. It may well include anglophone responses.

While the regional patterns of support are similar, it is noteworthy that Bibby reported considerably lower levels of support for bilingualism from his 1985 study using a much smaller sample (N = 1,200). Reginald Bibby, 'Bilingualism and Multiculturalism: A National Reading,' in Leo Driedger, ed., *Ethnic Canada: Identities and Inequalities* (Toronto: Copp Clark Pitman, 1987), 60. Unfortunately, Bibby did not report his questions so that systematic comparison of the two sets of responses is not possible.

17 Churchill and Smith, 'The Time Has Come,' 5. See also Tables 2 and 3 in *Language and Society* 19 (April 1987).

18 See Table 4, *Language and Society*, 19 (1987), n.p.

19 The poll was conducted for the *Globe and Mail* and CBC News, during June and July 1990. The sample consisted of 1,595 respondents. An English-speaking

person was defined as someone whose *home language* is English. The results were reported in the *Globe and Mail* (9 Aug. 1990), A4.

20 Reported in a Decima poll conducted in spring 1990, a few months prior to the CBC/*Globe* poll. In response to the question, 'Would you strongly support, support, oppose or strongly oppose the adoption of a French-only law in your community?,' 66.2 per cent of Quebec francophones were opposed or strongly opposed. These data were reported in *Decima Quarterly* 41 (1990), though the particular categories were analysed for me by Robert Burge at the Centre for the Study of Democracy at Queen's University.

21 *Language and Society* 19 (1987), Tables 2 and 3. The support levels are, respectively, 74%, 74%, and 71%. One other item nearly meets the criterion. Of Canadians 63% believe that minority language residents of a province should be entitled to postal services in their own language. The 1965 study analysed by Pool is broadly comparable only on the first item, regarding federal government services. In that instance, support was consistently over 80% in all groups. See Pool, 'Mass Opinion,' 489.

22 *Language and Society* 19 (April 1987), Tables 2 and 3. Unfortunately, these results cannot readily be compared with the Pool study, which examined individual electoral districts. In terms of regions, however, Pool did compare Quebec results with the rest of Canada collectively, and observed the same pattern. The highest levels of acceptance for language entitlements is almost invariably from Quebec – in sharp contrast to the image generated by all the publicity surrounding Bill 101.

23 Stacy Churchill and Anthony Smith concluded that 'a new consensus on matters of language policy is in the making, and the young are on its leading edge,' in 'The Emerging Consensus' *Language and Society* 18 (Sept. 1986), 9. See also Paul M. Sniderman, Joseph F. Fletcher, Peter H. Russell and Philip E. Tatlock, *The Clash of Rights: Liberty, Equality, and Legitimacy in Pluralist Democracy* (New Haven: Yale University Press 1996), Table 7.1B on 196. While they asserted that age does not significantly influence support for official bilingualism, their evidence indicates that 81% of the under 30 group consider it important, while only 69% of those over 30 share that opinion.

24 D'Iberville Fortier, 'Bilingualism and Canadian Values.' Notes for the Falconbridge Lecture delivered by the Commissioner of Official Languages at Laurentian University, Sudbury, 26 Nov. 1985, 11.

25 'Bilingualism Bylaw Splits Kapuskasing,' *Globe and Mail* (30 April 1986), A8.

26 'The Loss of Language,' *Globe and Mail* (5 Dec. 1985), A6.

27 Ibid.

28 Task Force on Canadian Unity, *A Time to Speak: the Views of the Public* (Hull: Minister of Supply and Services, 1979), 21.

29 Ibid., 265.

30 'The Third Language,' *Globe and Mail* (9 March 1987), A6. The treatment of and attitudes towards third languages is highly pertinent to my analysis as well; see Chapter 7.

31 The first published report from the project addressed the language rights entrenched in the Charter, specifically minority language education, mobility rights and rights to *federal* government services. See Paul M. Sniderman, Joseph F. Fletcher, Peter H. Russell, and Philip E. Tetlock, 'Political Culture and the Problem of Double Standards: Mass and Elite Attitudes toward Language Rights in the Canadian Charter of Rights and Freedoms,' *Canadian Journal of Political Science (CJPS)* 22(2), (1989): 259–84. I take issue with their analysis in my, 'Explaining Support for Language Rights: A Comment on "Political Culture and the Problem of Double Standards,"' *CJPS* 23(3), (1990): 531–6. I have drawn freely from this article in what follows. See also the response from Sniderman et al., 'Reply: Strategic Calculation and Political Values – The Dynamics of Language Rights,' *CJPS*, 23(3) (1990): 537–44. Their original article was followed by a book length study of Canadian political values. See Sniderman et al., *Clash of Rights*. My discussion here draws upon both publications, but focuses more on the findings in Chapter 7, 'The Politics of Language and Group Rights' of the book. Their study is based on a 1987 national sample of 2,084 and an elite sample of 1,002.

32 Sniderman et al., *Clash of Rights*, Table 7.1A, 195.

33 Ibid. The data are reported in Figure 7.2, at 201 and their commentary on it, 197–201.

34 These figures are drawn from Sniderman, et al., 'Political Culture,' Table 2 at 267. The results on federal government services were not reported in *Clash of Rights*. See n5 of Chapter 7, at 275.

35 These figures are drawn from Sniderman et al., *Clash of Rights*, Tables 7.3A and B, at 206–7. They also appear in their 'Political Culture,' in Table 3 at 269. In the latter, the support figures reported combine the 'yes' and 'qualified yes' responses, whereas I present only the figures for the 'yes' responses.

36 Ibid., Figures 7.4 and 7.5 at 211, 214 respectively.

37 Ibid., 203.

38 Ibid., 64–9.

39 See Churchill and Smith, 'The Time Has Come,' 4–8, for a discussion of the findings of a 1985 poll on language attitudes in Canada. These two language rights had the highest overall levels of support, at 74% of the national sample.

40 See Sniderman et al., 'Political Culture,' Table 5, at 272. The relationships are reported for anglophones only. Somewhat surprising is the finding in the citizen sample that the relationships are marginally negative between freedom of

association and expression and minority language education, while support for silence is marginally positive. This suggests that the complex of attitudes underlying support for these different rights are imperfectly understood and require more detailed consideration.

41 Sniderman et. al., *Clash of Rights*, 233.

42 The Swiss patterns are discussed in significant detail in Kenneth D. McRae, *Conflict and Compromise in Multilingual Societies: Vol. 1 Switzerland* (Waterloo: Wilfrid Laurier University Press, 1983), Chap. 2. McRae did not report on attitudes on language rights in Switzerland, nevertheless, the behaviour patterns are so different that one would expect a very different set of attitudes as well.

43 Sniderman et al., 'Political Culture,' 275–6.

44 Ibid., 277–8.

45 Sniderman et al., *Clash of Rights*, 225.

46 Ibid.; see Figure 7.9 at 227 and the discussion at 225–8.

47 A majority for both groups endorsed the mobility principle in general (i.e., equal treatment in hiring decisions) and local preference in hiring decisions also; this is a notable inconsistency.

48 Ibid., 233.

49 Ibid Figure 7.10B, 230. This survey was conducted for the Canadian National Election Study of 1988. The statement and its options was as follows: 'A business in Quebec should ... (1) have the right to put whatever language it wants on signs outside a building; (2) accept that Quebec is basically French and put only French on signs outside its building.'

52 Ibid., 230–1.

53 Ibid., 232–4.

3

Legislating National Language Rights in Canada

The right to learn and to use either of the two official languages should be recognized. Without this, we cannot assure every Canadian of an equal opportunity to participate in the political, cultural, economic, and social life of this country.[1]

Pierre Elliott Trudeau

Government legislation, and judicial interpretations thereof, play an essential role in defining the practice of rights in society. In this chapter the evolution of the status of language in the Canadian federal government will be analysed to determine the relationship between public perceptions and the conception of language rights that emerges in government legislation. Federal legislation has progressively extended beyond the limits of the social practice, while the constitutionally entrenched language rights remain firmly within it.

Beginnings to the BNA Act

The history of language rights in Canada is one of gradual evolution from informal custom to constitutional entrenchment. For much of Canadian history, language rights have been based in custom and only indirectly in law. The issue arose in 1763 with the acquisition by England of the French colonies in North America. The use of French in the courts was officially permitted in the territory of Canada by providing francophone juries for disputes among francophones and mixed juries for mixed cases (anglophone versus francophone). The persistence of the French civil law embodied in the Quebec Act of 1774 reinforced this tendency and strongly implied that French could be used in the courts, though this was not explicitly stated.

Similarly, the existing political institutions, specifically the appointive legislative council in Lower Canada, adopted practices accommodating the French language, such as maintaining debates and records, and publishing regulations in both languages. Although English was to be the only language of statutes in the assembly of the newly created Province of Canada in 1840, these restrictions on the use of French were eradicated in 1848, and the equal status of French was effectively affirmed.[2] During the period from 1840 to 1848, French continued to be used in the debates of the assembly and in the courts. To a limited extent, prior to Confederation, governmental institutions established practices of recognizing the legitimacy of the French language for some legislative and judicial activities.

From Confederation to the 1960s, language rights were defined by the provisions of the British North America (BNA) Act. Section 133, the sole provision on language, states:

Either the English or the French Language may be used by any Person in the Debates of the Houses of the Parliament of Canada and of the Houses of the Legislature of Quebec; and both those Languages shall be used in the respective Records and Journals of those Houses; and either of those Languages may be used by any Person or in any Pleading or Process in or issuing from any Court of Canada established under this Act, and in or from all or any of the Courts of Quebec.

The Acts of the Parliament of Canada and of the Legislature of Quebec shall be printed and published in both those Languages.

These provisions had the effect of embedding pre-existing political practices in the constitution, so that they now constituted legal rights. Two features of Section 133 were striking. It accorded public recognition to both the English and French languages, and it imposed a mandatory requirement regarding their use in the records and legislation of the federal Parliament and the Quebec legislatures.[3] In this respect, the languages themselves possessed the rights, rather than individuals or groups.

Section 133 also implicitly asserted an individual right to the choice of either English or French in the legislature and courts through its provision that either language 'may' be used. This right to use either language applied to all Canadians, whether or not they belonged to one of the associated linguistic groups, further emphasizing that it is the languages, rather than the individual members of the groups who speak them, that are accorded rights. For that reason, it is rather wrongheaded to suggest, as does one commentator, that Section 133 represented an early recognition of collective rights in Canada.[4] Nor did it recognize individual language rights because it did not, as the Royal Commission on Bilingualism and Biculturalism noted, 'Guarantee language rights of citizens in their various contacts with the state.'[5]

This last point emerges from a consideration of the variety of government endeavours that were not covered by Section 133. Basically, many areas of both federal and Quebec government administrative activity were untouched by this section – the development and implementation of by-laws and regulations by administrative tribunals being an important case in point. More generally, there were no constitutional requirements governing the provision of services at any level of government, from federal to municipal. The status of the languages in the courts was far from clear, in relation both to their scope (were they to encompass bodies exercising quasi-judicial authority, such as the Tax Appeal Board?) and to their language of operation. More important, although individuals might be entitled to present their cases in their mother tongue, there was no apparent obligation on institutions to respond in the same language.[6] Individuals were entitled to the assistance of an interpreter under federal law, however, the judge decided whether it was actually required. If required, the government assumed the cost of such services in criminal cases, but not in civil ones.[7] A 1986 Supreme Court decision indicated that although individuals may speak either French or English in the courts, this did not create a duty on the court to either understand or respond in that language.[8] On balance, the notion of language rights was at most nascent in these practices, and qualified by numerous restrictions as to their use.

During the debates on the adoption of the Confederation proposal, French-Canadian representatives objected to the use of the word 'may' in Section 133, arguing that it was merely permissive and not mandatory, and thus did not create any obligations on the state regarding the use of French in Parliament and the courts.[9] Their objections were apparently intentionally ignored, because the mandatory 'shall' was added for the journals and records, but no changes were made to meet their other concerns. Not surprisingly, the federal Parliament conducted its business as a unilingual English institution until simultaneous translation was adopted in 1958.

Nevertheless, over the years, a number of practices were adopted by Parliament to accommodate the two principal languages. In accordance with the Standing Orders of Parliament, the language in which the prayers are read at the beginning of each daily session alternate daily between English and French, subject to the linguistic capabilities of the Speaker; further, the Deputy Speaker must possess a fluent knowledge of the official language that is not that of the Speaker. The latter practice ensured that each Member of Parliament would at least be understood by the official object of their communications, the Speaker. Similarly, the practice of reading each duly seconded motion aloud in both languages ensured that each Member of Parliament would at least understand what he or she was voting on, even if not a word of the accompanying debate had been understood. These examples illustrate some of the ways in which the voluntary practices of Parliament extended considerably beyond the minimal requirements of Section 133.[10]

In relation to the provision of services to the Canadian public, the federal government addressed the matter by way of piecemeal reform. In 1934 the House of Commons passed a bill establishing a translation service for the federal government, as 'the first practical example of the need to ensure that federal institutions spoke to all Canadians in both official languages.'[11] A more substantial reform occurred in 1938 with the 'Lacroix amendment,' whereby the federal government adopted the administrative policy that an individual must be able to speak the language of the majority of the government's clientele in the area of the appointment before said individual may be hired. This reform followed in the wake of an uproar stemming from the dispatch of unilingual anglophone labour conciliators to Quebec to settle a labour dispute among francophones.[12] Although it was largely ignored, the Lacroix amendment was the first official recognition of the need for both languages in the provision of government services. Bilingual stamps and bilingual cheques were eventually introduced in the 1960s. Each of these changes were ad hoc amendments that did not constitute a framework for the development of a system of language rights.

Furthermore, subject to the specific provisions of Section 133, jurisdiction over language matters occupied a 'constitutional vacuum,' that left both Parliament and the provinces free to enact language legislation within their respective spheres of jurisdiction, largely unhampered by any specific language rights possessed by Canadian citizens overall.[13] For these reasons the B and B Commission concluded, 'The section [133] is not intended to secure fully the linguistic rights of the French-speaking or English-speaking minorities in Canada. At best it represents embryonic concepts of cultural equality, and it cannot be expected to provide for the many complex situations that must now be faced.'[14] Such language rights as did exist were 'generally based on custom, practical considerations, political expediency, or result from the exercise of incidental jurisdiction.'[15] Thus, the sole explicit provision concerning language in the BNA Act was an extremely modest foundation for a regime of language rights.

Denominational Schools and Language Rights in Education

The other linguistically relevant section of the BNA Act was its treatment of denominational schools. Section 93 of the act provided that provinces were prohibited from passing laws that would 'prejudicially affect' the rights and privileges of previously established denominational schools. This section secured the existence of certain types of schools, that is, *religious* schools, and was not particularly directed at schools aimed at the preservation of a particular language or culture. In the province of Quebec, at least, this point hardly mattered. There it was widely understood, especially by the French-speaking community, that language, culture, religion, and education were intrinsically related. Since there was a strong relationship between religious denomination and language at the time, this right to denominational schools indirectly supported a right to education in one's mother tongue. The Manitoba Schools Crisis, however, quickly demonstrated the inadequacy of Section 93 in the protection of denominational schools, let alone minority language educational rights.

In 1890 the Manitoba legislature passed a law establishing a non-sectarian school system and specified that only those schools conforming to its standards would receive public funding. One of those standards involved a substantial reduction in the amount of time devoted to religious instruction during school hours. The regulations struck at the very heart of the Roman Catholic schools, which had always assigned high priority in their curriculum to religious indoctrination. Since the Roman Catholic schools were unwilling to accept such a limitation, they would be deprived of public funding, while still being taxed to support the non-sectarian system. The French-Canadian minority in Manitoba challenged this act in the courts, on the ground that it prejudicially affected the status of their denominational schools. The courts ended up supporting the position that the imposition of such additional financial burdens did not infringe on the educational rights of the group.[16] The case demonstrated just how limited was the protection offered denominational schools by Section 93 of the BNA Act.

Section 93 offered even less protection to language rights in education.

In 1917 an Ontario court (in *Ottawa Separate Schools* v. *MacKell*, 1917, A.C. 62) ruled that the language in the BNA Act conferred educational rights on religious denominations and not on linguistic or ethnic groups.[17] The same point would be reiterated more than sixty years later when the Protestant School Board of Montreal challenged Quebec's Bill 101.[18] In short, the informal recognition of language rights in education had clearly ceased to be operative.

What little linguistic protection that Section 93 did offer would be supplanted in 1982 by the substantial entitlements entrenched in Section 23, the minority official language education rights clause, of the Canadian Charter of Rights and Freedoms. However, the question of denominational schools would ultimately return to the political agenda in the 1990s – in a very different context. In an increasingly secular society, non-denominational public schools have become the rule rather than the exception in the public school system. In the few provinces where the denominational school system is still prominent, it is now subject to overwhelming pressures for abolition on the grounds that it is inefficient and too costly. Newfoundland held a referendum in September 1995, in which a modest majority voted to abolish its denominational school system. The federal government then passed a constitutional amendment resolution to exempt Newfoundland from the requirements of Section 93.

The Quebec government has submitted a similar resolution to the federal government. In addition, the Quebec government has drafted a legislative bill (Bill 109) to replace the denominational school system in Quebec with a linguistically based system.[19] This has predictably created an intense debate centred about eligibility for the English language system.

There has been broad support in principle for a linguistically based school system in Quebec for some time, so that itself is not the issue. Neither is it a question of language rights per se. In his statement to the House of Commons in support of the constitutional amendment, the Honorable Stéphane Dion, federal Minister of Intergovernmental Affairs, emphasized that, 'Section 93 guarantees only the existence of denominational administrative structures in Montreal and Quebec City ... but it does not protect language rights.'[20] The issue is primarily one of community membership, or more specifically, of who is to be considered a member of the English-speaking community of Quebec for purposes of participating in its school system. This clearly illustrates that language rights have ceased to be relevant to the debates on denominational schools.

Legislating Language Rights

With the advent of nationalist stirrings in Quebec, the federal government made a commitment to develop a comprehensive language policy. It struck a royal commission to examine the language question and to propose appropriate policies to redress perceived problems. The B and B Commission proposed 'a new concept of an officially bilingual country in which the two official languages will have new rights and better guarantees.' Official bilingualism was proposed as a policy that 'evolves from the sum of the rights expressly guaranteed to English and French by laws protecting their use.'[21]

The underlying principle was that of an 'equal partnership' between the English and French language communities. As a concept, 'equal partnership' had several dimensions. One of those was a commitment to language rights for both English and French speakers throughout Canada, so that each would be able to use their respective language in dealing with the state. Another dimension sought a more equitable balancing of the costs and benefits of Canadian political life for the two language groups, which required greater political autonomy for Quebec. This latter element was given a generally hostile reception outside Quebec and was never adequately developed, with the result that 'equal partnership' disappeared from the debate over official bilingualism.[22]

In justifying its proposals, the B and B Commission indicated that the basis for the privileged position of English and French rested not on their historical claims, but rather on their existence as complete societies (or nearly so) within Canada, meaning that most Canadians were able to live their lives within these language communities.[23] This general approach is consistent with the framework of language rights discussed earlier, a framework which emphasized the grounding of such rights in an ongoing linguistic community. However, the commission's explanation opened an avenue for criticism of the principle, because the proposition was progressively less true for francophone communities the further one travelled from the borders of Quebec. Recognizing this difficulty, the B and B Commission emphasized that the principle of equality itself was an essential grounding for these rights. Addressing the claims of francophone minorities outside the 'bilingual belt,' the commission averred, 'We believe that these French-speaking minorities have indisputable rights by virtue of the principle of equality, and that provinces consequently have certain immediate obligations to them.'[24] Thus, the feasibility of provision of the services associated with language rights was the sole question to be determined.

In developing its policy recommendations, the B and B Commission addressed this issue of feasibility in relation to the territoriality versus the personality principles. The principle of territoriality requires that language rights be recognized on the basis of territorial boundaries. Government services were to be available in the language of the majority of the people in the given territory. That would mean that in Quebec, government services would be French; in Manitoba, in English. The personality principle, on the other hand, recognizes an individual entitlement to government services in one's official language, independent of the territory in which one resides.[25]

Taking as its guiding principle the equal partnership of the two linguistic communities, the B and B Commission rejected the territorial approach, arguing, 'It would deprive minority groups *en bloc* ... of essential language rights.' The general goal was to ensure that 'wherever similar conditions are found similar services will be offered.'[26] The 'bottom line' was feasibility. So long as there were sufficient numbers of people to warrant the service, then it was imperative that it be provided. On this basis, the commission urged those provinces that had substantial official language minorities (New Brunswick, Ontario, and Quebec) to become officially bilingual and the remainder to commit themselves to the provision of bilingual services as they deemed appropriate. It is noteworthy that the commission insisted that, in provinces with an English-speaking majority, such as Ontario and New Brunswick government services must be available in English even in those parts of the province with a large French majority (and vice versa for Quebec). Thus, the commission maintained, the majority language must be available everywhere and the minority language where feasible.[27]

In its analysis of the conditions necessary for equality for the two language communities in Canada, the B and B Commission strongly emphasized the importance of education in one's own language. 'The school,' it insisted, 'is the basic agency for maintaining language and culture, and without this essential resource neither can remain strong.' Accordingly, the commission recommended that 'the right of Canadian parents to have their children educated in the official language of their choice be recognized in the educational systems.'[28]

Any comprehensive system of language rights must include the basic right to an education in one's own language. However, the question arises whether there is a right to a *choice* of language of instruction. This formulation poses the curious prospect that English-speaking British Columbians could assert a right to a French-language education. Since the basis for this right is the entitlement to preserve one's traditional language, the right should be more properly understood as an *option* right for the members of the official language communities, that is, the opportunity should be available to receive an education in one's mother tongue. It is not a right to receive an education in the official language that is not one's mother tongue. Typically minority language community members may at their discretion choose the other language school system. This is precisely what some anglophone Quebeckers have chosen for their children and, similarly, what many francophones outside Quebec have done. Although they may choose to participate in the other language school system, their right to do so does not flow from their language rights. All the same, governments may well choose to encourage second language education for reasons of national policy.

Official Languages Act (1969)

The major recommendations of the B and B Commission for federal language policy were embodied in the Official Languages Act (OLA) of 1969. Section 2 of the OLA (1969) declared that English and French are the official languages of Canada and 'possess and enjoy equality of status and equal rights and privileges as to their use in all the institutions of the Parliament and Government of Canada.'[29] With this section, the government recognized a duty to provide services in both official languages where numbers warrant and in head offices of the federal government. In conjunction with Section 2, the federal government made a commitment to increase opportunities for individuals to work in the French language in the federal government and to increase the percentage of francophones in the ranks of the federal public service to achieve equitable participation. It also attempted to develop, with provincial agreement, a plan for the provision of government services in both official languages in designated bilingual districts across the country.[30]

Strictly speaking, it would be more correct to say that the set of language entitlements, rather than language *rights*, expanded dramatically in the federal domain, as citizens did not explicitly have a *right* to these language services. This characteristic highlights a certain continuity from the BNA Act to the OLA (1969), in that the associated language rights are not readily claimable by individuals or groups. In fairness, it should be emphasized that the federal language policy was self-consciously limited to areas of federal jurisdiction and that the government ultimately sought to entrench a more comprehensive set of language rights, binding on both levels of government, in the Constitution itself.[31]

In terms of justifying these policy innovations, the federal rationale was based not on any theory of language rights, but on grounds involving principles of equality, pragmatism, and considerations of national unity. Three years before the passage of the legislation, Prime Minister Lester B. Pearson justified the introduction of bilingualism in the public service as 'part of its fundamental objective of promoting and strengthening national unity on the basis of the equality of rights and opportunities for both English speaking and French speaking Canadians.'[32] This statement makes clear that the justification for language rights is 'goal based' rather than 'rights based.'[33] Specifically, language rights were treated as instrumental to the broader end of national unity. This goal was to be achieved by making the federal government more accessible to French-speaking Canadians, by enabling them to 'have a fair and equal opportunity to participate in the national administration and to identify themselves with, and feel at home in, their own national capital.'[34] Pearson's successor, Prime Minister Pierre Trudeau, implicitly invoked a similar rationale for federal language policy when he stated, 'We are dealing with straightforward political and social realities ... If only because of sheer force of numbers, either group has the power to destroy the unity of this country. Those are the facts ... These facts leave Canada with only one choice, only one realistic policy: to guarantee the language rights of both linguistic communities.'[35]

However, in explaining why failure to respect language rights was so disruptive, Trudeau graphically illustrated the importance of language rights for the *individual* (and sketched a compelling groundwork for a regime of language rights) when he remarked, 'but that is exactly why limiting a person's use of his language can cause in him such a trauma, because you are interfering with something almost as basic as breathing.'[36] This does not lead Trudeau, however, to formulate a case for individual rights to language.[37] Trudeau's rationale for language rights was obviously restricted to the Canadian federal context. If we were to apply Trudeau's line of reasoning to the Quebec provincial scene, where the anglophone population constitutes but a small portion of the electorate, we would conclude that there is no basis for recognizing language rights for the English-speaking community there.

Four years later (1977), in the wake of considerable anglophone hostility to its language legislation, the federal government issued a statement of its rationale and principles for Canada's official language policy. It maintained that French and English were the official languages of the country and were to enjoy equality of status in the various activities of the federal government. In general, the government recognized a responsibility on the part of both federal and provincial governments to preserve the linguistic heritage of the country. It echoed Prime Minister Trudeau's basic rationale in asserting that 'Canada cannot continue to exist as a single country unless the English and French languages are accepted and recognized as the official languages of the country.'[38] It further echoed Trudeau in its use of oxygen as a metaphor for the significance of language to the individual, when it stated, 'It is a structure and an environment, like the air we breathe. When it is healthy we don't notice it. When it deteriorates, we are all affected by it.'[39] Despite this richly suggestive metaphor, the document did not expand upon a normative rationale for recognition of language rights.

The conclusion to be drawn from these various statements on federal language policy is that language rights were conceived and justified primarily in terms of *political necessity*.[40] They were *not* justified in terms of civil or political rights. Instead, they were inspired by a commitment to accord French language speakers, where feasible, the same opportunities to use their language in interaction with federal government institutions as were universally enjoyed across Canada by English speakers. The precise status of these opportunities received remarkably little attention. Meanwhile, the powerful metaphors invoked suggested the paramount importance of language to the individual, inviting comparison with conventional human rights. A distinct ambiguity has thus existed in the official discourse of language rights in Canada.

Task Force on Canadian Unity

If the federal language policy was supposed to resolve the national unity issue in Canada, its short-term effects were notably modest – if not counterproductive. Language issues were strikingly intense during the 1970s, both federally and within the province of Quebec. Nationally, negative public reaction to federal implementation of the language legislation gave the government pause for thought. Anglophones were angered by the rapid expansion of bilingual positions, while francophones were disappointed by the lack of progress in making French a language of work in the federal administration. This was exacerbated by 'Les Gens de L'Air' controversy, wherein the federal government, pressured by anglophone air pilots with significant support in English Canada, rescinded the decision of the transportation agency permitting the use of French in cockpit/control tower communications – much to the chagrin of Québécois.[41] In Quebec, the development of language legislation assigning priority to the French language was a standing contradiction to the federal policy and was greeted with consternation in much of English Canada.

In response, the federal government struck a task force to advise it on further policy initiatives required to reinforce national unity. Although its principal focus was on the place of Quebec in Canadian federalism, it nevertheless devoted significant attention to the language question (See Table 3.1). In 1979 the Task Force on Canadian Unity recommended entrenchment of the principle of equality of rights and status for the two official languages in the federal government. This would include rights to federal government services and to radio and television services in both official languages, and their equal status as languages of work within the federal administration. At the provincial level, the task force urged initiatives for extending the recognition of language rights to minority official language education, essential health and social services.

Rights to education in either official language were supported for citizens of both official language groups. The task force report stated, 'We firmly believe that children of all Canadian citizens who move to another province should continue to have access to educational services in the language, be it French or English, in which they would have obtained them in their former province of residence.'[42] In regard to Quebec, a distinction was made between English-speaking Canadian citizens and English-speaking immigrants. The former would have access to English language education in Quebec; the latter would not. The argument offered in support of the distinction focused on its utility for national unity, specifically a concern to avoid interfering with Quebec's efforts to assimilate immigrants to the French language, and it was, therefore, consistent with the official rationale for national language policy.[43]

The task force's proposals simultaneously broadened and diluted the concept of language rights. They offered a considerable expansion of the language rights recognized to that point, especially in regard to essential health and social services and access to radio and television services.[44] At the same time, their careful distinctions among legislative jurisdictions and resultant entitlements raised challenges concerning the status of such rights.

The right to government services in either official language is a case in point. The task force report proposed to entrench such rights in the

TABLE 3.1
Task Force on Canadian Unity Language Proposals[a]

---

1   The principle of the equality of status, rights and privileges of the English and French languages for all purposes declared by the Parliament of Canada, within its sphere of jurisdiction, should be entrenched in the constitution.

These purposes should include:

i   The equality of both official languages in the Parliament of Canada;
ii   the right of members of the public to obtain services from and communicate with the head offices of every department, agency or Crown corporation of the Government of Canada, the central administration in the National Capital Region, and all federal courts in Canada in either of the official languages. Elsewhere, members of the public should be able to obtain services from and communicate with the central administration in both official languages where there is significant demand, and to the extent that it is feasible to provide such services;
iii   the equality of both official languages as languages of work in the central administration in the National Capital Region, in all federal courts, and in the head offices of every department, agency or Crown corporation of the Government of Canada. Elsewhere, the usual language or languages of work in central institutions should be the language or languages of work normally used in the province in which the central institution is operating. This recommendation is subject to the previous recommendation concerning the languages of service;
iv   the right of any person to give evidence in the official language of his or her choice in any criminal matter;
v   the right of every person to have access to radio and television services in both the French and the English languages;
vi   the availability in both official languages of all printed material intended for general public use.

2   Each provincial legislature should have the right to determine an official language or official languages for that province, within its sphere of jurisdiction.

3   Linguistic rights should be expressed in provincial statutes, which could include:

i   the entitlement recognized in the statement of the provincial first ministers at Montreal in February 1978: 'Each child of a French-speaking or English-speaking minority is entitled to an education in his or her language in the primary or secondary schools in each province, wherever numbers warrant.' This right should also be accorded to children of either minority who change their province of residence.
ii   the right of every person to receive essential health and social services in his or her principal language, be it French or English, wherever numbers warrant.
iii   the right of an accused in a criminal trial to be tried in his or her principal language, be it French or English, wherever it is feasible.

4   Should all provinces agree on these or any other linguistic rights, these rights should then be entrenched in the constitution.

TABLE 3.1
(*Concluded*)

5   The provinces should review existing methods and procedures for the teaching and learning of both French and English and make greater efforts to improve the availability and quality of instruction in these languages at all levels of education.

73 The entrenched collective rights should include the language rights listed in recommendations 1, 2, and 4 and the right of Parliament and provincial legislatures to adopt special measures to benefit native peoples.

[a]Task Force on Canadian Unity, *A Future Together*, (Otttawa: Minister of Supply and Services 1979) 121–2, 132. The numbers are those of the recommendation in Chapter 9 of the document.

federal government wherever there was significant demand. However, the suggested linguistic rights within the provincial sphere were limited to education, criminal trials, and health and social services. These were described as 'basic rights,' strongly suggesting that rights to government services in one's language were of lesser importance.[45] Although the proposed list represented critical components of a commitment to language rights, the omission of broad government services was a striking inconsistency. How could one maintain that a francophone in New Brunswick is entitled to French language services from the federal government, but not equally entitled to such services from the provincial government? Any rights-based case for the former would surely apply with equal force to the latter.

Obviously, a New Brunswick example is more intuitively compelling than an Alberta one, where the tiny francophone minority would presumably fail to meet a minimum size requirement. This underscores the point that a constitutionally entrenched language right to provincial government services would likely have very selective impact, since most provinces would be more like Alberta than like New Brunswick. Nevertheless, a statement indicating the circumstances under which provinces ought to acknowledge rights to provincial services in either official language would have been in keeping with the principle stated. On the other hand, the task force viewed these elements as sufficiently important to individuals to merit recognition. Beyond that, its proposals regarding provinces echoed the national practice of language rights accepted by Canadians, as identified in Chapter 2.

This does not mean that the task force was indisposed to constitutionally entrenched language rights for provincial linguistic minorities. On the contrary, the task force emphasized its goal of stimulating the development of a social consensus on language rights *prior* to their entrenchment in a constitution. It judged that 'French-speaking minorities will make more headway as a result of social consensus and provincial legislation than they would from constitutional guarantees at this time.'[46] Beyond that, the central issue for the task force was not language rights, but national unity. These proposals are best understood as an accommodation of linguistic sensitivities in Quebec and, to a lesser extent, the other provinces. Within this context, the task force report was politically judicious in balancing the recognition of language rights and the acceptance of such rights in the various political constituencies across Canada. Although it recognized a short list of language rights as 'basic rights,' it ultimately opted for an approach that encouraged their evolution through the practices of Canadian politics.

Entrenching Language Rights in the Charter of Rights and Freedoms

In 1982 a major constitutional reform initiative culminated in the introduction of the Canadian Charter of Rights and Freedoms, a controversial document that has galvanized debates that still rage over the role of constitutionally entrenched rights in Canadian society. Although the language rights sections of the Charter were a secondary matter of attention at the time – at least in English Canada – there are some indications that they were a principal impetus in the entire initiative. In 1980 Prime Minister Trudeau explained the need for the Charter to a Quebec City audience as a political necessity to enable the government to entrench a set of language rights. The Charter thus functioned as a 'Trojan horse' to English Canadians to make them accept language provisions deemed necessary for Trudeau's design for national unity.[47]

The language provisions of the Canadian Charter of Rights and Freedoms considerably expanded the scope of language rights (see Table 3.2). In the Charter, English and French were recognized as the official languages of Canada and accorded equal rights and privileges in all the institutions of the federal government and the provincial government of New Brunswick, as well as in the courts of each entity. The Charter also recognized *individual* rights to the use of *either* official language, but on an expanded basis. It included the right to receive available government services from head offices of the federal government and other offices where there was 'significant demand.' This was an individual right of all Canadians, only indirectly linked to the existence of linguistic groups.

However, it expressed the same limitation noted in the task force recommendations in that it applied to only one provincial government. Obviously, this reflected the lack of consensus among the provinces for such commitments and the constitutional fact that the provinces would control the administration of such rights.

Not all Charter language rights took the form of individual rights. An exception occured in Section 23, in relation to minority language educational rights, where the specified right may be claimed only by those Canadian citizens whose mother tongue is that of the official linguistic minority of the province of residence, or where their children already have such access (subject to the precondition of sufficient demand). In this case, group membership is significant in at least three ways: the claimant must have membership, first, in an official linguistic group; second, in an official *minority*; and, finally, in a group sufficiently large to warrant the service in the first place, that is, a functioning community.

The group character was reinforced by a further distinction between minorities in Quebec versus those in the rest of the country. Outside Quebec, the only requirement concerned mother-tongue language; inside Quebec, there was a further requirement that one had received one's primary school instruction in Canada in English or French.[48] Thus, individuals in similar circumstances possessed different rights depending on their geographic location. Once again the special features of a group (in this case long-standing residents versus immigrants) determined the possession of such rights. Strictly speaking, these were the only groups who had constitutionally entrenched rights to an education in a particular language. However, these groups were simply categoric in that they did not involve organization or activity by the members. The group, as such, did not control or determine the availability or exercise of these rights. In practical terms, Section 23 of the Charter simply ensured that all Canadian citizens would have access to education in their (English or French) mother tongue throughout the country, where numbers warrant.

On balance the character of these language rights was best captured by Patrick Monahan's assessment when he asserted,

Language freedom, as defined by ss. 16 to 23, is neither wholly individualist nor wholly communitarian. Instead, a complex and symbiotic relationship between individual autonomy and community values is posited. Community is both a prerequisite for individual freedom and a corollary of it. The complex and delicate linkage between individual and community is reflected most clearly in those pro-

TABLE 3.2
Canadian Charter of Rights and Freedoms[a]

Language Clauses

16(1) English and French are the official languages of Canada and have equality of status and equal rights and privileges as to their use in all institutions of the Parliament and government of Canada.

(2) English and French are the official languages of New Brunswick and have equality of status and equal rights and privileges as to their use in all institutions of the legislature and government of New Brunswick.

(3) Nothing in this Charter limits the authority of Parliament or a legislature to advance the equality of status or use of English and French.

17(1) Everyone has the right to use English or French in any debates and other proceedings of Parliament.

(2) Everyone has the right to use English or French in any debates and other proceedings of the legislature of New Brunswick.

18(1) The statutes, records and journals of Parliament shall be printed and published in English and French and both language versions are equally authoritative.

(2) The statutes, records and journals of the legislature of New Brunswick shall be printed and published in English and French and both language versions are equally authoritative.

19(1) Either English or French may be used by any person in, or in any pleading in or process issuing from, any court established by Parliament.

(2) Either English or French may be used by any person in, or in any pleading in or process issuing from, any court of New Brunswick.

20(1) Any member of the public in Canada has the right to communicate with, and to receive available services from, any head or central office of an institution of the Parliament or government of Canada in English or French, and has the same right with respect to any other office of any such institution where

(a) there is significant demand for communications with and services from that office in such language; or

(b) due to the nature of the office, it is reasonable that communications with and services from that office be available in both English and French.

(2) Any member of the public in New Brunswick has the right to communicate with, and to receive available services from, any office of an institution of the legislature of New Brunswick in English or French.

21 Nothing in sections 16 to 20 abrogates or derogates from any right, privilege or obligation with respect to the English and French languages, or either of them, that exists or is continued by virtue of any other provision of the Constitution of Canada.

22 Nothing in sections 16 to 20 abrogates or derogates from any legal or customary right or privilege acquired or enjoyed either before or after the coming into force of this Charter with respect to any language that is not English or French.

23(1) Citizens of Canada

(a) whose first language learned and still understood is that of the English or French linguistic minority population of the province in which they reside, or

(b) who have received their primary school instruction in Canada in English or French and reside in a province where the language in which they received that

TABLE 3.2
(*Concluded*)

Language Clauses

instruction is the language of the English or French linguistic minority population of the province, have the right to have their children receive primary and secondary school instruction in that language in that province.

(2) Citizens of Canada of whom any child has received or is receiving primary or secondary school instruction in English or French in Canada, have the right to have all their children receive primary or secondary school instruction in the same language.

(3) The right of citizens of Canada under subsections (1) and (2) to have their children receive primary and secondary school instruction in the language of the English or French linguistic minority population of a province

   (a) applies wherever in the province the number of children of citizens who have such a right is sufficient to warrant the provision to them out of public funds of minority language instruction; and

   (b) includes, where the number of those children so warrants, the right to have them receive that instruction in minority language educational facilities provided out of public funds.

59(1) Paragraph 23(1)(a) shall come into force in respect of Quebec on a day to be fixed by proclamation issued by the Queen or the Governor General under the Great Seal of Canada.

   (2) A proclamation under subsection (1) shall be issued only where authorized by the legislative assembly or government of Quebec.

[a]Constitution Act, 1982, enacted by the Canada Act, 1982 (U.K.), c.11, Schedule B.

visions which make the exercise of individual rights expressly contingent on the presence of community.'[49]

When examined with regard to its language provisions (see Table 3.2, Sections 16–23), Canada's Charter of Rights and Freedoms clearly reflects the then-existing national agreement on the practice of language rights. As was evidenced in the previous chapter, a national acceptance has evolved of three components of language rights: federal government services in both official languages, minority language education, and health and social services. The Charter embraced the first two components, but not the third. In relation to government services, it recognized language rights where they were already legislatively acknowledged, federally and in New Brunswick. They were, however, extended by virtue of their new form as *constitutional rights*, and by their *individual* character. Second, the right to minority language education established a right that previously existed only as a series of federal–provincial agreements on funding minority language education. However, a consensus had already been achieved by the provinces in support of minority language education in the St Andrews meetings in 1978. In this respect, this constitutional provision also mirrored emerging practice in Canadian society. Nevertheless, the entrenchment of the minority's right to education in its own language enabled official language minority groups to make use of constitutional support to advance their claims. In terms of the survival of official language minority groups throughout Canada, this was probably the most important innovation of the Charter.

Thus, the language provisions in the Charter were an organic outgrowth both of prevailing public attitudes and political consensus that reflected the existing practice of language rights in Canada.

Bill C-72 (1987)

The Task Force on Canadian Unity had proposed that language of work should form part of the entrenched language rights. The Charter, however, did not address that domain. In addition, the existing constitutional provisions regarding the language of the courts proved highly controversial. The courts had tended to apply restrictive interpretations of the right to use either official language in the courts. These issues would be addressed in 1987 in Bill C-72, as revisions to the Official Languages Act.

Bill C-72 had the important consequence of expanding the meaning of existing language rights and of extending the scope of their implementation.[50] Prior to the introduction of these revisions, the Commissioner of Official Languages had submitted to Parliament a set of proposals designed to amend the Official Languages Act, a central feature of which was a proposal to *personalize* language rights. It involved 'a *personal right* to be served in either language that would complement the existing institutional obligation to provide the service' and 'formal recognition of the *right of federal employees* to carry out their duties in the official language of their choice, subject to certain conditions.'[51] Both principles figured prominently in the new legislation.

An important illustration of this personalization of language rights in Bill C-72 was the specification that the courts have a duty to use the language chosen by parties to the proceedings conducted before it. Once these choices are made, the court must select judges or presiding officers for particular cases who are at least 'receptive bilinguals' in the chosen language or languages . This provision applied throughout Canada without qualifications regarding 'significant demand' or linguistic minority concentrations. In addition, at the request of a party to any proceedings, the court was now required to provide simultaneous interpretation of the proceedings and ensure that any person giving evidence can be understood in the official language of her or his choice.[52]

These provisions significantly expanded the scope of the meaning of a right to a trial in either official language. They also specifically corrected the restrictive interpretation of language rights in courts as developed by the Supreme Court (discussed in the following section). The individual parties to a proceeding became the holders of the right and controlled the decision regarding the language of court proceedings.

This right to be understood in court has occasioned considerable controversy over its impact on appointments to the bench. The concern has repeatedly been expressed that this meant that all future federal court judges would have to be bilingual, a charge repeatedly denied by government spokespersons.[53] The provision instead required that the courts, like the public service itself, maintain an institutional capacity to function in both official languages. Although some judges must be bilingual, most need not be. In fact, the courts had already made considerable progress in their capacity to offer trials in French throughout the country prior to the drafting of Bill C-72.[54] Consequently, although it constituted an important innovation in the expansion of language rights, it too could be described as a formalization of an existing practice.

Right to Work in Either Official Language

Another area where Bill C-72 expanded language rights was in relation to the language of work within the civil service. More specifically, it represented a culmination of a developing trend since the passage of the original OLA (1969). The issue first emerged in the research of the B and B Commission, which found serious discontentment among many francophone witnesses, who complained, 'I have to hang up my language with my coat when I go to work.'[55] In its report, the B and B Commission argued that real equality of opportunity for both language groups required an equal opportunity to work in their own languages. Accordingly, the commission proposed that the government establish French Language Units throughout the federal public service wherever feasible. The principal if not exclusive language of work was to be French to ensure that a full range of career opportunities would be available to both official language groups. Although the commission initially justified the policy on the grounds of the creation of an equal partnership between both official language groups in the federal public service, it ultimately couched its recommendation in the form of language rights when it urged that the Commissioner of Official Languages have responsibility for 'the language rights of public servants.'[56] The straightforward interpretation of their intent is that they were recommending the creation of a set of legal rights to language of work without claiming that these were in any sense fundamental human rights.

This issue was first broached in a statement to the House of Commons on the government's bilingualism policy by Prime Minister Pearson, who indicated the government's intention of ensuring that 'a climate will be created in which public servants from both language groups will work together toward common goals, using their own language and applying respective cultural values, but each fully understanding and appreciating those of the other.'[57] To implement the policy, designated French Language Units were created. However, the lukewarm reaction of francophone public servants, who feared that they would form linguistic ghettoes and career dead ends, led ultimately to the abandonment of this policy.

As noted, already, the issue of language at work was emphasized in the report of the Task Force on Canadian Unity, which insisted, 'It is not only a matter of equal opportunity to secure employment in the federal administration, for example, but the ability, once hired, for both English- and French-speaking Canadians to work in their own language. Too many francophones still do not enjoy this opportunity;'[58] To redress the problem, the task force recommended that the equality of both official languages as languages of work in the federal government be entrenched in the Constitution. However, their proposal was carefully confined to the National Capital Region and head offices of federal government departments. It proposed that the language of work in federal institutions in the various provinces should be the usual language of work in those provinces. This would mean, for example that it would be French in Quebec, but English in Ontario and most other provinces.

The 1988 reforms to the OLA actively embraced a qualified concept of a right to work in either official language. The preamble of Bill C-72 asserted that individuals 'should have equal opportunities to use the official language of their choice' within federal institutions. It did not use the language of rights, but that of equality. However, Section 34 stated that federal employees 'have the right to use either official language *in accordance with this part*' (my emphasis).

The qualification was more important than the general assertion. Although it ostensibly expressed a right to language of work, the exercise of this right occurred within a two-tier system, determined by the demographic character of particular regions. In the National Capital Region and prescribed areas of bilingual services, the act specified that federal institutions must ensure that work environments were conducive to work in both official languages, including support services, supervisory staff, and work instruments (Sections 35 and 36). In these areas, employees would have a basis for claiming a right to work in either official language. The second tier consisted of the non-bilingual areas, where federal institutions would have a responsibility to ensure that the treatment of the minority language for that area is comparable to the treatment of the other official language in the reverse circumstances.

The former qualification ensured that the content of the right to language of work was defined by Cabinet regulations. Accordingly, the regulations themselves were as important as the governing legislation. The latter qualification subtly changed the content of the right to work in an official language. What the individual actually would possess was a right to *equal treatment* of their language in comparable circumstances. This is a far cry from a straightforward individual right to work in the official language of your choice. In both instances, the right was a creature of government policy – and effectively subordinate to it.

If the right to work in one's (official) language were to be viewed as a basic language right, it would exhibit some important difficulties. Such a formulation tends towards the *strong* form of a language right, as *a right to live one's life* in a language. As such, it requires significant justification that is largely absent in Bill C-72. There are immediate complications with such a right. Imagine a francophone public servant in Sussex, New Brunswick, insisting that her right to work in French be respected. Imagine an anglophone public servant in Quebec City demanding the same right.[59] Each case has a certain quality of perversity about it, stemming from the fact that the demand occurs outside the context of a substantial language community to sustain the claim. How credible can such a claim be if the individual otherwise would have to live her or his daily life in the other official language? Several additional problems arise with this particular right in relation to conflicting rights between parties.

Conflict initially arises between the right to work in one's preferred official language and the right of the public to receive government services in their preferred language. This issue was dramatized when a francophone federal civil servant in Ottawa responded in French to an anglophone doctor in British Columbia.[60] Although the civil servant ultimately apologized, the case illustrates the fundamental clash of rights here, resolvable only by a formal hierarchy of rights claims. Such a hierarchy has always been understood to be part of the system. A Treasury Board document stated, 'If a public servant must be bilingual in order to serve the public in both official languages, it is clear that his or her "right" to work in the official language of choice is more restricted than that of other employees whose functions do not require them to serve the same public.'[61] Therefore, the worker's language rights must be subordinate to the citizen's language rights.[62] This is presumably justified on the grounds that individuals are hired to perform services to the public, and performance of those services in a language inaccessible to that public is simply a failure to provide that service.

On the other hand, the special exemptions granted to unilingual employees approaching retirement age whose positions were designated bilingual creates the situation where a significant number of staff are not able to provide the services their position requires. In this instance, the seniority rights of public servants override the public's right to service in their preferred official language.

A second difficulty is that this language right is inherently incompatible with the language rights of those co-workers who speak a different language. One example concerns a conflict between two officials within the federal civil service about the language of communication between them. In response to the question of whether or not a Cabinet Minister's request for oral and written communication in his own language interfered with the right of civil servants to work in their preferred language, the Official Language Commissioner stated that 'the minister's right is indisputable,' but emphasized that the bilingual capacity of the senior civil service should minimize such conflicts.[63] Unfortunately, the commissioner did not elaborate on the basis for the indisputability of minister's right. If the answer is to be found in the conventions of ministerial responsibility, whereby the staff of individual departments are simply collective agents of the minister, then that is a decisive argument, but nevertheless a fairly limited case.

If the answer is to be found in the hierarchical distribution of authority in conventional bureaucratic organizations, and the general notion that subordinates must defer to their superiors in the structure, then what we are facing is a competing principle that will often override the assertion of a right to work in an official language of one's choice.

Some of these problems were in fact recognized early in the discussion surrounding the notion of this language right. 'The "language right" of an employee to be supervised in his preferred official language,' noted one Treasury Board document, 'becomes the "language obligation" of his supervisor.'[64] This principle reverses the conventional hierarchical principle of organizations, since the preferences of those lower in the hierarchy determine the linguistic obligations of their supervisors. What, then, is the status of the supervisor's right to work in the language of her choice? Here again, the hierarchy of language rights reflects the responsibilities of the positions. Where a supervisor is charged with direction of a staff primarily working in French, proper performance of the supervisor's job requires the use of French. The responsibilities of the positions thus constitute an important limiting condition on the right to work in the language of one's choice.

This was the understanding conveyed by the Conservative government in the debates preceding its passage. Responding to criticisms about the potentially open-ended nature of this right, Doug Lewis, the minister responsible for the Treasury Board, responded,

I think the right has to be understood in the context of the Bill which requires federal institutions to provide certain types of services to public servants in both official languages in certain regions and to create work environments conducive to the use of either official language in such regions. Therefore, the employee's right to choice of language of work is linked to these institutional duties.[65]

It would appear that the right to use the language of one's choice depends on the region where one works and/or the responsibilities of one's position. For francophones, this means that the right to work in the language of one's choice applies primarily to the so-called bilingual belt – the National Capital Region, Quebec, and parts of Ontario and New Brunswick. Outside this area, 'the language of internal administration is the official language of the majority of the population of the province in which the office is located.'[66] This means that the right to work in one's own (official) language is more akin to a *special right*, granted to individuals who meet a set of specific conditions.

This particular language right represents an intersection point between concerns for rights and equality, with the latter emerging as the primary concern. As outlined earlier, language rights are founded on the importance of the language for individual and cultural identity. In this context, it is doubtful that a claim can be made for a right to work in one's *choice* of official language; rather a right would have to be formulated as a right to work in one's *mother tongue* official language. At the same time, this language right is concerned about *equality of opportunity* within the public service, which is enhanced by enabling employees to function in the language of greatest facility for them, thus equalizing opportunities to demonstrate competence. However, given that bilingualism is a highly prized skill, individual employees might well wish to cultivate skills in the other language. Thus, excluding the choice of languages of work potentially limits the opportunities for advancement of public servants. In the same way as many francophones declined to work in the French Language Units in the 1970s for reasons of restricted job mobility, so francophones might choose to function in English again. One could hardly justify imposing a requirement that they work in their mother tongue.

If there is a right to work in the official language of one's *choice*, certain perverse consequences can arise in some instances. Suppose a francophone insisted that he wanted to perform his work in English. If many francophones chose a similar option this would effectively eliminate French as a language of work by collective individual choice – defeating the purpose of the recognition of such a right! This claim would bear no connection to the justificatory framework for recognizing language rights. It would be consistent with a concern for equality of opportunity.

In his 1992 annual report, the Commissioner of Official Languages commented that the 'language of work objectives were the poor relations of the Official Languages Act.'[67] The phrase aptly describes the status of the right to work in one's choice of official languages. Although the inclusion of such a language right in federal legislation implies that it is an important right, the attendant qualifications subordinate it to various policy and organizational requirements. These considerations suggest the conclusion that the right to work in an official language is in fact a rather tenuous right at best, subject to override by the other components of language rights and the requirements of organizational life. This is, however, largely how it must be, because the attempt to give the concept real teeth would generate substantial, if not insoluble, problems of implementation in a balanced manner. Finally, such a concept does not form part of the practice of rights as currently recognized in Canada, so that its formal recognition as a language right is dubious both in principle and in practice. It is best viewed as a commitment to enhance the equal status of the two official languages within federal administration.

Legislative treatment of language rights, and even more so the implementation of language rights, is rife with ambiguity. As this discussion demonstrates, a consistently expansive approach has been taken to the substance of language rights in government legislation. Some new rights have been created, including minority language education, the right to work, and the right to be served in either official language. In addition, the content of several long-standing language rights have been radically enlarged. The original right to use English and French in the federal courts of Canada – though not necessarily to be understood except via translation – has been expanded to include a right to have a criminal trial by a judge able to function in one's preferred official language.

In these respects, language rights have gained ground dramatically in the federal domain. The ambiguity surfaces in relation to their rationale and qualified assertion. Although they are generally based on a commitment to equal treatment of the two official languages under similar circumstances, the circumstances are rarely similar and thus the achievement of equality is an ongoing challenge. Furthermore, language rights are nestled within a network of administrative principles that necessarily constrain, and in some cases subordinate, the priority assigned these rights.

Judicial Interpretation of Language Rights

The constitutional entrenchment of language rights has created an additional domain for the articulation of the status of language rights through judicial interpretation. The inclusion of language rights within the Charter of Rights and Freedoms created expectations that it would have a substantial impact upon the status of language rights in Canadian society. One observer described the Charter language rights as 'Canada's first attempt to provide comprehensive constitutional guarantees to protect the English and French languages,' but noted that they were nevertheless 'marvellously ambiguous.'[68] Judicial interpretation would thus play a crucial role in defining the content of language rights in Canada.

Somewhat curiously, the introduction of the Charter coincided with a retreat by the courts to a narrow interpretation of language rights. In the 1970s the Supreme Court embarked on a more expansive reading of Section 133, a process that reached its zenith in the *Manitoba Language reference*, where the Supreme Court maintained,

The importance of language rights is grounded in the essential role that language plays in human existence, development and dignity. It is through language that we are able to form concepts; to structure and order the world around us. Language bridges the gap between isolation and community, allowing humans to delineate the rights and duties they hold in respect of one another, and thus to live in society.[69]

Clearly, language rights were judged by the Supreme Court to be foundational elements of self-identity, citizenship, and community, and thus worthy of substantive interpretation. Somewhat ironically, this ringing endorsement of the importance of language rights was offered in defence of a rather modest set of constitutionally entrenched rights. However, such rhetoric could clearly provide a basis for an expansive approach to the interpretation of language rights.

The view expressed in the Manitoba reference, however, was not characteristic of the subsequent trend of the courts' decision making. In reviewing six decisions involving language rights, one legal scholar described a pattern of narrow interpretation whereby the courts 'uphold rights where their existence is unquestionable in the Charter or other parts of the constitution,' but otherwise 'interpret language rights narrowly.'[70]

The cases of the *Société des Acadiens* and *MacDonald* were more typical of the Supreme Court's approach in the Charter era. The question in the former case was whether the right to use either official language in judicial proceedings, as stated in Section 19(2) of the Charter, included the right to be understood in that language, meaning that court officers must be fluent in that language. In *MacDonald*, the point concerned the issuing of a speeding ticket in Quebec in French only, which the plaintiff challenged as a violation of Quebec's obligations under Section 133 of the Constitution Act, 1867. In *Société des Acadiens*, the majority on the Supreme Court restated its view of the distinctive character of language rights: 'Legal rights tend to be seminal in nature because they are rooted in principle ... Language rights, on the other hand, although some of them have been enlarged and incorporated into the Charter, remain nonetheless founded on political compromise.'[71] Broadly speaking, the court's assessment was consistent with the established practice of language rights in Canada, though somewhat overstated. It is rather intriguing that language rights in the Charter, unlike the fundamental freedoms and legal rights that are the acknowledged 'seminal rights,' are *not* subject to the Section 33 override clause in the Charter.[72] Presumably, a case could be made that this suggests a rather different weighting of the relative importance of the two sets of rights noted above – one that assigns constitutional priority to language rights. In addition, the capacity of governments to override legal rights and civil liberties via Section 33 renders all these rights creatures of political compromise. However, these themes were not pursued in the various opinions offered.

As a lower order of right, the court generally has been disinclined to adopt a 'broad and generous approach' to the interpretation of the content of language rights as it had in relation to other legal rights. Here again, the perception that language rights were a product of political compromise led the majority of the court to assume that the wording of the language rights sections precisely reflected the framers' intent, and thus to adopt a narrow reading of their content. The majority reasoned that the absence of wording specifying the right to be understood in the official language of one's choice was grounds to conclude that it was not part of this right. The choice of the verb 'use' rather than the verb 'communicate' was taken to be indicative of a restrictive intent. Similarly, in *MacDonald*, the majority maintained that although Section 133 *permitted* the use of either official language in court proceedings, it did not *require* the use of both. Accordingly, governments were empowered to adopt whatever practices they deemed appropriate regarding the language of court proceedings.

A notable exception to these views was Judge Bertha Wilson, who argued, in minority opinions in both cases, that the language rights acknowledged in the Charter necessarily impose duties on governments for their implementation. The right to speak a language in the courts implies a right to be understood and therefore places a corresponding obligation on the government to ensure that the court can understand the languages uttered within its bounds.[73] Judge Wilson urged the Supreme Court to adopt a 'progressively expansive' interpretation of this language right that would embrace a right to be understood by the court directly in the official language of one's choice.[74] Judge Wilson's opinion was flatly contradicted by the federal government's submission to the court in the *Société des Acadiens* case, insisting that 'a broad and generous interpretation of language rights cannot be used.' One legal scholar concluded that the court majority took its lead from this federal government position, thus spelling the end of any expansion of language rights through the Charter.[75]

Minority language education rights is the major exception to this relatively cool reception by the courts to language rights. Initially, Section 23 of the Charter was used to overturn section 73 of Quebec's Bill 101, which limited access to its English education system to those whose parents or siblings were educated in English in Quebec (the Quebec clause). Section 23 of the Charter guaranteed Canadian citizens access to minority language education systems where they are in a minority in a particular province (the Canada clause). The court declared that the Quebec Clause completely negated the Canada clause without sufficient justification, and the offending section was overturned.[76] However, the judge emphasized the absence of compelling evidence and argument concerning the detrimental effects of the Canada clause on the position of the French language in Quebec, strongly implying that these elements could have been grounds for sustaining the position of the Quebec government. Subsequently, francophone minorities would find ample support in Section 23 for their efforts to obtain French language education outside Quebec.[77]

The courts have been relatively receptive to Section 23 minority language education rights. However, they have been inclined to view them as something other than fundamental rights. The prevailing judicial view is reflected in the following comment made by the Supreme Court:

Sec. 23 of the Charter ... is not a codification of essential, pre-existing and more or less universal rights that are being confirmed and perhaps clarified, extended or amended, and which, most importantly, are being given a new primacy and inviolability by their entrenchment in the supreme law of the land. The special provisions of s. 23 of the Charter make it a unique set of constitutional provisions, quite peculiar to Canada.'[78]

This comment underscores the ambiguous constitutional status of our language rights. Lacking the weighty history and established legitimacy of traditional civil rights, they are nonetheless judged to be centrally important to Canadian political life.

The Charter language rights, as defined by judicial interpretation, are to be viewed as a demonstration of political compromise, rather than as inherent rights. Their content is thus to be determined by their expression in government legislation. Insofar as the Charter is concerned, this is largely in response to the accepted practice of language rights in Canada. As a result, both the constitutional status of language rights and the judicial interpretation thereof derive from the practice of language rights in Canada. The explicit language rights embedded in the Constitution continue to be treated as the stepchildren of political accommodation, and their content continues to be treated with considerable trepidation by the courts. Thus, unlike some other dimensions of the Charter, the courts have followed, rather than led, political opinion about language rights in Canada.

Conclusion

In the federal domain there are two streams of development at work with regard to the substance of language rights. The constitutional stream of language rights is closely patterned on the Canadian practice of language rights (with the notable omission of rights to hospital services), and it reflects a weak promotion model. The language rights now entrenched in the Constitution are those widely accepted by the public as important rights. Despite their relatively privileged position within the Constitution, they are nonetheless treated by the courts as legal rights emerging from political struggle, rather than as equivalent to conventional civil and political rights.

The legislative stream of language rights follows a more expansive list, approximating a strong promotion model. As reflected in the extension of language rights in the courts, the pattern is towards increasing the scope of language rights already accepted. The commitment is somewhat tentative, as witnessed in the treatment of the language of work provisions, but the course of development is consistently expansive. In pursuing this course federal policy has inescapably confronted difficulties arising from the inherent tensions of conflicting language rights. This expansive approach is in significant conflict with the existing practice of rights in Canada, and it forms the basis for the emerging debate about the future of language rights in Canada.

A certain irony exists in that this expansion of language rights occurs despite both the federal government and the courts continuing to view language rights as the product of political compromise and therefore of a subordinate status to conventional human rights. The pattern here is not entirely consistent. Both federal government commentaries and some court decisions have offered views to suggest that language rights are more fundamental. However, it remains the case that 'political compromise' is the prevailing justification for these rights in the federal Canadian domain.

Notes

1 Pierre E. Trudeau, *Federalism and the French Canadians* (Toronto: Macmillan, 1968), 56.
2 Royal Commission on Bilingualism and Biculturalism, Report, vol. 1, *The Official Languages* (Ottawa: Queen's Printer, 1968), 41–6. See also Frank R. Scott, 'Language Rights and the Language Policy in Canada,' *Manitoba Law Journal* 4 (2) (1971): 243–57.
3 The mandatory element was the product of pressure from certain French-Canadian members who were concerned about the permissive wording of earlier drafts. See B and B, *Report*, vol. 1, *The Official Languages*, 48.

4 Evelyn Kallen, *Ethnicity and Human Rights in Canada* (Toronto: Gage, 1982), 217.

5 B and B, *Report*, vol. 1, 54.

6 For an overview of the history of language use policy in the federal administration, see B and B, *Report*, Book 3, *The Work World*, Part 2.

7 B and B, *Report*, vol. 1, 60.

8 The case in question is cited as, *Société des Acadiens du Nouveau-Brunswick Inc. et al.* v *Association of Parents for Fairness in Education et al.*, [1986] 1 *Supreme Court Reports*, 549.

9 B and B, *Report*, vol. 1, 47–8.

10 See Claude-Armand Sheppard, *The Law of Languages in Canada*. Studies of the Royal Commission on Bilingualism and Biculturalism, no. 10 (Ottawa: Information Canada, 1971), for a more detailed presentation of these practices, 292.

11 Hon. David Crombie, Secretary of State, in Canada, House of Commons, *Debates*, 9 Feb. 1988, 12794.

12 The incident is reported in B and B, *Report*, Book 3, 104.

13 See Sheppard, *Law of Languages*, Chap. 13 for an overview of Canadian law and practice regarding official languages. He maintained, 'There is a constitutional vacuum in Canada with respect to jurisdiction over languages,' 292.

14 B and B, *Report* vol. 1, 55.

15 Ibid.

16 See the chapter by Cook in Ramsay Cook, Craig Brown and C. Berger, eds., *Minorities, Schools, and Politics* (Toronto: University of Toronto Press, 1969) The controversy is discussed more extensively in my 'Majorities and Minorities: Henri Bourassa and Language Rights in Canada,' doctoral dissertation, University of Minnesota, 1980.

17 For an extensive analysis of this case, see George M. Weir, *The Separate School Question in Canada* (Toronto: Ryerson Press, 1934).

18 The court case in question was the Protestant School Board of Greater Montreal versus the Attorney-General of Quebec (1976). The decision is discussed in the context of the evolution of legal decisions on denominational schools in Quebec in Pierre Foucher, *Constitutional Language Rights of Official-Language Minorities in Canada* (Ottawa: Minister of Supply and Services, 1985), 75–94.

19 Quebec National Assembly, An Act to amend the Education Act, the Act respecting school elections and other legislative provisions (Bill 109), second session, 35th legislature.

20 See House of Commons, *Debates* 134 (161) (22 April 1997), 10031. The constitutional amendment was required to revoke the impact of Section 93, subsections (1) to (4) on Quebec, as had been requested by the Quebec govern-

ment. Since the amendment affected only the province of Quebec, it could be treated as a Section 43 amendment to the constitution, so that only the federal government and the province in question need approve the change.

21 B and B, *Report*, vol. 1, 74.

22 For an overview of this concept and its demise, and the impact of the B and B Commission, see Michael Oliver, 'The Impact of the Royal Commission on Bilingualism and Biculturalism on Constitutional Thought and Practice in Canada,' *International Journal of Canadian Studies* 7–8 (Spring–Fall) (1993): 315–32. The mandate of the commission instructed it to address the matter in terms of equality. Some passages hinted at a disposition to develop a human rights framework for policy, e.g., the observation that 'we are not asked by our terms of reference to deal with these fundamental rights,' in B and B, *Report*, vol. 1, xl.

23 Noted by Oliver, 'Impact of Royal Commission,' 320. Oliver reported that the commission defined 'society' as 'a complex of organizations and institutions sufficiently rich to permit people to lead a full life in their own language.'

24 B and B, *Report*, vol. 1, 98.

25 For an elaboration of these language policy options, see K.D. McRae, 'The Principle of Territoriality and the Principle of Personality in Multilingual States,' *International Journal of the Sociology of Language* 4 (1975): 33–54.

26 B and B, *Report*, vol. 1, 73, 74, xliii.

27 Ibid., 103.

28 Ibid., 122–3.

29 Official Languages Act, 1968–69, *Revised Statutes of Canada 1970*, c.O-2, s.2.

30 The ambitious plan to designate bilingual districts foundered on the twin shoals of provincial intransigence and the peculiarities of the minority language population distribution in the country. For an informative analysis of the failure of this scheme, see Kenneth D. McRae, 'Bilingual Language Districts in Finland and Canada: Adventures in the Transplanting of an Institution,' *Canadian Public Policy* 4 (3) (1978): 331–51.

31 'The bill does not, of course, amend the constitution. I have often stated my belief that such amendment is necessary to guarantee the fundamental language rights of our citizens, and this is one of the subjects which is before the continuing conference on the constitution.' Statement by Prime Minister Trudeau, in House of Commons, *Debates*, 1st session, 28th Parliament, vol. 2 (17 Oct. 1968), 1483.

32 B and B, *Report*, Book 3, 353. The original statement was presented in the House of Commons (6 April 1966).

33 A goal-based theory is concerned with the welfare of any individual only insofar as that contributes to some generally desirable state of affairs. A rights-

based theory places the individual at the centre of the evaluation. The distinction originates with Ronald Dworkin's, *Taking Rights Seriously* (Cambridge: Harvard University Press, 1977), 172, and was applied by Marsha Hanen, 'Taking Language Rights Seriously,' in Stanley French, ed., *Confederation: Philosophers Look at Canadian Confederation* (Montreal: Canadian Philosophical Association, 1979), 307–9. I would take issue with Hanen's assertion that the federal policy is properly characterized as rights based, on the basis of the prime minister's statement noted above.

34 Rt.Hon. Lester Pearson, 'Statement of Policy Respecting Bilingualism,' House of Commons, *Debates* (1st session, 27th Parliament, (6 April 1966), 3915. This central concept of linguistic equality is examined in Chapter 6. Here I focus on the evolution of language rights per se within the federal domain.

35 Canada, House of Commons, *Debates* (31 May, 1973),4303.

36 Ibid.

37 Prime Minister Trudeau nevertheless viewed language rights as 'fundamental,' sufficiently important to deserve constitutional entrenchment. See his statement in Canada, House of Commons, *Debates*, 1st session, 28th Parliament, vol. 8 (17 Oct. 1968), 1483. See also the speech from which the introductory quotation is drawn.

38 Government of Canada, *A National Understanding*, 41.

39 Ibid.,73.

40 This pattern of government justification also helps explain public perceptions about language rights reported in Chapter 2. The widespread view that language rights are primarily based on the preservation of national unity is completely consistent with the message presented by the federal government on their behalf.

41 This controversy is examined in considerable detail in Sanford F. Borins, *The Language of the Skies: The Bilingual Air Traffic Control Conflict in Canada* (Montreal: McGill-Queen's University Press, 1983).

42 Ibid.

43 Ibid. This distinction is critically examined in Chapter 4.

44 It is somewhat curious that the Task Force on Canadian Unity proposes an individual right to access to radio and television services in *both* official languages. Presumably, this means that unilingual English-speaking Albertans have a right to these services in French. This is difficult to relate to the theoretical justification for language rights elaborated here, since it would neither help preserve the English language community in Alberta nor reinforce individual self-identity. In all likelihood, it would be viewed as little more than a curiosity by them. They may well have meant to say that all Canadians are entitled to these services in their official language.

45 Task Force on Canadian Unity, *A Future Together: Observations and Recommendations* (Hull: Supply and Services, 1979), 53.

46 Ibid.

47 This explanation is offered in Ken McRoberts, *English Canada and Quebec: Avoiding the Issue* (North York: Robarts Centre for Canadian Studies, York University, 1991), 15.

48 This is the 'Canada clause' of the task force proposal.

49 Patrick Monahan, *Politics and the Constitution: The Charter, Federalism and the Supreme Court of Canada* (Toronto: Carswell, 1987), 112.

50 House of Commons, Bill C-72, *An Act respecting the status and use of the official languages of Canada*, 2nd session, 33rd Parliament (first reading, 25 June 1987, passed 7 July 1988).

51 Commissioner of Official Languages, *News Release* (11 Feb. 1986).

52 See *Official Languages Act*, c. 31 (4th Supplement) of the *Revised Statutes of Canada, 1985*, Part III.

53 For instance, a much-criticized article in a Western Canadian magazine claimed that 'the new bill also insists that within five years, all federally-appointed judges, other than those on the Supreme Court of Canada, be fully bilingual.' 'English Isn't Good Enough,' *Alberta Report* (1 Feb. 1988), 12. The federal Conservative government was sufficiently alarmed by this article that it published a letter in Western publications rebutting its arguments, which was signed by all Western Canadian Cabinet Ministers.

54 According to the Official Language Commissioner, much remains to be accomplished. In 1995, Victor Goldbloom pointedly remarked, 'The manner in which the Criminal Code provisions concerning the language of trials has been implemented since 1990 seems to be unequal and in some cases sporadic from one region of the country to another.' See Commissioner of Official Languages, *Language Rights in 1995* (Ottawa: Minister of Supply and Services, 1996), 7.

55 B and B, *Report*, Book 3, 3.

56 Ibid., 287.

57 Ibid., Appendix B, 'Statement of the Right Hon. Lester B. Pearson Regarding Policy Respecting Bilingualism in the Public Service (House of Commons, 6 April 1966), 352.

58 Task Force on Canadian Unity, *A Future Together*, 50.

59 An anglophone employee in Verdun, Quebec, has successfully filed a complaint that, among other things, internal communications and meetings were in French only. The case is briefly noted in Commissioner of Official Languages, *Language Rights in 1995*, 2.

60 Commissioner of Official Languages, *Annual Report 1984*, 52.

61 Canada, Treasury Board, *Revised Official Languages Policies in the Public Service of Canada* (Sept. 1977), 4.

62 Official Language Commissioner, *Annual Report 1984*, 52.

63 Ibid., 73.

64 Treasury Board, *Language Reform in Federal Institutions*, Mimeograph (1979), 14.

65 Hon. Doug Lewis, House of Commons *Debates* (9 Feb. 1988), 12766.

66 Treasury Board, *Language Reform* 14. The principle does, however, have broader impact across the country. It also means that the federal government is committed to providing work instruments, such as technical manuals, in both official languages for unilingual employees working throughout the country. This addresses a standard complaint among francophones that they were often unable to perform their work in French, even in francophone areas.

67 Commissioner of Official Languages, *Annual Report 1992* (Ottawa: Minister of Supply and Services, 1993), 48.

68 Joseph Eliot Magnet, 'The Charter's Official Languages Provisions: The Implications of Entrenched Bilingualism,' *Supreme Court Review* 4 (1982): 170.

69 Supreme Court, *Reference Re: Manitoba Language Rights* [1985] 2 *Supreme Court Reports*, 347.

70 Ian Greene, *The Charter of Rights* (Toronto: Lorimer, 1989), 207. Mandel observed a more self-consciously political role for the court. See Michael Mandel, *The Charter of Rights and the Legalization of Politics in Canada* (Toronto: Thompson, 1994) , Chap. 3. This narrow conception would appear to be contradicted by the judgment in the *Ford* case concerning Quebec's Sign Law, Section 58 of Bill 101, in which the court assessed the validity of the Quebec requirement that all commercial signs be only in the French language. However, the *Ford* decision reflects an expansive reading of 'freedom of expression' rather than 'language rights' as such. That case is examined in some detail in Chapter 4.

71 The quotation is from the case, *Société des Acadiens du Nouveau-Brunswick Inc. et al.* v *Association of Parents for Fairness in Education et al.* [1986] 1 *Supreme Court Reports*, 549. I have drawn it from Greene, *Charter*, 191. The second case concerning bilingual summonses is cited as *MacDonald* v *City of Montreal et al.* [1986] 1 *Supreme Court Reports*, 460. See his Chapter 7, 'Language Rights' for a useful summary of these and other Supreme Court decisions regarding language rights since the Charter.

72 McRoberts made the same point and further maintained that the language rights clauses are in fact the *raison d'etre* of the charter itself. *English Canada and Quebec*, 15.

73 Judge Wilson, *MacDonald* v *City of Montreal,* 521–4.

74 See Greene, *Charter,* 190–4.

75 Joseph Magnet, 'Comments,' in David Schneiderman, ed., *Language and the State: The law and Politics of Identity* (Cowansville, Que: Les Éditions Yvon Blais, 1991), 146. The federal position is quoted on 144.

76 The case is cited as *A.-G. Que.* v *Association of Quebec Protestant School Boards et al.,*[1984] 2 Supreme Court Reports, 66.

77 See Wayne MacKay, 'Minority Language Educational Rights Vindicated,' in David Schneiderman, ed., *Language and the State,* 123–40 . His discussion, however, emphasized that Section 23 is a useful, but not necessarily decisive, resource in the face of an intransigent provincial government.

78 *Quebec Association of Protestant School Boards et al.* (1984), 10 Dominion Law Reports (4th), 321 at 331; quoted in Pierre Foucher, *Constitutional Language Rights of Official Language Minorities in Canada* (Ottawa: Minister of Supply and Services, 1985), 347.

4

Quebec: Collective Rights to Language

We are Québécois ... At the core of this personality is the fact that we speak French. Everything else depends on this one essential element and follows from it or leads us infallibly back to it.[1]

René Lévesque

For much of Quebec's history, language policy was a product of Section 133 of the BNA Act and the customs surrounding Section 93, whereby denominational schools were effectively divided on English and French lines. Coupled with that, the government adopted a *laissez-faire* approach to access to these schools, the result being that individual families chose which system to attend. Similarly, it has been the practice to provide health, social, and government services in both English and French.[2] Except for Sections 93 and 133, no language rights were embodied in legislation, but, insofar as these rights were recognized, it was by long-standing customary practice. In essence, Quebec's unofficial language policy has offered language services only recently entrenched as language rights at the federal level.

It is ironic, then, that the achievement at the federal level should coincide with a striking rejection of such an approach within Quebec. Quebec's La Charte de la Langue Française / Charter of the French Language, popularly known as Bill 101, represents a significant deviation from the federal approach, in that it ostensibly asserts a collective rights approach to language. Subsequent Quebec legislation retreated to a more balanced interplay of individual and group rights regarding language. A detailed consideration of the issues that arise from the orientation of Bill 101 reinforce the conclusion that language rights are not collective, but group rights, and that their formulation in Bill 101 reveals serious limitations to such an approach.[3]

Bill 101 was the culmination of efforts for more than a decade to resolve language problems within the province of Quebec. These problems arc multifaceted, involving economic aspects (the disproportionately low income levels of francophones and their inadequate representation in the higher ranks of business), demographic aspects (fears that francophones may become a minority in at least Montreal as a result of the assimilation of immigrants to the English language), and philosophical (a desire to accord French speakers legal guarantees of linguistic rights). In addition, Bill 101 is an important symbolic gesture, related to the perception that the French language is the very essence of Québécois identity. The legislation thus was a symbolic assertion of the Québécois personality in all aspects of Quebec life. As a result, Bill 101 was an attempt to achieve certain policy goals regarding the status of the French language in Quebec as well as a statement about language rights. Both aspects must be kept in focus in an assessment of its content.

The Rationale for Bill 101

The preamble of Bill 101 clearly indicated its double purpose of goal orientation and rights assertion. As a policy, it stated the government's commitment 'to see the quality and influence of the French language assured." However, the preamble of Bill 101 was somewhat confusing about the basis of language rights, as it offered distinct lines of reasoning for the claims to language rights of different language groups within Quebec society. The claims of the French language were based on the existence of a French-speaking majority and the French language as 'the instrument by which that people has articulated its identity.'[4] The native peoples of Quebec, the Amerindian and the Inuit, also have recognized language rights, although the explanation for them was that these groups are the original inhabitants of this land. No mention was made of language rights for the English-speaking minority. This point was underscored by the chapters on fundamental language rights, the five clauses that asserted only rights to use and to be served in the French language.[5]

Bill 101 was initially intriguing because it asserted individual rights on the basis of collective rights. Bill 101 recognized a series of language rights in relation to the French language for all citizens of Quebec. These are individual rights insofar as every person had the right to be educated, to receive goods and services, and to work in French. This included Quebec residents who are *not* French speaking. In regard to non-French-speaking Quebec residents, Bill 101, recognized in its preamble, 'the right of the Amerinds and the Inuit of Québec, the first inhabitants of this land, to preserve and develop their original language and culture.'[6] In the ensuing text, the legislation recognized the right of the appropriate persons and organizations to use Cree, Inuktitut, and Naskapi, and exempted the Indian reserves from the application of the act (Sections 87, 88, and 95–7).

A comparison of the treatment accorded these distinct groups reveals serious inconsistencies in the understanding of a human right. Although the argument for the pre-eminence of the French language makes pointed reference to its majority status, the legislation's recognition of Amerindian and Inuit minority language rights demonstrated that majority status is not a necessary condition of language rights. Once we move beyond the sheer emphasis on numbers, the rationale begins to reveal serious flaws. If the argument for language rights rests upon its contribution to the articulation of cultural identity, then the same argument can be used to advance a claim to language rights on behalf of both English and Native groups. Yet it was not used to advance such a claim. Since it was not, the preamble effectively suggested that the contribution to cultural identity is not a sufficient basis for language rights. As a result, we are returned once again to the difference of numbers, that is, majority and minority status.

The argument of prior inhabitance as the basis of a language right is one with significant limitations. It is meaningful only if the original language has been preserved, in which case an argument from cultural identity would be equally applicable. Moreover, the mere fact of prior inhabitance seems a curious basis for recognizing language rights, bearing no recognizable relationship to conventional arguments for human rights. Finally, its application carries implications that contradict the thrust of the argument. If original inhabitance of territory is the basis of a right, then even the French language group does not have language rights. On the other hand, if the right arises from the process of settling an area, then presumably any group who originally settled an area can legitimately claim such rights. Yet no such provision was made for the descendants of English settlers in the province of Quebec. William Watson emphasized the anglophone claim for inclusion on this score when he observed, 'It is not obvious why a century's head start on English and several millennia's lag behind the languages of the original inhabitants should confer moral primacy.'[7] That no provision has been made for English descendants indicates that the authors of Bill 101 correctly perceived that prior inhabitance is not a strong basis for language rights. Thus, the legislation failed to offer a coherent argument for treating the preservation of one's language as a fundamental human right.[8]

The error lies more in the attempt to draw distinctions in language rights than in the basic view. The preamble to Bill 101 captured the core of a justification in emphasizing that language rights are based on membership in a language community and on the contribution of that language to personal and cultural identity. The problem rests primarily in the particularistic application of the principle, restricting it to the French language group. The Inuit and Amerindians, who are relatively isolated from French and English groups and have sustained their traditional language, are in a very strong sense a relatively independent community with a distinct culture. The English language residents also constitute an ongoing community, though it is not as independent and territorially isolated.

This assertion of an apparently 'individual rights' approach raises interesting questions. How can there be individual rights regarding language that do not apply to all individuals; that apply to Québécois, Amerindians, and Inuit, but not to other non-French-speaking inhabitants of Quebec? In fact, an 'individual rights' approach to the status of the French language was rejected as 'trivial,' because it does not address the central problem of the French language in North America, namely, 'protecting the existence of an original culture and developing it to its fullness.'[9] Here the focus is on the collectivity rather than the individuals it comprises. This orientation is central to the rationale for these rights, actually treating them as collective rights, that is, rights which can be claimed only by peoples, not individuals. In his speech introducing the legislation, Camille Laurin stated,

From the beginning, French has been the language of the people of Québec, taken overall as a collective entity – which does not mean that many other mother tongues cannot exist or be used in private life and in the activities of individual ethnic groups. But the Amerindians and the Inuit are the only ones who from a certain point of view can consider themselves as peoples separate from the totality of Québécois and in consequence insist on special treatment under the law. All other groups are the descendants of immigrants of full rights and duty and thus co-heirs to the juridico-political and socio-cultural tradition common to the people of Québec.[10]

Thus, the Québécois and the Native peoples both possess the critical characteristics of being original inhabitants of the land, and, as well, respectively being collectivities in the sense of shared history, traditions, language, and institutions. Interestingly, anglophones, who have a two-hundred-year history in the province of Quebec, are regarded as immigrants who are welcome to partake of the prevailing culture, but not recognized as entitled to make claims on behalf of their own culture.

When we look at the treatment accorded the Native peoples, it is surprising how little Bill 101 accorded in the way of language rights for this group. This was simply an assertion of *toleration* rights, rather than a commitment to preserve these languages on the part of the Quebec government. None of the basic rights regarding the French language were extended to these languages, despite these languages being those of collectivities having the same features as the Québécois. The major difference between the two groups is one of numbers – French has been the language of the majority. Ultimately this offers a majority-rule basis for the claim to language rights of the French language. More important, it tends to undermine the assertion that being a collectivity entitles a group to substantive language rights.

The analytical problems concerning the basis of language rights are reflected in two interrelated problems in Bill 101. It implicitly denied a right to the English language, even in the *weak* form, while advancing a *strong* claim for French language rights. In its regulation concerning the use of the French language in public life, Bill 101 dramatically altered the relative positions of language groups in Quebec. It asserted a strong language right for French-speaking citizens by ensuring that French will be 'the language of communication, work, commerce and business' within the province of Quebec.[11] Citizens may demand goods and services, and the opportunity to live and work in the French language. Obviously, this is a right of a particular language, and not of all languages. As a result, English-speaking residents were presented with duties corresponding to this recognized right, duties that are not reciprocal. The logical extension of this view was underscored in a recent commentary advocating reforms to language policy in Quebec which, after defining Quebec as a francophone society, maintained that 'businesses and public and private organizations operating in the Quebec market should be able to serve their Quebec clientele in French at all times,' including in anglophone neighbourhoods in Montreal. The commentator further insisted that any anglophone elected official or employee who is unable to do so should be dismissed.[12] Anglophones therefore bear the total duties of recognizing the language rights of the francophone majority – without corresponding rights of their own.

The position of the English language in Quebec is one of substantial ambiguity. Certain limited language rights and some privileges are accorded English-speaking residents. They are entitled to an education in their maternal language. However, this right was accorded on a selective basis – to those English-speaking residents of Quebec (prior to August 1977) who were educated in English in that province. Beyond the realm of education, the restrictions on use of the English language are wide-ranging. The attempted abolition of English as a language of the legislature and the courts, and the prohibition of English commercial posters and traffic signs are the most striking examples.[13] In relation to government services, there was no clearly recognized right in Quebec to deal with one's provincial government in the English language. Public institutions were permitted, but not required, to communicate with individuals in languages other than the official language. The basic approach was aptly summarized in Section 89 of Bill 101, which stated: 'Where this act does not require the use of the official language exclusively, the official language and another language may be used together.' The silence of the law, rather than its content, defines the boundaries of English language use. The language of Bill 101 never conveyed the notion that the use of English is a right.[14] This is a further illustration of the particularistic character of the concept of language rights developed in Bill 101.

This restriction of English language use is a necessary consequence of the internal conflict between rights and duties, where a strong claim to a French-language right is admitted. The right to live one's life in one's native language requires that others forego the same right for their language. Bill 101, however, resolved this dilemma in philosophically unacceptable ways, by effectively denying that English-language residents have any language rights.[15] Thus, there is no internal conflict of equal language rights because one party to the conflict simply has none. This is not an adequate solution. Language rights, to be human rights, must be universal or else they are not rights at all. If language rights are acknowledged to be rights, then the effort to realize them must necessarily seek a just balance between competing claims.

Further issues arise through an examination of the complex of individual and collective rights claims in Bill 101. Although Bill 101 assigned individual language rights to francophones, the assignment of duties entailed by those rights was decidedly ill-defined. The legislation made a clear distinction between individuals and organizations. It assigned positive duties to communicate with individuals in French to public institutions, quasi-public institutions, and business firms in Quebec (Chapter 2, Section 2). Beyond that, the duties must be inferred from the substance of the rights. For example, Sections 4 and 5 specify that 'workers have a right to carry on their activities in French' and 'consumers of goods and services have a right to be informed and served in French.' These sections are best interpreted in the context of the francization provisions for business firms. Bill 101 exempted firms with fewer than fifty employees from this requirement. This suggests that the duties in relation to workers and consumers fall primarily on relatively large organizations rather than individuals per se. Presumably the organizations in question would be able to perform the required duties without the necessity of all members of the organization being required to speak French. However, given the broader goal of making French the language of internal communication in most businesses, ultimately the duty of communicating in French would extend to all organization members.

Outside these firms, the duties imposed on individuals were of a negative rather than a positive sort. French-speaking workers were entitled to refuse to function in any language other than French. An English-speaking person (such as customer or worker) had no right to demand services in English. If accorded, it was a privilege under the complete discretion of the French speaker. Does the non-francophone have a positive duty to speak French to the francophone? The law was not designed in such a way as to suggest this conclusion. No legal remedies were established to enforce such behaviour, as there were for business firms, for instance. To do so, of course, would clearly infringe on an individual's freedom of expression. More to the point, the shift in emphasis between Sections 2 and 5 and 3 and 4 is highly instructive. Whereas Section 2 asserted a right to be communicated with in French, and Section 5, a right to be served and informed in French, Sections 3 and 4 assert the right to speak French, rather than to be spoken to.

These were the issues of a court case that concerned the provision of medical services in French. A French worker complained that, although he received his medical services in French from the doctor, the medical report he requested for submission to the Workers Compensation Board was in English. The court concluded that, since the appellant had failed to request French language services immediately upon contact, he had effectively renounced his right to such service. In its judgment, the court stated that the duties generated by Section 5 of Bill 101 were not absolute, but dependent on the active exercise of the right by the consumer. In addition, the court indicated that the provider of services was obliged to make services available in French, without specifically requiring that the provider of such services herself be bilingual.[16] This judgment has the effect of limiting the duties of non-francophones regarding the language of service, while placing a greater burden on francophones to demand their rights.

It used to be said that the English and French of Quebec meet only in the realms of business and politics. To the extent that this remains true, Bill 101 ensured that French will dominate in those realms, but it has turned a blind eye to other domains. However, Bill 101 has occasioned a noticeable shift in the balance of duties regarding interpersonal language use. Anglophones report that they are much more likely now to attempt to communicate in French in casual encounters with francophones than they were in the past.[17] Apparently, the formal recognition of rights for the French language has inspired a perception of duties among anglophones in relation to its use *vis-à-vis* francophones.

Two points emerge from these requirements. First, language rights are clearly akin to social rights, such as the right to an education, in that the relevant duties can only be reasonably assigned to governments and organizations rather than to individuals, as these duties would involve substantial burdens for individuals. Second, these requirements assert a strong promotion approach to language rights for Québécois, in that Bill 101 was designed to ensure that they can 'live their lives' in French. In this respect Bill 101 differs from all other language legislation in Canada. In consequence, French language rights involve collisions with either the rights or interests of non-French-speaking minorities. French language rights do not conflict with the language rights of non-francophones in Quebec, as non-francophones in Quebec are not perceived to have any language rights.

Both the White Paper on language and Laurin's statement took pains to reject the argument advanced by the anglophone minority that the English language enjoys 'acquired rights' in Quebec. Both documents emphasized the irrefutable constitutional fact that there is no such status recognized in existing law, beyond the limits of Section 133 of the BNA Act. Accordingly, in Quebec the English language enjoys certain liberties and privileges, but no rights.

For the most part, Bill 101 expressed a toleration-oriented language policy towards minority languages. The policy towards English can be regarded as a weak promotion one, as Quebec maintains an English language public education system and at least permits the use of English in the provision of government services.[18] Nevertheless, the broader point remains that there are no recognized rights to the English language with which Bill 101 might conflict. However, conflicts about individual rights have arisen in at least two ways.

One individual right affected by Bill 101 is the right not to be discriminated against on the basis of, among other things, language. Section 35 of Bill 101 stated that licences to practice the professions in Quebec will only be issued 'to persons whose knowledge of the official language is appropriate to the practice of their profession.' Does such a provision constitute discrimination on the basis of language? Marsha Hanen argued that it does not because 'the feature with respect to which the discrimination is occurring is not an unalterable feature of an individual's constitution, such as sex, or skin colour: one can, after all, learn another language, or at least one's children can.'[19] The final clause of this quotation suggested strongly that such a requirement has a discriminatory effect, in which case it would represent a violation of the right to non-discrimination.

Recent experience in Quebec has shown that much turns on how much knowledge is appropriate. Several instances emerged of individuals who were perfectly capable of performing certain jobs in French, yet incapable of passing the language test.[20] Consequently, the requirement was redefined such that a series of successfully completed high school and university French language courses was considered adequate. As French language instruction is readily available in the secondary and postsecondary educational institutions, the French language requirement poses a smaller hurdle to access to such jobs and thus could not be viewed as discriminatory. Even if the conflict with individual rights is satisfactorily resolved, the end result will be simply a minority language policy of toleration, far less than the English minority desires.

Commercial Signs and Freedom of Expression

The most discussed conflict between individual and collective rights in Bill 101 concerns restrictions on public signs. Section 58 of Bill 101 specified that all signs, posters, and commercial advertising in Quebec must be exclusively in the French language. Section 59 exempted religious and political messages from this requirement. Thus, Bill 101 attempted to avoid substantive restrictions on freedom of speech, while restricting the form of the speech itself.

This attempt was ultimately undermined by expansive readings of the meaning of 'freedom of expression' by successive courts and other judicial bodies. In ruling unconstitutional this provision of Bill 101, the Supreme Court of Canada viewed language as an integral component of the fundamental right of freedom of expression. The court observed, 'Language is so intimately related to the form and content of expression that there cannot be true freedom of expression by means of language if one is prohibited from using the language of one's choice.'[21] The right to express oneself in the language of one's choice is therefore a fundamental component of freedom of expression. This right is notably different from the other Charter language rights in that, like freedom of speech itself, freedom to express oneself in the language of one's choice is a *liberty*, which thereby places constraints on what governments may do to limit the right, without imposing on governments duties to facilitate its implementation. On the other hand, the *Charter* does enumerate language rights that constitute positive entitlements for individuals with corresponding duties for governments – for example, the provision of government services and minority language education. This was emphasized by the court when it observed, 'The respondents are asserting a freedom, the freedom to express oneself in the language of one's choice in an area of non-governmental activity, as opposed to a language right guaranteed in the Constitution.'[22] This strikingly illustrates the point that the court interpreted the issue as being outside the realm of language rights as such.

It is worth emphasizing that Bill 101 had carefully exempted religious and political messages from these requirements, precisely on the grounds that these constituted the traditional domains of freedom of expression. This constitutional subtlety was overridden by the court's expansive reading of freedom of expression, to include commercial signs, especially company names and advertising. In the case of signs, the court decision found Section 58 in contravention of the Quebec Charter of Rights and Freedoms as well as of the Canadian Charter of Rights and Freedoms.[23] It found that, while the government might require the use of French on public signs, it could not ban the use of other languages in conjunction with it. In explaining its decision, the Supreme Court of Canada, maintained,

Commercial expression, like political expression, is one of the forms of expression that is deserving of constitutional protection because it serves individual and societal values in a free and democratic society ... commercial expression ... plays a significant role in enabling individuals to make informed economic choices, an important aspect of individual self-fulfilment and personal autonomy.[24]

The court acknowledged the importance of protecting the French language in Quebec, yet it concluded that the Quebec government had failed to establish the necessity of *French-only* signs, as opposed to bilingual signs with French being the more prominently displayed.[25] On the other hand, the court's support for the individual right of freedom of expression did not extend to a defence of unilingual English commercial signs. Put another way, the court decided that freedom to express one's commercial name and message in the language of one's choice was compatible with a *mandatory* requirement (in Quebec) that one express oneself in a different language (French) as well.

The court's reasoning attracted significant criticism. Michael Mandel, for example, condemned it as a defence of economic power against popular sovereignty. Although agreeing that 'commercial expression' is important to society, Mandel viewed it as an unwarranted inference to conclude that it deserves constitutional protection.[26] Other observers viewed the decision as a consistent application of liberal, individualist values to Charter rights, including language rights. Claude Jean Galipeau insisted that, albeit indirectly, 'the Court followed in spirit the language rights contained in Sections 16–23 of the Canadian Charter and Section 133 of the Constitution Act, 1867.' Galipeau also suggested that the decision reflects a consistent application of the broad conception of freedom of speech, extending beyond conventional political speech, that has emerged in recent court decisions.[27] Subsequently, a similar argument and conclusion would prevail in yet another decision concerning commercial signs in Quebec, by the United Nations Human Rights Committee.[28]

The Supreme Court's apparently balanced approach nevertheless indicates that commercial expression is not *simply* an extension of the principle of freedom of expression. Take, for example, the court's endorsement of a requirement that public signs be bilingual. Could one imagine as defensible a parallel requirement that, before one gave a speech on a current issue in public in English in Quebec, one was required to either repeat it immediately in French, or else to distribute a written French translation of it?[29] Such a requirement would be condemned as posing a 'chilling effect' on free speech for anglophones in Quebec. For a unilingual anglophone, or even one modestly fluent in French, the time and effort required to produce a translation would discourage all but the most committed from uttering a word. By the same token, if the medium of expression inevitably colours the message, then a requirement that one present it in another language raises a distinct possibility of message distortion arising from a possibly cruder grasp of the instruments of communication, that is, vocabulary, syntax, and idiom.[30] Most would consider such requirements a serious limitation of freedom of expression applied to political speech, yet the Supreme Court of Canada endorsed precisely this position for commercial signs. Clearly, there is something significantly different about commercial signs that warrants toleration of mandatory bilingualism. Is the difference sufficiently great as to cast doubt on the validity of including commercial signs as a component of freedom of expression?

Leslie Green argued that an understanding of the expressive function of language would support the court's decision. One important basis of freedom of expression is that it provides opportunities for individuals to engage in expressive acts, understood as 'attempts to get others to understand or share some proposition or attitude'[31] Green further maintained that 'the use of a language may have an expressive function without regard to subject matter.'[32] For example, he noted that a decision to erect a unilingual English commercial sign in Quebec might well be an expressive act par excellence – a political protest or a statement of the preferred status of the English language. Since this expressive element may emerge in any context of communication, Green concluded that one must adopt the broadest conception of the domain of free speech. However, such an example addresses the ancillary features of the specific focus of commercial communication. 'Drink Coca Cola' is a typical example of commercial messages. It constitutes an 'expressive act' in a relatively narrow sense, of attempting to influence the economic behaviour, that is purchasing activity, of others. It does not, however, enter into a form of dialogue that is a characteristic feature of political discourse. It does not attempt to persuade anyone about values to share, issues to address, or identities to embrace.

On Green's account, the message, 'Drink Coca Cola,' is accorded the same status as the message 'End Apartheid.' The latter message has traditionally been seen as intrinsically more important and therefore deserving of constitutional protection. To put it another way, the modes of expression relevant to our assertions of citizenship and of artistic and religious expression have been viewed as the central dimensions of freedom of expression. Extending freedom of expression to commercial advertising risks trivializing the very concept, by equating freedom of expression with commercial expression, that is, something not central to self-expression.

On the other hand, the argument has been made that for some people commercial speech is indeed important – more important, say, than the speech embodied in newspaper editorials or political pamphlets.[33]

Although such views may be disputed, they nevertheless serve as a reminder that even commercial signs are a form of communication that requires some subtlety in the delivery of message, which, in turn, speaks to the importance of the opportunity of communicating in one's own language. This suggests that commercial expression serves a significant social or community function. However, this line of argument is not readily persuasive as to why commercial expression falls within the domain of freedom of expression.

Although the case for viewing commercial signs as a component of freedom of expression may be less than air-tight, the case for the restriction of other languages is decidedly shaky. The primary justification of this restriction turns on its importance for the survival and development of the 'French fact' in Quebec. It is readily understandable that public signs must include French, but the necessity for the absence of other languages is not so apparent. Such was the conclusion of the Gendron Commission, which examined language issues in Quebec for the Quebec government, and proposed that the *inclusion* of French be obligatory on signs in the public and parapublic sectors, with the French language to take precedence.[34] The commission did not extend this proposal to the private sector or suggest excluding languages from signs.

The court emphasized the absence in the government's brief to the court of any evidence documenting the necessity for a provision to exclude other languages from commercial signs. Although government rationales have emphasized the importance of doing so, little evidence has been presented regarding the anticipated impact on the francophone population or of the negative effects of the unilingual English or bilingual signs. Various commentaries on the necessity of unilingual French signs acknowledged its irrelevance to the survival of the French language, emphasizing instead its role in assuaging francophone psychological insecurities on linguistic matters.

After stressing the significance of such threats to the French language as the low birthrate of francophones, allophone assimilation to the anglophone community, and the attractions of English-speaking products for young francophones, one commentator observed that 'to keep English off commercial signs would not solve any of these problems, of course, but putting it back would give the threat a painful symbolic reality.'[35] The necessity for unilingual signs stems rather from the desire to send strong signals to immigrant groups that there is only one official language in the province. The Conseil de la Langue Française, a provincial government-appointed advisory body on language policies, urged the premier to reinstate French-only commercial signs, on the ground they 'indicate clearly to visitors and immigrants that only one language is official in Quebec: French.' The council emphasized, 'Bilingual signs would carry a totally different message. By putting French and English on an equal base, it would signal immigrants that they can choose whichever language they prefer.'[36]

Indeed, the linguistic assimilation of non-French-speaking immigrants in Quebec has been a central issue in the language debate of the province for the past three decades. Success on this front is essential for eliminating potential threats to the dominance of the French language, though it must be emphasized that French has been and remains the first language of more than 80 per cent of Quebec citizens.

In fact, the demographic strength of the French language in Quebec has improved marginally in the past decade.[37] Consequently, it is difficult to believe that bilingual signs constitute a threat to the French language, since they are compatible with the government's expressed purpose, to allow francophones to 'live their lives' in the French language. The presence of English on such signs is far less threatening to the French language than, for example, the availability of English-language records and films.[38] More to the point, Québécois generally support the notion of bilingual signs as the fairest policy, strongly suggesting that they do not find bilingual signs threatening to their cultural identity.[39] These considerations suggest that unilingual signs primarily serve as a *symbolic* buttress to broader policy purposes of linguistic assimilation and are not actually necessary in the defence of the position of the French language itself.

The second line of argument offered in support of unilingual signs is that it is a manifestation of collective rights. In response to the 1988 Supreme Court decision, the Liberal government in Quebec passed Bill 178, which reinstated the main elements of the sign laws but invoked Section 33 of the Charter of Rights and Freedoms (the 'override clause') to protect the legislation from court challenges. Bill 178 required French-only on exterior signs, but permitted bilingual signs within stores so long as the French language was the more prominently displayed.[40] The latter provision represented a softening of language regulations in Bill 101, much to the chagrin of many Québécois nationalists.

In defending his decision to use the override clause, Premier Robert Bourassa invoked the importance of collective rights for francophones over the individual rights of anglophones in linguistic matters:

At the end, when a choice had to be made between individual rights and collective rights, I arbitrated in favour of collective rights, by agreeing to invoke the not-withstanding clause.

I repeat that I am the only head of government in North America who had the moral right to follow this course, the only political leader of a community which is a small minority.

Who can better, and who has more of a duty to protect and promote the French culture if not the Premier of Quebec? But I made this decision with enormous reluctance.[41]

Premier Bourassa obviously considered that he was protecting a collective right for the survival of the French language. His position is reinforced by at least one Anglo-Canadian academic, Reg Whitaker, who criticized the Supreme Court decision for 'threaten[ing] a delicate and complex balance between individual and collective rights.'[42] But what was the content of the collective right being invoked to justify these practices?

Although there has been much discussion of collective rights to the French language, there has been remarkably little attention to specifying their content. One commentator suggested that it is 'the right of a cultural group to protect itself, a group right to self-preservation.'[43] Recalling the discussion in Chapter 1, collective rights are justified as a means of preserving a cultural structure as a context of choice for group members. Collective rights are ultimately grounded on a commitment to equality of respect for individuals. Given the centrality of language to Québécois culture, language certainly must count as a legitimate focus of efforts at cultural preservation. However, where such efforts affect other cultures, they must also be judged by other criteria. One of these is the equality principle, whereby the status and rights claimed on behalf of the collectivity can be extended to other groups as well. Another is the criterion of consistency, that is, whether the measures taken accord equality of respect for all individuals. These are decidedly problematic in regard to the sign provisions.

Bill 101 entailed a *strong* sense of French language rights in recognizing francophones' right to live their lives in French. However, Bill 178 suggested a more expansive interpretation of these rights. Presumably, bilingual signs would be sufficient for the strong sense of language rights – for self-preservation, insofar as individuals would always have French available to them in conducting their affairs. Bill 178 went beyond this to ensure the absence of other languages from public visibility. Accordingly francophone collective rights must entail a right to a totally French linguistic environment, a right to *not see* any other language. It requires the active suppression of other languages. It is therefore a remarkably intolerant right, that cannot be shared by other language groups in the society. In this regard, it violates the elements of both equality and consistency. Not only can it not be extended to other language groups in society, but it involves a denial of equal respect for those other language groups.[44]

Bilingual signs with mandatory French, on the other hand, demonstrate equal respect for all language groups. This requires recognition of the French character of Quebec society, while allowing room for other languages. The exclusive use of French for signs is a peculiar collective right in that, unlike other candidates that assert positive rights to do or control something, this one confers a negative right to prevent something – in this case the appearance of any other language in public.

One might counter that the collective right is a positive right, to wit, the right to decide the languages of the community. Reg Whitaker argued that the issue is fundamentally one concerning sovereignty: 'Language is a sovereignty issue in Quebec in that it revolves around the sovereign right of the Quebec community, through those political institutions under its control, to legislate the priority of the French language within the boundaries of the community.'[45] At issue here is power itself, rather than a particular goal such as preservation of the culture. This construction of the issue is false in that it implies that sovereignty as such does not admit limits to the exercise of its power. This ignores the role of constitutions, and charters of rights, in defining the limits of state power. One would hardly maintain that judicial override of a law making it a crime to dye one's hair represented an assault on the sovereignty of the Canadian people. Similarly, it is possible to challenge particular manifestations of the effort to establish the priority of the French language, without denying the 'sovereignty' of Quebec political institutions.

Second, there is a conflation of the concept of sovereignty with the specific collective right of cultural preservation that is the justification for such language legislation. This conflation gains much of its force from the conspicuous denial of the presence of other language groups that form part of the Quebec community. Once these groups are acknowledged, this assertion of sovereignty takes perverse forms. The anglophone minority in Quebec jointly shares in a collective right to ban its own language. This recalls Rousseau's paradox of the general will, whereby criminals willed their own executions! Once the linguistic diversity of Quebec society is acknowledged, this assertion of collective rights as sovereignty is seriously inadequate to the defence of the language legislation.

In short, the concept of 'collective rights' to language presented in relation to Quebec language legislation is seriously flawed. These considerations lead to the conclusion that the sign provisions are not defensible on the ground of protection of francophone collective rights and are excessive restrictions of linguistic expression in other languages.

Whether one found their conclusions persuasive, these various judicial decisions firmly established that the sign provisions of Bill 101 intruded on the individual right of freedom of expression. They did not assert any positive or substantive language rights for the anglophone community, but simply identified a negative right, a zone, the private realm, within which governments could not reasonably intrude. The judgments made clear that the Quebec government was free to enact whatever measures it saw fit for the public sector.

Partly in response to judicial decisions critical of its policy, the Quebec government introduced Bill 86, to amend Quebec's language policy to accommodate these individual rights. In introducing the legislation, Claude Ryan, the minister responsible for these policy areas, presented Bill 86 as an issue of resolving a conflict of rights, and indicated that he was firmly on the side of individual rights:

It's the old problem of trying to reconcile individual rights with collective aspirations ... I have no hesitation in stating that, as a basic principle in a liberal democracy, individual rights come first. They are the foundation upon which must rest the recognition of collective rights. The collective rights, to me, are acceptable and necessary to the extent that they are the extension of genuine individual rights.[46]

In regard to public signs posted by private entities, the amended Section 58 of Bill 101 specified that government regulations shall determine when languages must be unilingual French, bilingual, or possibly unilingual in a language other than French.[47] The intention of the government was to distinguish between on-site signage and billboard advertising. All publicly owned corporations in Quebec (for example, Hydro-Quebec) would be required to use only French on billboards or within public transportation systems. For private companies, billboards would still be required to be unilingual French. External (on-site) signs could be in French plus another language, so long as the French portion was twice as prominent as the other language.[48] By putting the restrictions in regulations rather than in the law, it was expected that the regulations would be safe from court challenges. This compromise would avoid the complaints of small businesses serving a clientele in their immediate communities but still ensure that Rue Ste Catherine was not awash in English language bill-boards of large-scale corporations.

A noteworthy feature of this provision is that it largely ignores the ratio-nale of the various judicial decisions. The United Nations Human Rights Committee, for example, had categorically asserted that *all* forms of com-mercial communication were covered by the freedom of expression rights, and, therefore, one could not make the distinctions offered here. In that respect, the provision still violated the individual right of freedom of speech as understood by the courts. For those inclined to doubt that com-mercial expression is included within constitutionally protected freedom of expression, this represented a more acceptable accommodation of the respective priorities of the two major language groups within Quebec.

These conflicts arose over traditional individual rights transgressed by Quebec language laws. The question needs to be asked – should Quebec anglophones have specific language rights and if so, which ones? Prior to an analysis of that question, it is useful to review Québécois public opin-ion on the matter.

Public Opinion on Language Rights in Quebec

Since the early 1970s, francophone opinion in Quebec has been decid-edly more supportive of some recognition of English than government policy would indicate. However, this opinion is both volatile and consid-erably ambiguous. A Quebec poll conducted in 1974 revealed that only 18.9 per cent of francophones preferred a policy of French unilingualism. Approximately one-half (47.6 per cent) supported a priority status for French with some recognition of English, and another third (32.3 per cent) supported equal status for French and English.[49] Subsequent polls demonstrated a continuation of this distribution of opinion. A 1983 Sore-com poll indicated that 72 per cent of the francophone population believed that a language other than French should be permitted on signs and that 65 per cent agreed that government services should be available in English. Michael Goldbloom, the president of Alliance Québec, emphasized that 'the inescapable conclusion arising from this poll is that a consensus exists between the English-speaking and the French-speaking communities – which is not reflected in Bill 101.'[50]

More strikingly, the 1985 Canadian Facts poll of Canadian public opin-ion indicated that Quebeckers have the highest level of support for minority language services in the country. More than 80 per cent of

Quebec respondents supported the notion that schools, hospitals, post offices, and department stores should provide services in the minority language, and more than 70 per cent supported the same for provincial governments and business services.[51]

More recently, Québécois opinion continues to be supportive of bilingual public signs. A Decima poll in the spring of 1990 indicated that two-thirds (66.2 per cent) of Québécois were opposed to laws prohibiting languages other than French on signs in their communities.[52] This is consistent with a CROP poll in January 1993 which reported that 68 per cent of Quebeckers, and 64 per cent of Québécois supported bilingual signs. In explaining the majority support for bilingual signs, the analysis suggested that 'there is widespread concern over the unfavourable image the ban on English has given the province.'[53] Two 1996 polls (March and April) indicated that Québécois consider the present language law, which permits some bilingual signs, as appropriately severe and view the state of the French language as improving.[54] In short, these polls portray a continuing pattern of support for some recognition of English in Quebec society.

On the other hand, there are ongoing indications of ambiguity in this apparent support. A 1984 Sorecom poll indicated that a plurality of francophones (42 per cent) believed that Bill 101 limited English language use to an appropriate degree, while 29 per cent thought it too much.[55] Similarly, a 1986 poll found that 46 per cent of Québécois support unilingual French signs, and 75 per cent support the preservation of Montreal's 'French face.'[56] The ambiguity is highlighted in two 1989 findings regarding Québécois views of the sign laws. A Decima poll reported that Québécois were evenly split on the subject of Bill 178, with 50.2 per cent favouring it and 49.8 per cent opposed.[57] Yet another 1989 survey indicated that 70 per cent of Quebec francophones agreed with the proposition that 'A business in Quebec should accept that Quebec is basically French and put only French on signs outside its buildings.'[58] There is considerable variation, to say the least, between the two sets of opinions. This is not to say that they are contradictory. One might well believe that individuals should be entitled to put other languages on signs, but nonetheless prefer that they not do so. At a minimum, this suggests that the expression of public opinion is highly sensitive to the nuances of the question. Furthermore, anxieties about the position of the French language are an important ingredient in attitudes towards toleration of other languages in Quebec public life.

These various polls indicated substantial and continuing public support for the provision of English language services and a measure of tolerance of English in the public face of Quebec. At the same time, there was ongoing concern for the protection of the French language and for the preservation of its symbolic priority in Quebec society. The ambiguity remains and is a permanent feature of the language issue in Quebec. However, subject to those considerations, Québécois opinion is strongly supportive of English minority language rights. This fact has tended to be ignored in government legislation and has remained submerged in the public debate that has transpired.

Language Rights of Quebec Anglophones

The previous discussion has proceeded on the implicit assumption that the anglophone community in Quebec is entitled to language rights. Precisely what those rights ought to include has been a subject of sporadic debate. In the wake of Bill 101, Quebec anglophones have tended to denounce it as a denial of 'traditional rights' to their language. A recent exchange between a Quebec anglophone and a Québécois nationalist revealed the tenor of this debate. William Watson's protests about restrictions on English language rights earned the retort from François Vaillancourt that 'the implication is that anglophones have a right to live and work solely in English in Montreal and to impose the burden of bilingualism mainly on francophones'[59] Anglophones, the Québécois nationalist further insists, must become bilingual before a useful dialogue is possible. Although Vaillancourt opposed the active suppression of languages, at no point did he recognize any language rights for minorities. Although this is an uncharitable interpretation of Quebec anglophone demands and an inaccurate portrayal of the linguistic picture in Quebec, it is a reminder that the English minority in Quebec once enjoyed unrivalled linguistic privileges. One could live one's life as if the French fact did not exist. This extraordinary privilege reminds us that the mere existence of privileges does not create rights to them. Accordingly, talk of the 'traditional rights' of Quebec anglophones requires careful specification.

While not claiming to offer an exhaustive list, Watson sketched the main elements of anglophone demands: 'English Quebecers would wish to maintain a variety of rights: their right to educate their children in English at public expense equal to whatever was being spent on French children; their right to their own publicly funded universities and social and cultural institutions; and their right to use the English language — including the right to put English on commercial signs.'[60] Although not explicitly stated, the 'right to use English' is not simply a toleration right but also promotion oriented, presumably including entitlement to government services in English. These should, Watson insisted, be entrenched in a constitution. This is a substantial list, extending considerably beyond the acceptable practice of language rights in Canada – even within Quebec.

The question thus arises, does the anglophone minority meet the conditions for recognition of language rights? The criteria identified earlier emphasize the size of the community, the commitment of its participants to its survival, and its status as an indigenous language. There can be no question of the status of English as an indigenous language in Quebec, extending over two centuries. Its claim to recognition on this score is as strong as the claims of French.

In relation to the criterion of size, the anglophone community rests in an ambivalent position. Defined by mother tongue, the anglophone community is a declining element in Quebec society, constituting 9.2 per cent of the 1991 Quebec population (down from 10.9 per cent in 1981). If defined by home language, the English-speaking community is still only 11.2 per cent of the Quebec population (down from 12.7 per cent in 1981).[61] Although there is no specific minimum percentage for such recognition, these figures approach the outer limits of a legitimate claim for a comprehensive list of language rights.

Yet two considerations counter this relatively small size in favour of some recognition. The anglophone community is geographically concentrated in the Montreal area and the Eastern Townships, which greatly increases the practicality of provision of the services associated with language rights. Second, the anglophone community forms part of the larger English language community in Canada as a whole. As such, its prospects for survival as a community within Quebec are virtually assured. However, a continued decline in its demographic presence in Quebec could well jeopardize its legitimate claims.

More generally, there is an important sense in which anglophone claims of 'traditional rights' are surely valid. One of the criteria used in judging whether a group is entitled to rights is whether there is an established tradition in the society for treating the group separately. Obviously, there is a long-established tradition within Quebec of provision of the language services demanded. With English language institutions already in place, it would be strikingly unjust to withdraw them. It would also be particularly easy to translate existing provisions into legal and/or constitutional rights. This is not to say that all of the above-quoted set deserve legal recognition.

In wake of the dramatic decline of elementary school enrolments in the English language school system, a right to English language postsecondary institutions ceases to be credible. Similarly, a right to separate English language institutions is in some cases credible only because of their present provision. Obviously, they do not justify an equal status of English with French as official languages within Quebec. The attempt to eliminate such status in Bill 101 has been implicitly endorsed by the Task Force on Canadian Unity's recommendation that Section 133 of the BNA Act be amended to permit provincial discretion in such matters. However, the anglophone community can legitimately claim the right to government services, health and social services, and education in English as *rights*. This is not as fulsome a list as Quebec anglophones have traditionally enjoyed, albeit informally, but it is consistent with their present demographic position and the practice of language rights in Canada. In fact, Quebec language policy has developed significantly to recognize most of these entitlements as rights.

Minority Language Education

Under Bill 101 English-speaking residents of Quebec are entitled to an education in their maternal language. However, Bill 101 made a sharp distinction between resident English-language groups and immigrants. All English speakers who were Quebec residents as of 26 August 1977 are entitled to such an education, as well as those who sustain their Quebec residency and receive English-language instruction within the province.[62] All those moving to the province of Quebec subsequent to the passage of the law in 1977 must have their children educated in French. This includes English-speaking individuals whether from other Canadian provinces or any other part of the world.

This feature of the law has drawn sharp criticism. For example, W.R. Lederman argued that this constitutes a violation of the historic right of the anglophone minority in Quebec. As an alternative he suggested that 'the right to attend the anglophone school system in Quebec should obtain for any children whose mother tongue is English, wherever the family comes from in the English-speaking world and whenever they come.'[63] As a compromise, Lederman suggested that English residents must be bilingual, but yet have unlimited access to English-language education.

The question of access has only become more pressing with the consequences of implementation of Bill 101. In wake of the limitations it imposed, enrolment in the English language schools has declined relentlessly, to the point where there are now more French language schools in Ontario than there are English language schools in Quebec.[64] Although the 'Canada Clause' expanded potential access to the English language schools, there has been a net emigration of English-speaking people from Quebec over the past twenty years, with a consequent reduction in enrolments. To offset this downward spiral, the anglophone community lobbied for reforms to Bill 101 to allow immigrants from all English language countries to enrol.

In 1992 a provincial government appointed Task Force on English Education concluded that 'access to English-language schooling must be widened to include all immigrant children who were educated in English or whose parents come from English-speaking parts of the world.'[65] It argued that such a change would have a negligible impact upon enrolment in French language schools – about a 1 per cent reduction – while substantially increasing English language school enrolments (about 20 per cent). Such a change was necessary to improve the survival prospects for the English school system and, by extension, the English-speaking community within Quebec. The Task Force insisted, _

The idea that the English-speaking community of Quebec is not threatened because of the North American context in which we live begs the question. The 'Englishness' of individual Quebecers may not be threatened, but Quebec's English-speaking community as a working part of the larger Quebec society cannot function without the requisite human resources to make its collective contribution. If it is prevented from renewing itself, it will simply fade away.[66]

Sharing similar concerns, Alliance Québec, the anglophone and allophone lobby group, adopted a resolution at its 1993 convention 'calling for the right of all Quebeckers to freely choose the language of education of their children.'[67] This would have permitted the allophone group and francophones unlimited access to the English system as well, and significantly redistributed the enrolments between the two systems. In effect, it would have rescinded the education provisions of Bill 101.

Despite concurring with the thrust of Lederman's proposal, I would argue that it rests on an insufficiently established premise. Language rights are acknowledged in some charters of human rights, however, such recognition is not obviously in conflict with the educational provisions of Bill 101. For example, the International Covenant on Civil and Political Rights states that linguistic minorities in a community with other members of the group shall not be denied the right to use their language (Article 27).[68] This does not apparently entitle such groups to educational facilities in their own language. Thus, the assertion of language rights in this matter requires careful attention to the philosophical bases of such recognition.

The discussion about the conditions under which language rights hold stated that membership in an ongoing community and a sharing of language and culture were required. This basis determined that immigrants to a new cultural community do not possess a claim to language rights. Under these principles, Bill 101 appears to be too restrictive of access to English language education, while Lederman's proposal may be too broad. The extent of these respective excesses turns on the issue of community membership. Who may legitimately claim membership in the local English community? In its White Paper on language policy, the Quebec government maintained that 'parents who studied in English schools in Quebec can legitimately be thought to belong to the linguistic community which created and maintained this system of instruction. These parents are in a way the heirs of the English schools.'[69] This, however, is entirely too narrow a conception of the English linguistic community. It is the language, not the schools themselves, that defines this community. At a minimum, English-speaking residents of any part of Canada can legitimately claim to be part of a larger English-Canadian cultural community with the English-speaking Quebeckers. Thus, they ought to be entitled to claim the same language rights as the English language residents of Quebec. Bill 101 fails to draw proper distinctions between English Canadians moving to Quebec and, say, Spanish-speaking immigrant from Chile.

On the other hand, it is not obvious that an English language mother tongue is a sufficient basis to claim membership in the Quebec English language community. Focusing on shared traditions and cultural heritage may allow the argument that immigrants from the British Isles or the United States, for example, are sufficiently similar in culture that they should be included in this extended community. At this point, however, a commitment to shared history, experience, and interaction as a definition of community is left behind. Moving further afield, an African or Asian immigrant whose mother tongue is English likely shares little else in relation to the English-Canadian cultural community. Thus, Lederman's proposal for unlimited access to the English language education system goes beyond the bounds that the principle undergirding language right admits.

At a minimum, then, English Canadians moving to Quebec should on these principles have a recognized right of access to English language education.[70] Non-Canadian English-speaking immigrants do not have as strong a claim to these language rights. However, where such access does not threaten the dominance of the French language, and yet helps preserve the English language community, it is a reasonable extension of the promotion-oriented commitment to minority language education. With some qualification, the task force's proposal that access be restricted to immigrants from English-speaking parts of the world meets these dual requirements. A recent survey of the international distribution of languages indicates that English is widely used in over thirty countries around the world. This poses the potential for significant redistribution of students in the Quebec education system. However, if only those countries where English was the dominant language were included, the list would be reduced to a dozen countries, overwhelmingly comprising Anglo-American democracies that share a broadly similar culture.[71] Unhappily for the Quebec English school system, these countries are also a diminishing source of immigrants to Canada. What is consistent with principle may be insufficiently effective in practice.

Finally, non-English-speaking immigrants cannot claim any language rights in regard to the language to which they will assimilate. In relation to the principles undergirding language rights developed here, there is no basis for the assertion of rights to choice of language of instruction. The same applies to the Alliance Québec proposal for free choice regarding the language of education.

The passage of the Canadian Charter of Rights and Freedoms in 1982 effectively expanded the minority language education provisions of Bill 101 to include the 'Canada Clause' (Section 23) which ensured that individuals educated in English in Canada have a right to access to the English language school system in Quebec. The courts have endorsed the view that the Charter overrides Bill 101's minority language provisions.[72] In 1993, Bill 86 amended Bill 101 to conform to Section 23 of the Charter. Bill 86 also included provisions easing access to the English language school system for special cases; disabled children most notably benefited from these changes. Anglophone parents who enrolled their children in the francophone school system were permitted to retain their rights to the English language school system.

These changes were considerably less than those sought by the anglophone community. Although the government was initially favourably disposed towards the task force recommendation on access, it was keenly aware of polls indicating that a majority of Québécois would oppose any move to increase access to English schools.[73] Clearly, francophone support for minority language education rights was limited by concerns to protect the position of the French language in Quebec. Accordingly, the government chose to limit itself to the 'housekeeping' changes already noted. Nevertheless, official recognition by the Quebec government of the 'Canada Clause' marked an acceptance of a broader notion of the English language community.

The issue of community membership will continue to bedevil the education debate in Quebec for the foreseeable future. At this writing, the Quebec government has drafted legislation (Bill 109) to replace the denominational school system in Quebec with a linguistically based system.[74] This has predictably created an intense debate with the issue of community membership as a central element. Who may be counted as a member of the English-speaking community in Quebec for purposes of voting in school board elections and paying taxes to support an English language school system? Is it only those whose children are eligible under Section 23 of the Charter to attend the English language school system? (the Parti Québécois government proposal), or is it 'the Quebec community of English expression,' that is, those who consider themselves members of the English language community (the position endorsed by the Liberal opposition in Quebec and the English language community itself)?[75]

The latter position is consistent with present practice in Quebec, where individuals may choose which system they wish to support through education taxes and school board elections. With the proposed changes, many people who presently choose to pay taxes to the English language school system would be required to support the French language system. This creates the perverse anomaly that many individuals who are strongly integrated in the anglophone community would not be permitted to support its institutional infrastructures. For example, one schoolteacher, who has taught in English education for twenty-seven years in Quebec, is ineligible to vote in the school board elections where he works because he received his own education in French.[76] More broadly, those without children would be automatically assigned to the voting lists for the French language schools.

The problem here is that real communities are not defined by administrative criteria, in this case eligibility for participation in a particular school system. As Quebec Liberal leader Daniel Johnson remarked, 'Canadian citizens in Quebec who come from the United States and various countries of the British Commonwealth have been here among us for a long time and consider themselves legitimate and full-fledged members, as Quebecers, of the Quebec anglophone community.'[77] The proposed system flies in the face of these real psychological attachments and networks of community ties that are the foundations of community life. For that reason, there is much merit in a compromise proposal whereby parents without children in school could choose the system in which they would vote and pay taxes. The PQ government has to date resisted demands that it adopt the compromise proposal, apparently out of a concern that this could become grounds for future courts to mandate expanded access to the English language system in Quebec.[78]

This debate is not simply one about the proper boundaries of the English-speaking community in Quebec. The stakes in this debate are considerable. The proposed changes would have a significant impact in redistributing resources from the English language to the French language school system. The already beleaguered English school system would face greater financial hardships compounding the difficulties stemming from the drastic enrolment decline. Somewhat ironically, the legislation also would eliminate the present practice of the Protestant School Board providing French language instruction. Section 19 of Bill 109 stipulates, 'A French language school board shall provide educational services in French; an English language school board shall provide educational services in English.'[79] This change would further reduce the enrolment levels in the English language system.

In light of these developments, a broader notion of the English-speaking community in Quebec is an important basis for maintaining a viable English language school system in Quebec. Events may unfold to that end. Francophone opinion in Quebec is apparently sympathetic to that possibility. In addition, the Liberal federal government has insisted on a requirement of consensus within Quebec, carefully undefined, as a necessary precondition for its willingness to pass the required constitutional amendment resolution. These factors might well lead to a broadly acceptable compromise arrangement. However, the stresses upon the English language school system will ensure that it continues to be a focal point for policy debate.

Health and Social Services

The Quebec government passed two notable pieces of legislation affecting the status of the English language. In 1983 Bill 57 softened the impact of Bill 101 in relation to English language institutions by allowing these institutions to function internally, and with each other, in English, and by allowing continued use of English place names and street names where they were already established. It also allowed for the possibility of signs exclusively in another language for *foreign* ethnic groups. These changes came in the wake of strong complaints from the anglophone community that the existing law threatened the survival of English hospitals, which were experiencing increasing staff recruitment problems. They argued that they should be required to maintain 'institutional bilingualism' rather than 'individual bilingualism,' whereby promotion prospects for staff would depend on a bilingual proficiency.[80] These measures could not be described as an expansion of English language rights, but rather as a reduction in the intrusiveness of the French language upon the English-speaking community.

More significant in regard to language rights was the passage of Bill 142 in 1986, which stated that 'every English-speaking person is entitled to receive health services and social services in the English language' subject to availability.[81] One noteworthy feature of this wording was that it did not distinguish between English speakers and those belonging to the English language community of Quebec, as Bill 101 attempted to do.[82] This was a welcome recognition that certain services simply must be in the language of the client in order to be properly provided. Although it is not constitutionally entrenched, Bill 142 nonetheless created a legal right to such services in the province of Quebec and thereby marked an important advance in the status of English language rights in Quebec. Quebec thereby advanced considerably beyond the language rights recognized in the Charter, and was thus also considerably more generous towards its English-speaking minority than the other provinces were to their French-speaking minorities.

These measures, in conjunction with the passage of Bill 86, represent an increasing symbolic accommodation of the anglophone community, a recognition that anglophones belong to the Quebec community, while maintaining the essential policy thrust of Bill 101 to assure the French character of Quebec. They also ensure that, on balance, Quebec language policy is consistent with the practice of language rights in Canada, though less generous than Québécois opinion would endorse.

As indicated earlier, Canadian public opinion supports three elements of language rights – to federal government services, minority language education, and hospital services. Quebec opinion is considerably more generous, as it would include provincial services and services from business in this list.[83] In relation to those elements endorsed nationally, Quebec offers the most extensive minority language education system available anywhere in Canada, including postsecondary education. By the same token, Quebec supports the most extensive array of health and social service institutions in the country for its official language minority.

In contrast to these relatively generous legislative components, Quebec language policy does not explicitly recognize rights to government services in English for the anglophone community. It allows their provision through its permissive exemptions regarding language use within provincial government institutions. On the other hand, it restricts English language services in municipal institutions to those with an anglophone majority. Both components deserve comment. In regard to provincial government services, the complaint is voiced that 'it is still difficult to obtain either written or oral information in English.'[84] This is partly because anglophones are remarkable mainly for their absence from the Quebec public service, a reality that will not change in the foreseeable future.[85] Although it is defensible to insist that the Quebec government need not offer bilingual services throughout the province, it is obviously indefensible to maintain that the 600,000 English-speaking citizens in the Montreal metropolitan area do not warrant such consideration.

Similarly, the requirement that English signage and municipal services shall only be available in communities with an English-speaking majority is an unreasonably restrictive approach to language rights, though quite consistent with the logic of the broader policy itself. As noted at the outset, the majority status of French serves as the principal justification for the official status of French and the exclusion of other languages. Thus, it is at least logically consistent that the only recognition of English would occur in those institutions where it formed the majority. However, the perversity of such an approach was graphically demonstrated in the community of Rosemère.

Bill 101 permitted communities with an anglophone majority to post bilingual street signs. As of the 1981 census, the anglophone portion of Rosemère had slipped to just under 50 per cent. Accordingly, the language authorities, prodded by complaints from a few residents, proposed to force the community to post unilingual French signs. The francophone mayor of Rosemère, Yvan Deschênes, protested the office's decision, and held a plebiscite in the town on retaining bilingual status. In the plebiscite (held 12 April 1992), 78 per cent voted to keep bilingual status (there was a 40 per cent turnout rate).[86] However, the Office de la langue française authorities were adamant, emphasizing that the legislation did not require consideration of community preference on the subject. The picture that emerged was one of a tolerant francophone majority willing to retain an English language presence, but being stymied by a rigid law enforced by equally rigid bureaucrats. This was a significant issue for the broader waning anglophone community as well, since the same prospect would likely be faced by more than a dozen communities with waning anglophone majorities in the near future. In the subsequent amendments to Bill 101, embodied in Bill 86, the majority status requirement was retained but the removal of entitlements to post bilingual signs became a discretionary decision of the government.[87]

Granted that there is a certain arbitrary quality to any threshold figure, nevertheless it is strikingly illogical that a 50 per cent concentration is adequate for recognition of a language, but 48 per cent is not.[88] This is particularly glaring when it is contrasted with the Gendron Commission recommendation that 10 per cent should be the threshold for provision of bilingual services.[89] The latter offered a generous approach to language rights; the former, a begrudging one. Clearly, a 48 per cent concentration – and even a figure significantly below this – meets the criteria for recognition of language rights developed earlier. In these communities, the English-speaking population constitute ongoing, well-established communities with deep roots in Quebec. Furthermore, it is readily feasible for municipal and provincial governments to provide services in English. It is equally reasonable that signage be bilingual where the English-speaking population is a significant component of a municipality. Finally, doing so does not in any way threaten the position of the French language in Quebec.

These criticisms notwithstanding, the Quebec government has conceded an important principle in asserting that anglophones have language rights to health and social services that extend beyond what is already constitutionally recognized, even if these rights have been historically accorded. Thus, Quebec language policy is consistent with the national practice of language rights in Canada.

Conclusion

The Quebec approach to the nature of language rights is distinctly different from what appears at first sight. Although it treats language rights as a right of the collectivity, analysis of the justificatory rationale reveals serious inconsistencies in its logic that stem from this formulation. In the final analysis, language rights in Quebec are group rights possessed by the group with the largest numbers. A reasonable claim exists for official recognition of language rights for the English language community, however, this is only partially reflected in Quebec legislation. Although Quebec policy has been excessively intrusive in very specific areas, such as commercial signs, it has simultaneously respected the array of language rights that are nationally recognized. The exception has been in minority language education, where Quebec applied a more restrictive set of entitlement criteria – subsequently discarded in Bill 86. With its inclusion of health and social services, Quebec language policy is consistent with national public opinion regarding language rights in Canada. However, there remains a striking gap between the generous regime of language rights endorsed in principle by the Quebec population and the guardedly supportive policy maintained by recent Quebec governments.

Notes

1 René Lévesque, *An Option for Quebec* (Toronto: McClelland and Stewart, 1968), 14.
2 Quebec history presents the surprising anomaly that, if anything, French was relatively disadvantaged in government services prior to 1920, when the Quebec government even printed its cheques in English. For an account of francophone efforts to overcome the disadvantaged position of French early in this century, see Susan Mann Trofimenkoff, *Action Française: French Canadian Nationalism in the Twenties* (Toronto: University of Toronto Press, 1975), Chap. 5.
3 The ensuing analysis of Bill 101 draws extensively upon my, 'Language Rights, Human Rights and Bill 101,' *Queen's Quarterly* 90 (2) (1983): 351–8.
4 Government of Quebec, La Charte de la Langue Française, *Revised Statutes of Quebec, 1977*, c.11, 1.
5 Ibid., c.2.
6 Ibid., c.11.
7 William G. Watson, 'A Comment,' in John Richards et al., *Survival: Official Language Rights in Canada* (Toronto: C.D. Howe Institute, 1992) 97 n4.
8 For an alternative explanation of the recognition of Amerindian and Inuit language rights, see Louis-Jacques Dorais, 'La loi 101 et les Amérindiens,' *Canadian Review of Sociology and Anthropology* 15 (1978): 133–5. Dorais suggested it is based on the 'noble savage' notions deriving from Rousseau. This is a particularistic basis for recognizing language rights that is not generalizable.
9 Government of Quebec, *Québec's Policy on the French Language* (Quebec: Éditeur Officiel du Québec, 1977), 32.

10 Camille Laurin,'Charte de la Langue Française / French Language Charter,'
    Canadian Review of Sociology and Anthropology 15 (1978): 122.
11 La Charte de la Langue Française, Sec. 100.
12 François Vaillancourt, 'English and Anglophones in Quebec: An Economic
    Perspective,' in John Richards et al., *Survival*, 75.
13 La Charte de la Langue Française, Secs. 7–13. These sections of Bill 101 have
    been ruled *ultra vires*. See Edward McWhinney, *Quebec and the Constitution
    1960–78* (Toronto: University of Toronto Press, 1979), Chap. 6, for an analysis
    of these decisions.
14 The commitment to minority rights was asserted in *Quebec's Policy on the French
    Language*, 34ff. A substantial part of this discussion was directed towards a
    denial of the notion of 'acquired rights' for the English language community.
    Coleman observed that the infrequent mention of the English language in
    Bill 101 was perceived, by some groups, to avoid 'the creation of legal rights
    for that language in place of the unwritten "privileges" that already existed.'
    See William D. Coleman, 'From Bill 22 to Bill 101: The Politics of Language
    under the Parti Québécois,' *Canadian Journal of Political Science* 14 (1981): 466
    n15.
15 See, for instance, Laurin, 'Charte,' 115–27.
16 See Gaston Cholette, 'Les droits linguistiques des Québécois sont-ils vraiment
    protégés par la Charte de la langue française,' *L'Action Nationale* 78 (1–2)
    (1988): 95–101.
17 Richard Y. Bourhis, 'The Charter of the French Language and Cross-Cultural
    Communication in Montreal,' in Richard Y. Bourhis ed., *Conflict and Language
    Planning in Quebec* (Clevedon: Multilingual Matters, 1984), 181–2.
18 There is some irony in the use of the word 'promotion' here, since the exist-
    ing policy represents a substantial erosion of previous levels of support and, in
    relation to education, virtually ensures a serious erosion in the size of the
    English language education system.
19 Marsha Hanen, 'Taking Language Rights Seriously,' in Stanley G. French, ed.,
    Confederation: Philosophers Look at Canadian Confederation (Montreal: Canadian
    Philosophical Association, 1979), 307.
20 The case of Joanne Curran, a fluently bilingual registered nursing assistant,
    who lost her job because of a failure to pass the written test was the most con-
    troversial case and led to substantial criticism of the test by prominent franco-
    phones. See 'Yes We Have No "ananas,"' *Maclean's* (2 Nov. 1981), 30.
21 An excerpt of the Supreme Court of Canada decision appeared in 'Language
    Is Not Merely a Means of Expression,' *Globe and Mail* (16 Dec. 1988), A7. The
    decision is reported as *Ford* v *A.G. Quebec*, [1988] 2 Supreme Court Reports,
    712. Beckton shared this line of reasoning in asserting, 'The prohibition

against other languages is such a basic requirement of form that it actually becomes a requirement of substance.' See Clare Beckton, 'Freedom of Expression (S.2{b}),' in Walter S. Tarnopolsky and Gérald A. Beaudoin, eds., *The Canadian Charter of Rights and Freedoms: Commentary* (Toronto: Carswell, 1982), 119. This discussion of commercial signs draws extensively upon my 'Rights in Conflict: Contemporary Disputes over Language Policy in Quebec' *International Journal of Canadian Studies* 14 (Fall 1996): 195–200.

22 Ibid., 752.

23 *Globe and Mail* (3 Jan. 1985), 1. The legal issues were discussed in a comparative context by F. Thibaut and Jean-Claude Amboise in 'L'étrange paradoxe d'une liberté devenue obligatoire: la loi 101 sur l'usage exclusif du français dans l'État du Québec,' *Revue du Droit Public* (1) (jan.–févr. 1987), 149–72.

24 'Language Is Not Merely a Means of Expression,' *Globe and Mail* (16 Dec. 1988), A7.

25 The suggestion that this decision was a political rather than a constitutional one, aided by the Bourassa government, is briefly argued in Michael Mandel, *The Charter of Rights and the Legalization of Politics in Canada* (expanded ed.) (Toronto: Thompson, 1994), 159–70.

26 Ibid., 160–1.

27 See Claude Jean Galipeau, 'National Minorities, Rights and Signs: The Supreme Court and Language Legislation in Quebec,' in Alain-G. Gagnon and A. Brian Tanguay, eds., *Democracy with Justice: Essays in Honour of Khayyam Zev Paltiel* (Ottawa: Carleton University Press, 1992), 66–84.

28 United Nations, Human Rights Committee, *Views Communications* (359/1989 and 386/1989) (31 March 1993). I address the arguments of their report in my, 'Rights in Conflict: Contemporary Disputes over Language Policy in Quebec,' in *International Journal of Canadian Studies* 14 (Fall 1996): 204–7. See also Fernand de Varennes, 'Language and Freedom of Expression in International Law,' *Human Rights Quarterly* 16 (1) (Feb. 1994): 163–86. The Canadian case is briefly discussed in the context of a review of cases involving language and freedom of expression.

29 A comparable incident occurred in the federal Parliament when the head of the Consumers Association of Canada was prevented from presenting a brief to the House of Commons Consumer and Corporate Affairs Committee because it wasn't available in French as well. The decision was overturned subsequently when a legal opinion was delivered to the committee that every individual and group has the right to address Parliament in either official language. For an account of the incident, see 'Group's Ouster for English-only Paper Rekindles Language Debate,' *Globe and Mail* (26 June 1989), A9; 'Ouster over English Notes Called Improper,' *Globe and Mail* (12 July 1989), A4.

30 This happens surprisingly often with commercial signs. One example is the Chinese translation of the first Coca-Cola advertisement in Chinese, wherein 'the real thing' was translated as 'bite the wax tadpole.' This is one of several examples reported in 'Wow, a Sporty, Five-Speed Matron,' *Globe and Mail* (3 March 1992), A17.

31 Leslie Green, 'Freedom of Expression and Choice of Language,' *Law and Policy* 13 (3) (July 1991): 226.

32 *Ibid.*, 217.

33 This argument was discussed by F. Thibaut and J.-C. Amboise,'L'étrange paradoxe,' 149–72.

34 *Commission of Inquiry on the Position of the French Language and on Language Rights in Quebec* (Gendron Commission), *Report* (Quebec: Éditeur Officiel du Québec, 1972), Recommendation 73.

35 Lise Bissonnette, 'A Case of déjà-vu in Quebec,' *Globe and Mail* (31 Dec. 1988), D2.

36 'Language Advisors Urge Bourassa to Preserve Sign Law,' *Globe and Mail* (14 Dec. 1988), A1.

37 For instance, the number of individuals who speak French as their home language in Quebec increased from 5,253,100 in the 1981 census to 5,651,800 in the 1991 census. In relative terms, this constitutes a growing percentage of Quebec's population, from 82.5 per cent in 1981 to 83 per cent in 1991. See Brian Harrison and Louise Marmen, *Languages in Canada* Cat. No. 96–313E (Scarborough: Statistics Canada, and Prenctice-Hall, 1994), 16–17.

38 See 'The Chanson Crisis,' *Globe and Mail* (5 April 1986), C1, C3. Apparently, music videos have had a powerful influence in increasing the visibility of anglophone music in Quebec, just as reduced quota requirements for air time have reduced the visibility of francophone musicians.

39 A 1987 survey conducted as part of the Charter Project (discussed in Chapter 2) reported that 57% of francophones (overwhelmingly composed of Québécois) disagreed that English should be prohibited from advertising to preserve French culture. See Paul M. Sniderman, Joseph F. Fletcher, Peter H. Russell, and Philip E. Tetlock, *The Clash of Rights: Liberty, Equality, and Legitimacy in Pluralist Democracy* (New Haven: Yale University Press, 1996), 220. Polls in Quebec have continued to indicate that the majority of Québécois endorse bilingual signs. For example, polls in 1993 reported that almost two-thirds of Québécois supported this option. See, for example, Lysiane Gagnon, 'Most Francophones Favour a More Tolerant Approach to Language Laws' *Globe and Mail* (6 Feb. 1993), D3; Rhéal Séguin, 'Reaction to Language Bill Unusual,' *Globe and Mail* (26 May 1993), A5.

40 'Language Bill Given Royal Assent,' *Globe and Mail* (23 Dec. 1988), A1, A5.

41 Benoit Aubin, 'Bourassa's Use of Charter Clauses Shows his Vision of Distinct Quebec,' *Globe and Mail* (22 Dec. 1988), A8.
42 Reg Whitaker, 'The Overriding Right,' *Policy Options* (May 1989): 6. See the counter argument in P.K. Kuruvilla, 'Quebec's Action Was Wrong,' *Policy Options* (May 1989): 7–8.
43 Nathan Brett, 'Language Laws and Collective Rights,' *Canadian Journal of Law and Jurisprudence* 4 (2) (July 1991): 347–60, 355.
44 The point was made rather provocatively by D'Iberville Fortier, when he observed, 'The salvation of French, in Quebec or elsewhere, must surely lie in positively asserting its own demographic weight, cultural vigour and innate attractiveness, and not in humbling the competition.' See Commissioner of Official Languages, *Annual Report 1987* (Ottawa: Minister of Supply and Services, 1988), 9. The remark elicited a unanimous vote denouncing his statement from the Quebec National Assembly on 24 March 1988.
45 Whitaker, 'Overriding Right,' 5.
46 'Bourassa Using Sign Language,' *Globe and Mail* (12 Dec. 1992), A5. Bill 86, An Act to Amend the Charter of the French Language, was introduced in the Quebec National Assembly on 6 May 1993 and received assent on 17 June 1993.
47 Bill 86, Sec. 18.
48 'Quebec Issues Draft Language Legislation,' *Globe and Mail* (12 June 1993), A5.
49 The provincewide poll was conducted jointly by the *Gazette, Le Devoir* and *Le Soleil,* in conjunction with the Quebec Institute of Public Opinion. Not surprisingly, 79.2% of anglophones and 65.6% of allophones advocated official bilingualism. See Michael B. Stein, 'Bill 22 and the Non-Francophone Population in Quebec: A Case Study of Minority Group Attitudes on Language Legislation,' in John R. Mallea, ed., *Quebec's Language Policies: Background and Response* (Quebec: Les Presses de L'Université Laval, 1977), 253.
50 Alliance Québec, press release (25 Oct. 1983), 2. These poll results are drawn from the press release.
51 'Data taken from the survey conducted at the request of the Commissioner of Official Languages by Canadian Facts in September–October 1985,' *Language and Society* 19 (April 1987): Table 3.
52 Reported in the *Decima Quarterly Reports*, no. 41. The results reported here are based on a Quebec regional sample (313 francophone mother tongue individuals in a Quebec sample of 385) from a national poll, and thus the error margins are substantial. These figures were compiled for me by Bob Burge of the Centre for the Study of Democracy at Queen's University from the Decima data.

53 Lysiane Gagnon, 'Most Francophones Favour a More Tolerant Approach to Language Laws' *Globe and Mail* (6 Feb. 1993), D3. The poll also showed substantial regional variations in support for bilingual signs. Québécois support was around 70% in the unilingual French parts of the province, but dropped to 59% among French-speaking Montrealers and to 55% in the Quebec City region.

54 Both polls were conducted by Léger and Léger for the *Globe and Mail*, first in March 1996 and then in April 1996. One of the authors interpreted the polls as indicating that 'Quebeckers believe "the French language is doing well in Quebec and there is no need to reopen the language laws."' See, 'French Language Secure, Quebeckers Say,' *Globe and Mail* (20 April 1996), A5. See also, 'Poll backs current language law,' *Globe and Mail* (23 March 1996), A4.

55 'Sondage auprès des Québécois par SORECOM (mai 1984) sur la question nationale et constitutionnelle,' *L'Action Nationale* 74 (4) (1984): 438.

56 'Coffee's en francais in Westmount Despite Growing Language Tensions,' *Globe and Mail* (19 May 1986), A5.

57 Results are reported in the *Decima Quarterly*, no. 37 (Spring, 1989). These figures were tabulated for me by Bob Burge. In this instance, Quebec francophones are defined by the language in which the interview was conducted.

58 This finding was part of the 1988 Canadian National Election Study, as part of a follow-up mailback questionnaire in early 1989. It is presented and discussed in Paul Sniderman et al., *Clash of Rights*, 230–2.

59 F. Vaillancourt, 'A Comment,' in Richards et al., *Survival*, 133.

60 William G. Watson, 'Separation and the English of Quebec,' in Richards et al. *Survival*, 123.

61 See Brian Harrison and Louise Marmen, *Languages in Canada*, Tables 1.2 and 1.3 at 8, 10 respectively.

62 Section 73 stated the conditions under which one is entitled to enter the English language educational system: 'Upon the request of their father and mother, the following individuals may receive their instruction in English: (a) a child whose father or mother received his or her elementary instruction in English, in Québec; (b) a child whose father or mother domiciled in Québec on 26 August 1977, received his or her elementary instruction in English outside Québec; (c) a child who, in his last year of school in Québec before 26 August 1977 was lawfully receiving his instruction in English, in a public kindergarten class or in an elementary or secondary school; (d) the younger brothers and sisters of a child described in paragraph *c.*'

63 W.R. Lederman, 'Securing Human Rights in a Renewed Confederation,' in Richard Simeon, ed., *Must Canada Fail?* (Montreal: McGill-Queen's University Press, 1977), 289.

64 For the year 1996–97, there were 418 primary and secondary schools in
    Ontario for the French language minority, and 334 in Quebec for the English-
    speaking minority. These figures are estimates provided in Commissioner of
    Official Languages, *Annual Report 1996* (Ottawa: Minister of Supply and Ser-
    vices, 1997), Table IV.1, 92.

65 Task Force on English Education, *Report to the Minister of Education of Quebec*
    (Jan. 1992) (Gretta Chambers, Chair), 5. The Task Force was established in
    Sept. 1991.

66 Ibid., 4.

67 'Ad Campaign Aims to Mobilize Opinion against Language Bill,' *Globe and
    Mail* (2 June 1993), A3.

68 See Canada, *The International Bill of Rights* (Ottawa: Ministry of Supply and Ser-
    vices, 1980). This document and others are available in Walter Laqueur and
    Barry Rubin, eds., *The Human Rights Reader* (New York: New American Library,
    1979).

69 Government of Quebec, *Quebec's Policy on the French Language* (Quebec:
    Éditeur officiel du Québec, 1977), 74.

70 The Canadian Charter of Rights and Freedoms in the Constitution Act, 1982
    acknowledged such rights for Canadian citizens.

71 See Jean A. Laponce, *Languages and Their Territories*, Anthony Martin-Sperry
    trans. (Toronto: University of Toronto Press, 1987), Table 22, 96–9.

72 'English in Quebec Defended in Court,' *Globe and Mail* (18 Aug. 1982), A5.

73 Lysiane Gagnon, 'Most Francophones Favour.' This is another area where
    Quebec opinion is highly volatile. A decade earlier, 72% of Québécois sup-
    ported the right of all English-speaking people in Quebec – whatever their
    place of origin – to send their children to English schools. This result was
    reported in Alain-G. Gagnon and Mary Beth Montcalm, *Quebec: Beyond the
    Quiet Revolution* (Scarborough: Nelson, 1990), 186. Data are from D. Monnier,
    La question linguistique: l'état de l'opinion publique (Quebec: Conseil de la langue
    française, 1983).

74 Quebec National Assembly, An Act to amend the Education Act, the Act
    respecting school elections and other legislative provisions (Bill 109), 2nd
    session, 35th legislature.

75 The latter phrase is used in the request to the federal Parliament for a
    constitutional amendment to Section 93. It is reported in "Amendment May
    Be Reviewed: PM,' *Gazette* (Montreal) (14 June 1997), A6. See the statement
    by Quebec Liberal Party leader Daniel Johnson, 'English Community
    Bigger Than That Defined by Bill 101,' *Gazette* (14 June 1997), B5. For an
    argument in defence of the government's proposal, see Michel Venne, "Le

droit de la minorité est restreint partout au Canada,' *Le Devoir* (10 June 1997), 1.

76 This and other examples are reported in 'Teacher Barred from Voting for Board that Employs Her,' *Gazette* (Montreal) (14 June 1997), A6. In another instance, an elementary school teacher who emigrated to Quebec in 1979 from the United States (and therefore received her own education in English outside Canada) to assume a teaching post in the English language system is also ineligible.

77 Daniel Johnson, 'English Community Bigger.'

78 'Liberals Back Off School Bill,' *Gazette* (Montreal) (13 June 1997), A1, A2. While the Education Minister Pauline Marois stated that the government had received legal opinions raising this concern, neither she nor her department officials were willing to release these opinions to the press.

79 Bill 109, Section 19. It went on to clarify that 'nothing in this section shall prevent the teaching of a second language in that language.' This clause permits second language instruction as part of the curriculum of each system. Incidentally, the irony consists in the fact that it is a language policy goal of the PQ government to integrate the anglophone and allophone populations into the communal language of Quebec.

80 See 'Hospitals Threatened by Quebec's Bill 101, MD Tells Study Group,' *Globe and Mail* (29 Oct. 1983), A3; 'PQ Curbs Language Abuses,' *Globe and Mail* (11 March 1983), A9. Bill 57, An Act to Amend the Charter of the French Language, 1983, c.56, was introduced 17 Nov. 1983 and received assent 22 Dec. 1983.

81 Bill 142, An Act to again amend the Act respecting health services and social services, 1986, c.106, was introduced 12 Nov. 1986 and assented to 19 Dec. 1986.

82 A point duly noted by the PQ opposition who unsuccessfully sought to amend the phrase to read, 'the English-speaking community.' They also objected that such legislation is not the proper vehicle for creating 'fundamental rights.' See 'PQ Offers Amendments to English-services Bill but Will Still Oppose It,' *Globe and Mail* (13 Dec. 1986), A4.

83 See Table 2.1 in Chapter 2.

84 Reed Scowen, *A Different Vision: The English in Quebec in the 1990s* (Don Mills: Maxwell Macmillan, 1991), 48.

85 For an informative overview of anglophone participation in the Quebec public service, see David Allnut, 'The Quebec Public Service,' in Gary Caldwell and Éric Waddell, eds., *The English of Québec: From Majority to Minority Status* (Quebec: Institut Québécois de Recherche sur la Culture, 1982), 227–36. Allnut

reported that as of May 1979 there were only 521 anglophones among the 73,185 employees of the Quebec government. He concurred with a colleague's observation that 'you almost have to become French' to work in the Quebec public service.

86 *Globe and Mail* (18 April 1992), A4.

87 See Section 10 of Bill 86, which amends Section 29.1 of Bill 101 to say that 'the Government may ... withdraw such recognition.'

88 To be sure, this illogic is surpassed by the anglophones in Kapuskasing, Ontario, as noted in another chapter, who rejected French language services in a municipality with a Francophone majority.

89 As noted in Scowen, *A Different Vision*, 131.

5

Legislating Language Equality: New Brunswick

On linguistic issues, there are no minorities in New Brunswick – only citizens equal before the law, only equal communities, only equal treatment of individuals and communities.[1]

Premier Frank McKenna

In 1969 New Brunswick became the first Canadian province to adopt its own regime of official language rights. Prior to the introduction of the legislation, the government issued a policy statement explaining its objectives in language matters. Its principle objective was 'to develop meaningful linguistic and cultural equality of opportunity in the public life of the province.'[2] It made explicit commitments to provision of government services in both official languages, bilingual government documents and publications, and education in both official languages. The statement also expressed an intention to imitate the federal government's policy goal of permitting both English and French as languages of work in the public service and of ensuring that the public service reflects the cultural and linguistic values of both language groups, presumably an oblique commitment to proportional representation.[3]

Committing to Equality

The legislation asserted the general principle that English and French were the official languages of New Brunswick and that they 'possess and enjoy equality of status and equal rights and privileges as to their use for such purposes.'[4] The content of this equality was not defined, with the result that its intended meaning must be gleaned from accompanying policy statements and the content of the legislation. The legislation was notably less ambitious than the policy statement. The wording was open to significantly different interpretations. Section 2 of the act stated, 'Subject to this Act, the English and French languages a) are the official languages of New Brunswick for all purposes to which the authority of the Legislature of New Brunswick extends, and b) possess and enjoy equality of status and equal rights and privileges as to their use for such purposes.'[5] The significance of the section turns on the relative priority assigned to the phrases, 'subject to this Act' and 'for all purposes to which the authority of the Legislature extends.' The former suggests that the boundaries of its application are specified in the ensuing clauses of the act; the latter invites an expansive interpretation that would have application to all the domains falling within provincial jurisdiction. Although a persuasive case can be made for the expansive interpretation, it is apparent that the more restricted sense was intended for the construction of the remainder of the act, and from the insistence of the government that it was merely acknowledging existing rights.[6]

In examining the sections of the act, what stands out is that the formal statement of equality was eroded in various ways, by the actual provisions. For example, the requirement that all statutes subsequently passed be printed in both official languages does not apply to an amendment to a pre-existing statute.[7] A casual perusal of the index of the New Brunswick *Hansard* for any session demonstrates that the vast majority of bills are amendments to existing legislation.

Similarly, the specification that documents and motions 'may be printed in either or both official languages' in conducting the business of the legislature (Section 5) is essentially *permissive* regarding the use of French. In the context of a legislature that overwhelmingly conducts its business in English, this virtually guaranteed a subordinate position for French. Subsequently, analysts would criticize the inadequacies of these provisions for effectively forcing francophone MLAs to conduct their work in English.[8] These features strongly suggest that the government interpreted equal status for the two languages to mean equal legal validity, without embracing a commitment to the equal use of the languages in the business of the legislature.

These provisions concerned the internal operations of the legislature. For the proverbial 'person in the street,' the most significant elements of the act were its assertions that education was to be in the (English or French) mother tongue of the pupils (Section 12); that both official languages could be used in the courts (Section 13); and that, upon request, government offices and agencies were required to communicate and provide available services in either official language (Section 10). For the most part, the significance of these measures was a moot point. Of the entire substance of the act, only five of its provisions were proclaimed promptly and these had virtually no effect on the expansion of official bilingualism in the province. The major substantive elements were made subject to future proclamation and/or to regulations to be later specified by the Cabinet.[9] The sections on the language of education and government services were among the last to be proclaimed in July 1977. It could reasonably be said that New Brunswick did not become officially bilingual until 1977.[10] Consequently, the main impact of the Official Languages Act was to make a symbolic statement of the equality of the official languages without making substantive advances towards achieving that goal.

In introducing the legislation, Premier Louis Robichaud had stated, 'It is the aim of the bill to give clear, unequivocal effect to provincial custom and convention.'[11] In its major thrust and omissions, it would appear that this government rationale was largely the case. In the areas of government services, the courts, and education, the legislation extended provincewide practices that had been informal, piecemeal, and regional. There were no recognized language rights in New Brunswick prior to 1969, nevertheless, a series of practices had developed that embraced the notion of official bilingualism. Government services were available in French in certain parts of the province; the French language was used in the courts on an unofficial basis; the Assembly had already adopted the practice of simultaneous translation of debates; and French was recognized as a language of instruction in the province.[12] The legislation's most striking omission was that it did not apply to municipalities, particularly given the fact that a student demonstration about the lack of bilingual municipal services in Moncton had been a catalyst to the emergence of the issue. Thus, the legislation was a reflection of the prevailing practice regarding language services in the province. The important innovation was that these practices were to be institutionalized as rights.

In the ensuing ten years, the desultory pace of implementation of language policy became an increasing source of frustration to the Acadian community. In the fall of 1979, the Convention d'Orientation Nationale, organized by the Parti Acadien and the Société des Acadiens du Nouveau-Brunswick, endorsed a greatly strengthened language policy that recognized their collective language rights and the need for independence for the Acadian region. In addition, the federal initiative regarding patriation of the Constitution and the development of a Charter of Rights and Freedoms imposed the necessity to reconsider existing policy on language rights.

Equality of Linguistic Communities

In 1981 the New Brunswick government passed two other pieces of legislation concerning the status of official languages. The first was Bill 88, a distinctive bill intended to recognize the collective rights of the two official linguistic communities. Jean-Maurice Simard, a prominent Cabinet minister in the Conservative government, explained its purpose:

The time has come to declare that there exist in New Brunswick not only individual rights but certain collective rights; to affirm that the Legislative Assembly is the protector of those rights; in particular, to make explicit in a declaration of the Legislative Assembly that there exist two official linguistic societies in New Brunswick, the English and the French; to impose a legal obligation on the provincial government to enhance the full development of each and ensure the equality of both. That is the purpose of this bill.[13]

Bill 88 affirmed the equality of status and the equal rights and privileges of the two official linguistic communities, and, in particular, it asserted a responsibility on the part of the government to protect that equality. More pointedly, it recognized that these communities had a right to 'distinct institutions within which cultural, educational, and social activities may be carried on,' and expressed a commitment by the government to promote the development of these communities.[14]

Bill 88 was a significant departure from the manner in which language equality had been debated to that point. Whereas the previous legislation had identified the languages themselves as the subjects of equality, Bill 88 focused on the linguistic communities. Beyond that, the sense of equality was necessarily transformed. Although Simard referred to an 'equality of status' between the two linguistic communities as acknowledged by the bill, it was quite unclear what that could mean for linguistic communities. The legislation did not propose to confer on them a 'legal personality,' such that they could act independently. Instead, the bill emphasized equality of use of the languages, as reflected in the commitment to 'distinct institutions' as a means for social, cultural, and linguistic development. An additional noteworthy feature of this proposal was that it made a commitment to provide and/or support non-governmental institutions for the provision of these services.

This attention to collective rights made Bill 88 potentially a historic turning point in New Brunswick politics. However, the bill was strikingly vague regarding the *content* of these collective rights. It neither specified what particular activities constituted such rights, nor conveyed either the authority or resources to support or administer them, nor suggested any mechanisms by which the linguistic groups could demand their delivery. Although its supporters pointed to the successful application of the principle of duality in the Department of Education, they hesitated to embrace the practice wholeheartedly, emphasizing, in words reminiscent of former Prime Minister Mackenzie King, that 'in many situations duality will be necessary, but we shall not necessarily require duality in all circumstances.'[15] Bill 88 appeared to promise much, but in fact it was a blank cheque that only the government of the day could write at its discretion. This would become particularly apparent in the discussion of "Motion 1."

This new direction in language equality was promptly reversed in Motion 1, a resolution to entrench language rights in New Brunswick in the Canadian Charter of Rights and Freedoms. It proposed a series of clauses for inclusion in the Charter, largely drawn from the content of the existing language legislation, and these were subsequently entrenched in the Canadian Charter of Rights and Freedoms. The provisions read as follows:

16(2) English and French are the official languages of New Brunswick and have equality of status and equal rights and privileges as to their use in all institutions of the Legislature and government of New Brunswick.

17(2) Everyone has the right to use English or French in any debate and other proceedings of the Legislature of New Brunswick.

18(2) The statutes, records and journals of the Legislature of New Brunswick shall be printed and published in English and French and both language versions are equally authoritative

19(2) Either English or French may be used by any person in, or in any pleading in or process issuing from, any court of New Brunswick.

20(2) Any member of the public in New Brunswick has the right to communicate with and to receive available services from any office of an institution of the Legislature or government of New Brunswick in English or French.[16]

This legislative initiative reverted the focus of the subject of equality to the individuals who are members of these language groups, rather than the collective entities. This is reflected in the requirements that individuals may demand services in either official language, and that individuals may use either language in the proceedings of government and the courts. Subsequently, these directions would be extended. In 1990 the New Brunswick Official Languages Act was amended to guarantee that each person who is a party to a proceeding in a court 'has the right to be heard by a court that understands, without the need for translation, the official language in which the person intends to proceed.'[17]

There were, however, some omissions from the Motion 1 initiative. Particularly noteworthy was the absence of any reference to the 'collective rights' recognized in Bill 88.[18] Somewhat ironically, Premier Richard Hatfield rejected an attempt by the opposition to include a clause recognizing collective rights on the ground that it would be inappropriate to mix collective rights in a section concerned with individual rights.[19] However, Hatfield made no effort to develop an equivalent clause in an appropriate place. Thereby an opportunity was passed over that would have created an enforcement mechanism for collective language rights.

Bill 88 and Motion 1 indicated that the government of New Brunswick had begun to develop a notion of language rights and to embody that concept in its language policy. At the same time, the government seemed to have been uncertain about the extent to which these entitlements were to be institutionalized in the province's administrative practices. The government flirted with the notion of collective rights, but failed to explore the implications of a right to distinct institutions. An opening had nonetheless been provided to a greatly expanded practice of language rights in New Brunswick, and this opening would be addressed in subsequent task force reports.

Implementing Language Equality

The principles embedded in Bill 88 were gone, but certainly not forgotten. They reappeared shortly in a decidedly more vigorous form. The New Brunswick Task Force on Official Languages (popularly referred to as the Poirier-Bastarache Report after its co-chairpersons, and hereafter so denoted) presented in March 1982 the most ambitious and comprehensive set of proposals for linguistic equality yet to appear in Canada. Its objective was 'the total integration of the Official Languages Act and bilingualism programs, as well as the integration of linguistic policy, to other policies of the province of New Brunswick.'[20] It called for a stronger commitment by the government to the provision of bilingual government services, the extension of such requirements to municipalities with more than 20 per cent of their population (or 1,500 people) who are French speaking, and, most controversially, the introduction of duality within the civil service to permit francophones to work in the French language in the civil service and to ensure equality of service in French. Moreover, the task force report extended these provisions in limited ways to the private sector, in relation to consumer rights (bilingual standard form contracts) and the rights of workers (bilingual safety signs in the workplace, collective agreements, and grievance procedures).

In developing its rationale, the Poirier-Bastarache task force took very seriously the notion that there were two *equal* languages in New Brunswick, and their recommendations encompassed a sustained effort to recognize that status throughout New Brunswick society. 'Equality of the two languages,' their report maintained, 'imposes the duty to serve the client in his own language without an intermediary.'[21] This was expressed in a commitment to equal quality of service, equal access to positions in the civil service, and the right to work in one's own language, the latter two being viewed as 'fundamental rights.'[22]

These principles served as the basis for the report's most controversial recommendation – that the provincial civil service be administratively restructured on the basis of linguistic dualism, with civil servants able to work in the official language of each division. Citizens would have the right to request services from either division, but communication would be in the language of work of that division.[23] Thus, the respective rights of the citizen and the civil servant would be simultaneously respected. Within each section, the civil service staff could be unilingual. Consequently the promotion ladder would normally include the prerequisite of bilingualism.

In response, the provincial government established an advisory committee to develop recommendations after soliciting public opinion on the report. In presenting its proposals, the committee noted that 'it is vital to identify the fundamental principles and objectives which will set the direction of linguistic policy and to set out the principal procedure for its implementation'[24] In particular, the major legislative initiatives of the previous decade were deemed important in identifying those principles. These included the federal Charter of Rights and Freedoms, Bill 88, and Motion 1. From this basis, the advisory committee developed four general principles to guide legislative reform of language policy:

1   The right of the citizen to receive equal services in the language of his or her choice
2   The opportunity for the civil servant to work in his or her language
3   Equitable representation of the two linguistic communities in the institutions of government
4   Recognition of linguistic regions[25]

In defining the content of language rights, the advisory committee used the term "right," in characterizing the right to equal services from government, as a 'fundamental right.' One additional use is noteworthy. It recommended that the government adopt the principle that 'every child has the legal right to an adequate education in the second language by means of the educational system.'[26] The committee did not use such terminology in relation to language of work as the Poirier-Bastarache report had. Instead the committee presented the four general principles as the basis for developing an effective regime of language rights. Nevertheless, its recommendations followed the basic direction of Poirier-Bastarache in regard to government services and equitable representation, albeit in moderate form. Their recommendations regarding municipalities and the private sector diverged substantially, however, resorting to persuasion rather than legislation.

The New Brunswick government chose to follow the lead of the advisory committee in interpreting language policy. In August 1988 it issued a statement of its official language policy, accompanied by an implementation guideline. This was followed in March 1990 by a report on the application of language policy.[27] In its 1988 policy statement, the government made a commitment to *equality of service* to both language communities and, furthermore, emphasized its commitment to expanding opportunities for civil service staff to work in either official language. These initiatives were claimed to follow from the Charter of Rights and Freedoms, the New Brunswick Official Languages Act, and Bill 88.

Equality of service was presented as based upon constitutional obligations flowing from the Charter, thereby possessing the character of constitutionally entrenched rights. The right to work in either official language was based on Article 2 of the New Brunswick Official Languages Act, delineating the equal status of the two languages, and it was further justified on the grounds of increasing productivity and efficiency in the public service. The implementation guideline accompanying this statement emphasized that the policy on language of work was 'secondary to the paramount constitutional obligation of the Government of New Brunswick to provide available services to citizens, in the official language of their choice.'[28] It was also subordinate in a second sense, in that the policies on language of service applied to all components of government institutions (including educational and health institutions, as well as public utilities), whereas the language of work provisions were to apply only to government departments and agencies.

Equality of service was the primary orientation of these documents. In this regard individuals were emphasized as the subjects of this equality. The policy on language of work however was more ambiguous. Although there was strong commitment to extend the use of French as a language of work in the public service, the rationale and mode of implementation indicated that this was primarily oriented to client service and represented a commitment to respect individual preferences of public servants rather than to equality of use of language as such. These documents never referred to a 'right' to work in an official language, nor did they recognize any right to equitable representation, nor make a commitment to it as a matter of policy.

Furthermore, no formal commitments were made to equitable representation in the public service; the preference was to assign positions on the basis of functional need. Thus, as part of the implementation process, government departments were required to identify the positions within their units in terms of the language skills necessary to perform various tasks. The result was that 25 per cent of all positions in the public service were designated 'bilingual essential' and 12 per cent were 'French essential,' producing a figure of 37 per cent of the public service that required French language skills.[29] This figure exceeded the share of the provincial population constituted by francophones, which was 33.6 per cent in the 1981 census.[30] However, since 7.1 per cent of the public servants whose mother tongue is English were either fluently or functionally bilingual, this policy might possibly result in a smaller share of the public service being filled by individuals whose mother tongue is French than would be warranted by a policy of equitable representation.[31] Although it did not embrace the principle of equal representation formally, the New Brunswick government effectively committed itself to a policy the consequences of which would have much the same results.

In 1993 the egalitarian emphases embodied in Bill 88 were revived. In preparation for the constitutional amendment package known as the Charlottetown Accord, the government of New Brunswick struck a commission to develop recommendations for it. In its 1992 report the commission endorsed the equality objective embodied in Bill 88 with some qualification. Although it particularly supported the necessity for distinct institutions for the two linguistic communities, it emphasized schools and community centres as the central elements of this duality. It pointedly excluded the apparatus of government from this proposal. It then proposed that the New Brunswick government initiate a constitutional amendment to the Canadian Charter of Rights and Freedoms, to specify that equality includes the right to distinct educational and cultural institutions.[32] At the request of the government of New Brunswick, Clause 16 of the Charter of Rights and Freedoms was amended to specify that the equal status of the two language groups included the right to separate schools and cultural institutions.[33] The text of the constitutional amendment stated:

[16.1](1) The English linguistic community and the French linguistic community in New Brunswick have equality of status and equal rights and privileges, including the right to distinct educational institutions and such distinct cultural institutions as are necessary for the preservation and promotion of those communities.

(2) The role of the legislature and government of New Brunswick to preserve and promote the status, rights and privileges referred to in subsection (1) is affirmed.[34]

This initiative confirmed the symbolic commitment of the New Brunswick government to linguistic equality as a central element of its language policy, without, it must be emphasized, moving beyond the character of policy embedded in its administrative commitments. The amendment further defined equal status to include entitlements to institutions to support the two communities, without making further claims about the relative status of the language groups.

In his opening remarks in the legislative debate in New Brunswick on the motion to amend the Constitution, Premier Frank McKenna insisted that the new provision demonstrated, 'On linguistic issues, there are no minorities in New Brunswick – only citizens equal before the law, only equal communities, only equal treatment of individuals and communities.'[35] He also emphasized that it would benefit both anglophone and francophone communities where they were the minority group in different parts of the province. At the same time, McKenna was careful to emphasize that the provision 'does not really deliver any new goods. It simply proclaims what we have achieved.'[36] Specifically it did not include the more controversial elements of the Poirier-Bastarache proposals – no duality beyond the education system, and no impact on the private sector. It made reference to cultural institutions, but these would only be provided upon demonstration of their necessity for the preservation of the linguistic community. Furthermore, the term 'linguistic community' itself was never defined and the only example given referred to a 'community centre,' which although controversial, was an already existing practice of the government.[37]

On the whole, these legislative initiatives indicate that the government of New Brunswick had begun to expand its notion of language equality, but at the same time appeared quite guarded about the extent to which the relevant entitlements were to be institutionalized in the practices of government administration. These different legislative initiatives and the subsequent policy proposals reflect different formulations of the substantive meaning and policy content of equality, though the general pattern is one of gradual expansion of the concept.

Whether this expanded understanding of the concept of equality is consistent with prevailing political attitudes in New Brunswick on linguistic equality remains to be determined. Although Premier McKenna went to considerable lengths to suggest that these amendments were endorsed by public opinion, this claim was sharply challenged by the opposition during legislative debates on the motion.[38] In fact, considerable evidence exists suggesting that these initiatives posed a direct challenge to public perceptions regarding language equality.

Public Opinion on Language Equality

One of the important questions regarding the recognition of language rights in New Brunswick concerns the disposition of public opinion towards their scope and content. The Poirier-Bastarache task force had conducted its own studies and drawn quite caustic conclusions about anglophone views on linguistic matters. These conclusions stand in marked contrast to the results of the various public opinion polls conducted over the past few years. These contradictions themselves deserve analysis. Beyond that, these sources offer insight into the public's approach to language rights, permitting us to assess the correspondence or lack thereof between public opinion and existing legislation. Analysis of public opinion on language equality reveals the puzzling pattern that anglophones in New Brunswick accept a policy of bilingualism, but not one of language equality.

Task Force Assessment

The Poirier-Bastarache report used two methods to elicit public opinion on language issues in New Brunswick. One was an analysis of material (for example, editorials, articles, and letters to the editor) in a 'representative sample' of local newspapers for the previous three years to determine francophone and anglophone opinion. This produced over 400 items, two-thirds of which were drawn from francophone publications. The second method involved in-depth interviews with seventy-seven community leaders from various regions of the province who were judged to be knowledgeable about the issues.[39] In presenting its analysis, the report used a selective approach to its interpretation of the results. Although the authors acknowledged that 'very frequently the opinions vary greatly within the same linguistic group,' the orientation adopted was that of identifying strands of thought in opposition to official bilingualism and exploring their logic, rather than attempting to assess the distribution of opinion in each linguistic community on each issue. For example, the report suggested that the 'one Canada' mentality 'is probably shared by most anglophones in New Brunswick,' without making any attempt to suggest a basis for this judgment.[40]

Similarly, the authors tended to rely on the perceived *implicit* logic of particular statements to present a presumed set of attitudes on the relevant issues. It postulated a quasi-Darwinian theory of linguistic evolution and struggle, however, it admitted, 'The articulate expression of such a strategy is found in only rare sources of information and it is by comparing the statements with each other that this impression is clearly derived.'[41] Consequently, the report, although offering appropriate explanations of its analyses, tended to place its emphasis on currents of thought that as often as not represent distinctive and *minority* perspectives, and even logical reconstructions, of attitudes on the situation.

In summarizing prevailing attitudes on language rights in New Brunswick, the Poirier-Bastarache report identified important differences of emphasis and acceptable scope for official bilingualism. It noted that increasing numbers of anglophones support a policy of language rights, but only in regard to the provision of government services to individuals in both official languages. Anglophones rejected, however, any implementation that imposes costs on themselves, such as extensive designation of bilingual positions in the civil service, a policy of proportional representation of linguistic groups, or the creation of French language work units within the provincial civil service. 'A good many' francophones, in contrast, viewed each of these practices as an important component of an effective policy of bilingualism, though access to government services is most widely supported among francophones as well.

As a concluding caveat, the task force report observed that there was a clear absence of consensus both within and between the two linguistic communities on the question of language rights, and the authors submitted that, 'The most radical Acadians find what they are looking for in the symbolic proposals of the Government, whereas the anglophones, even though suspicious, like many Acadians, also find what they are looking for, as do the most passive Acadians, in the inaction and lack of coercion in the linguistic and cultural policies of this Government.'[42] It could be said that there is a general acceptance of rights to government services in both official languages among both anglophones and francophones in New Brunswick. At the same time, there is substantial opposition among anglophones as well as a relative indifference among francophones to a remoulding of the civil service to achieve comprehensive bilingualism. This combination strongly suggests a limited opportunity for linguistic reforms.

The Evidence of Public Opinion Surveys

In 1978 a study of public opinion in Atlantic Canada was conducted for the Task Force on Canadian Unity. Subsequent secondary analyses revealed substantial support for French language services in New Brunswick. Although only 61 per cent of New Brunswick respondents supported the principle of bilingualism, nevertheless, between 71 and 76 per cent supported the propositions that (a) French speakers outside Quebec should be able to use their own language when dealing with government; (b) they should be able to have their children educated in French; (c) language rights should be guaranteed in New Brunswick in education and (d) in the courts.[43] At the same time, 85 per cent agreed with the statement that 'the French should have no more privileges than any other ethnic group.' This apparent inconsistency has been explained as a confirmation that the anglophone respondents viewed these as rights. As Perlin stated,

While [the denial of special privileges] may seem inconsistent with support for the entrenchment of French language rights, the inconsistency disappears if one makes the distinction between 'rights' as affording a protection to which all people are entitled and 'privileges' as granting something to which only some people are entitled. It appears that most members of the sample believe the ability of francophones to express themselves in their own language is a legitimate right and not a privilege.[44]

A significant additional conclusion suggests itself as well. These patterns indicate that anglophones observed a distinction between the entitlements of French-speaking individuals as opposed to francophone groups. Although French-speaking individuals are entitled to certain language services, this is not perceived to carry with it any group entitlements or claims to group status. This is significant for any claims to equality of groups.

The Canadian Unity Task Force study was distinctive in offering one of the strongest direct indications of a widespread public acceptance in New Brunswick that individuals are entitled to receive government services in their own language. The study did not examine whether this extends to services from business, or other essential services such as health care; however, responses to a 1985 national survey offer indirect evidence that this is the case. The 1985 survey of national opinion on language issues reported that 70 per cent of Atlantic Canadians agree that business services should be available in both English and French, ranging from a low of 62 per cent for services in department stores to a high of 78 per cent for hospital services. Although the study did not report results for New Brunswick separately, it is very likely that New Brunswick responses are broadly consistent with this pattern.[45] An analysis of these findings led its authors to conclude that 'the notion of access in both languages to the institutions of the private sector has seeped into the public consciousness by osmosis.'[46]

Two points are noteworthy about these findings. First, they suggest a broad support for services in both official languages from government, from public sector institutions providing essential services, and from private sector institutions. This would lead one to anticipate that there would be public support for some expansion of provincial language policy. The authors of the Unity Task Force study did not, however, use the language of rights in their questions, and therefore their investigations were not designed to establish the context in which the public views these language services. Second, the results were in marked contrast to the depiction of anglophone opinion presented in the Poirier-Bastarache report. Subsequent events and public comments, however, would offer an additional basis for assessing the respective validity of each task force's conclusions.

In a survey of anglophone opinion in New Brunswick in 1986, George Perlin reported a sharp decline in support for official bilingualism, from 58 per cent in 1978 to 46 per cent in 1986. Those who felt that provincial bilingualism policy had 'gone too far' had risen from 24 per cent in 1978 to 49 per cent in 1986. The view that francophones received better treatment from the provincial government than anglophones gleaned almost identical increased support – from 23 per cent in 1978 to 48 per cent in 1986. On the basis of these results, Perlin concluded that 'the whole regime of bilingualism in the province is threatened,' and this portends future developments nationally.[47]

These changes in anglophone opinion were doubtless a reaction to the language controversies of the early 1980s in New Brunswick. Anglophone opinion was increasingly inclined to perceive that implementation of official bilingualism was highly inequitable. This perception was not without some foundation. One observer remarked that an examination of education expenditures in New Brunswick reveals that francophone schools generally received higher funding levels than did anglophone schools.[48] In addition, federal government actions regarding its bilingualism policy fed this resentment. The federal plan to require all commissionaires at the Fredericton airport to become bilingual – which meant replacing a group of unilingual anglophones with bilingual individuals, probably francophones – was deeply resented and ultimately abandoned.[49]

A 1994 debate in the New Brunswick legislature illustrated the tenor of this problem. A Confederation of Regions (COR) member of the Legislative Assembly introduced a motion demanding that the provincial government redirect funding from the federal minority official languages program so that it 'may be spent to benefit all New Brunswickers, as opposed to only one community.'[50] Gregory Hargrove pointed to the fact that the Arts Council serving the French language community obtained dramatically higher levels of support than did its counterpart for the English language community, largely because it had access to federal funds. Similarly, subsidies could be obtained through this program to attract francophone doctors to serve the French language communities, but nothing was available to enable anglophone areas deprived of medical services to obtain English-speaking doctors. Therefore, the complaint was that the French language community was enjoying special benefits and preferential treatment. This was not equality as the COR MLA understood it.

Hargrove's understanding, incidentally, was modelled on the idea of equality as equal shares, rather than equal treatment in similar circumstances, or equal results. The English-speaking minority in Quebec was also being heavily subsidized by the federal program. This was noted and dismissed with the fact that French speakers are the minority in nine of ten provinces and therefore the beneficiaries most of the time. Medical services in New Brunswick were routinely being provided in English throughout the province, but were often not available in French. This fact was not even acknowledged as relevant. In short, the argument ignored the egalitarian point of the differential treatment – equality of service and compensatory measures for different circumstances – to effectively insist that all programs must distribute entitlements equally. To the extent that this attitude was widely shared, it represents a fundamental rejection of the egalitarian thrust of the government's language policy.

Public Comment

The responses from the surveys present one picture of public attitudes on these questions, but they tend to be abstracted from particular cases. It is important, therefore, to also look at what people say in the context of particular disputes, especially those where they themselves are participants. The results can often be strikingly different, as experience in New Brunswick tellingly illustrates.

At least on the surface, the survey results already discussed are in stark contrast to the anglophone hostility that greeted the Poirier-Bastarache proposals for the expansion of French language rights in New Brunswick. A journalist covering the public hearings on these new proposals pointedly remarked, 'Anglophones who are progressive on the question of language, if there are any in New Brunswick, have been noticeable by their absence during this debate.'[51]

The government arranged public hearings to provide an opportunity for public response to the proposals. The result was an overwhelming 512 briefs submitted to the advisory committee charged with overseeing the process and responding to the Poirier-Bastarache proposals. The various viewpoints were subsequently summarized in a report by the advisory committee.[52] It found that the majority of the English language briefs dealing with the issue (58.1 per cent) supported the principle of official bilingualism, and 29.4 per cent opposed it. Striking were numerous reservations about the propriety of equal status for the language of a minority group. The report noted that 'although the term "bilingualism" is frequently employed in the English briefs, the word "equality" rarely appears unless in a sentence which denies its possible achievement.'[53] The viewpoints on equality demonstrated that the majority status of anglophones was viewed by anglophones as an important reason why the two languages are not and cannot be equal. In short, English language briefs reflected the view that a policy of official bilingualism was separate from a policy of equality for the two languages, and support for the former could readily be combined with rejection of the latter. More pointedly, there were strong indications that anglophones rejected the concept of equal status such as is embodied in the earlier Bill 88. Although the advisory committee's report did not reflect on the issue, the term 'language rights' was also notable for its absence in the English language briefs that discussed the principles of official bilingualism. In sharp contrast, the French language briefs supported the principle of bilingualism unanimously and argued the case on the grounds of equality and protection of rights.

Disagreement on the foundations of the principle of language rights carry over into disagreements on its substance. The advisory report provided a good summary of the anglophone views when it stated,

While there was substantial support for government services in both official languages (75.6% of all briefs, though 55.3% of English-language briefs), there was a rejection of the right of civil servants to work in their own language (89% of English-language briefs) and of the concept of equitable representation of linguistic groups in the civil service (84% of English-language briefs) and of duality (95% of English-language briefs). One brief echoed many in stating, 'what we object to is the proposal that suggests that groups have a right to part of our public institutions as groups.'[54]

For many anglophones, bilingualism was adequately achieved by the provision of government services through translation or interpretation, rather than by direct provision of bilingual services. For francophones, reliance on translation and interpretation was an unacceptably inferior route to receipt of government services and did not reflect a commitment to equal status for the two languages. Such a commitment was reflected in the notions of equitable representation and duality. These options were, however, overwhelmingly rejected by anglophone groups. Equitable representation was rejected as reverse discrimination and duality was considered even more objectionable as a contribution to divisiveness.

Somewhat surprising, however, was the rejection of proposals that municipalities with significant linguistic minorities provide bilingual services. This would appear to be a simple extension of the principle of provincial government bilingualism. It tended to be rejected on the grounds of costs and the absence of demand for such services. A frequent refrain was the comment that few francophones are unilingual, therefore the service was unnecessary. The question of its relationship to the larger principle does not appear to have been addressed.[55] However, this finding does much to explain the reluctance of successive governments to include municipalities within the scope of the language policy.

Underlying much of the opposition to these proposals was its anticipated impact on the job prospects for anglophones in the civil service of the future. This was illustrated in reactions to the proposal to designate certain positions as bilingual that called for its implementation to be delayed 'until all children have been adequately educated in both official languages. The mere fact or [sic] suggesting that these positions be classified bilingual ... discriminates against all English-speaking citizens of New Brunswick.'[56] Delayed implementation seemed the only available remedy to the tension between acceptance of bilingual services and the rejection of its effects on the English language population. This concern was dramatically illustrated in the reaction of the CUPE local to plans to introduce French language services in the Saint John Regional hospital. A large advertisement in the local newspaper quoted various hostile remarks by union members, including the comments, 'Take the French and their language and send them back to Quebec' and 'Tell the people who want French to go live in a French country.'[57]

More broadly, however, there was a basic rejection of the notion that there are rights to the use of one's language on the job or to a particular share of positions in an organization. The right to work in one's language, was dismissed by an overwhelming emphasis on organizational efficiency as a paramount criterion, and the pragmatic observation that people should simply be pleased to have a job. The same feature was prominent in response to the question of designating certain positions as 'bilingual' in the civil service, or making bilingualism one part of the qualifications for appointment to the civil service. The dominant sentiment was that 'merit' should be the primary consideration, and it did *not* include a bilingual capability. Although there was an appreciation that *some* bilingual capacity was a functional prerequisite to official bilingualism, there were strong reservations about the need to introduce any substantial number of bilingual positions. Here again, the concern for job prospects was paramount in the anglophone reaction.

On the whole, each of these studies found partial reinforcement and important corrections in the others. The Poirier-Bastarache report tended to depict a disposition of anglophone opinion that significantly underestimated the degree of acceptance of official bilingualism, as is evidenced by the public opinion surveys. However, the Poirier-Bastarache report was accurate in its presentation of some of the limits to the acceptance of official bilingualism located in anglophone rejection of practices that affected their own employment prospects or asserted a notion of collective rights. In contrast, the public opinion surveys identified fairly substantial support for official bilingualism, but failed to elicit the qualifications that appeared in the briefs to the advisory committee. The briefs to the advisory committee, in turn, are broadly consistent with the surveys in documenting support for bilingualism, but more detailed in identifying the limitations to such acceptance than was the Poirier-Bastarache report.

Conclusion

At both the federal and New Brunswick levels, the official rationale for language policy has been explicitly based on principles of equality. The New Brunswick experience indicates that there are substantial grounds to question this approach as a strategy for acceptance of a practice of language rights. This analysis has emphasized the extent to which language equality remains not only essentially contested in principle, but also essentially muddled in legislative expression.

In the first place, there is conspicuous absence of consensus on the matter. Anglophones and francophones disagree sharply over the meaning and implications of language equality. The English-speaking public specifically rejects the notion that language rights involve *equal status* for the two languages and the related notion of equal representation of the two linguistic communities in the public service. At times it appears also to exclude the notion of an entitlement to an equal quality of service in each official language. In this last manifestation, one can only conclude that the anglophone commitment to language equality is at best tenuous, becoming progressively less firm as one moves from the abstract statement of principle to its concrete implementation.

Second, the anglophone public's notion of language equality emerging from these sources, is at odds with that operant in government legislation. The New Brunswick government, after various flirtations with other forms of equality, opted for a guarded expansion of its commitments. At the constitutional level, it recognized the equality of the two linguistic communities, but primarily in regard to entitlements to distinct institutions (schools and community centres) to support community development. At the administrative level, the New Brunswick government has ultimately settled on equality of service as the core meaning of language equality in New Brunswick. Beyond that, in implementing the policy it has opted to effectively adhere to proportional representation of language groups and significantly expand opportunities to use French on the job in the New Brunswick public service, without committing to these practices as elements of language equality.

This approach has the advantage of *greater* consistency with what public opinion claims as its understanding of official bilingualism. If the emphasis is on the right to government services and *equality of service* as the primary principles, then other practices can be advocated as a prerequisite to their realization. Such a strategy offers improved prospects for general acceptance. Whether this is sufficient to defuse the language controversy in New Brunswick is another matter. Even shorn of the most controversial proposals for linguistic equality, New Brunswick policy remains significantly in advance of anglophone public opinion. Thus, the more actively the government pursues these goals, the greater the public reaction is likely to be.

More generally, commitments to language equality appear to be the most divisive sources of conflict over language policy in Canada. The New Brunswick experience confirms that proposition and gives clear evidence that the uneasy truce continues. 'Plus ça change ...'

Notes

1 Premier Frank McKenna, New Brunswick, *Journal of Debates (Hansard)*, Session of 1992, vol. 11 (4 Dec. 1992), 4706.
2 Government of New Brunswick, *Statement on Language Equality and Opportunity* (tabled 4 Dec. 1968 by Hon. Louis J. Robichaud, Premier), 1.
3 *Ibid.*, 8.
4 Official Languages of New Brunswick Act (OLNBA), *Revised Statutes of New Brunswick, 1973*, vol. 4, c.O-1. While Quebec already had a regime of language rights in place, it was a product of the national constitution rather than of the Quebec legislature.
5 OLNB Act, c.O-1.
6 The issue of the appropriate interpretation of this section is discussed in Robert W. Kerr, 'The Official Languages of New Brunswick Act,' *University of Toronto Law Journal* 20 (1970): 483–5.
7 OLNBA, Sec. 7(2).
8 See Gérard Snow, *Les Droits Linguistiques des Acadiens du Nouveau-Brunswick*, Documentation du Conseil de La Langue Française 7 (Québec: Éditeur Officiel du Québec 1981), 35–45.

9 'OLNBA,' 482–3.

10 Task Force on Official Languages, *Towards Equality of the Official Languages in New Brunswick: Report* (Fredericton: Government of New Brunswick, 1982), 23–4. (Hereafter cited as Poirier-Bastarache.)

11 Premier L.J. Robichaud, *Synoptic Report of the Proceedings of the Legislative Assembly of the Province of New Brunswick 1969 Session* vol. 2, 493.

12 Robert Gill, 'Bilingualism in New Brunswick and the Future of L'Acadie,' *American Review of Canadian Studies* 10(2) (1980): 56–8.

13 M. Simard, New Brunswick, *Journal of Debates (Hansard),* vol. 16 (1980), 7069. According to then Premier Richard Hatfield, Simard had been advised by Michel Bastarache that such legislation was necessary to respond to the renewed emergence of Acadian nationalism. The comment from a personal interview was reported in Catherine Steele, *Can Bilingualism Work?* (Fredericton: New Ireland Press, 1990), 17.

14 An Act Recognizing the Equality of the Two Official Linguistic Communities in New Brunswick, *New Brunswick Acts 1981,* c.O-1.1. Bill 84, originally introduced in 1980, was renumbered Bill 88 in the course of its passage in 1981. It received royal assent 17 July 1981.

15 Hon. Mr Bird, New Brunswick, *Journal of Debates (Hansard),* vol. 16 (1980), 6666.

16 Hon. Mr Hatfield, New Brunswick, *Journal of Debates (Hansard),* vol. 1 (1981), 66–7.

17 New Brunswick, An Act to Amend the Official Languages of New Brunswick Act, *New Brunswick Acts 1990,* c. 49 (assented to 9 Nov. 1990). This reflected the impact of the 1988 federal initiatives regarding languages in the courts.

18 In fairness it should be noted that Motion 1 was passed prior to Bill 88. However, the latter was introduced in the previous year, and was therefore available as a resource for inclusion in the Charter package.

19 Hon. Mr Hatfield, *Journal of Debates,* vol. 1 (1981), 436. In fact, the government proposed an amendment that would include a section dealing with collective rights in the resolution once it was passed at some point in the future. It was not adopted. See ibid., 783.

20 Poirier-Bastarache, 29.

21 Ibid., 419.

22 Ibid., 411.

23 The concept of duality has been applied comprehensively in Belgium. For a detailed analysis of its operation, see Kenneth D. McRae, *Conflict and Compromise in Multilingual Societies* vol. 2, Belgium (Waterloo: Wilfrid Laurier University Press, 1986), 189–202.

24 Advisory Committee on Official Languages of New Brunswick, *Report,* (Fredericton: Government of New Brunswick, 1986), 96.

25 Ibid., 97.

26 Ibid., 104.

27 Government of New Brunswick, Board of Management *Official Languages Policy* (Aug. 1988); *Implementation Guidelines for the Official Languages Policy* (Aug. 1988); *Implementation of the Official Languages Policy: Report* (Feb. 1990).

28 Board of Management, *Implementation Guidelines*, 10.

29 Board of Management, *Implementation Report*, 10.

30 The francophone share of New Brunswick's population remained relatively stable in the 1991 census. Francophones, defined by mother tongue, were 34% of the population; 31.2%, if defined by home language. See Brian Harrison and Louise Marmen, *Languages in Canada* (Ottawa: Statistics Canada, 1994), Tables 2.2 and 2.3, 15, and 17.

31 These statistics on language fluency appear in Government of New Brunswick, Official Languages Branch, *Linguistic Profile of Employees in the Public Service* (Sept. 1986), 7, Table 4, 22. According to this profile, the number of employees whose first official language is French is 31.6% of Part I of the provincial public service, i.e., departments and agencies. *Ibid.*, 6.

32 New Brunswick, Commission on Canadian Federalism, *Report* (Fredericton: New Brunswick Commission on Canadian Federalism, 1992), 26–8.

33 'Controversial Language Law Hot Topic in New Brunswick,' *Globe and Mail* (30 Jan. 1993), A16. This amendment was part of the Charlottetown Accord package of constitutional reforms. Since New Brunswick was the only province to support the accord in the national referendum, Premier Frank McKenna interpreted the vote as an endorsement of the language reform.

34 Canada, House of Commons *Debates, Official Report (Hansard)*, vol. 132, no. 193, 3rd session, 34th Parliament, 15084 ff. The significance of this text as a recognition of community rights is discussed in Donald A. Desserud, 'The Exercise of Community Rights in the Liberal-Federal State: Language Rights and New Brunswick's Bill 88,' *International Journal of Canadian Studies* 14 (Fall 1996): 215–36.

35 Hon. Frank McKenna, *Journal of Debates (Hansard)*, Session of 1992, vol. 11, 4713. The resolution to amend the Constitution was Motion 89, passed 4 Dec. 1992.

36 Ibid., 4720.

37 Ibid., 4717. The Confederation of Regions (COR) MLAs, who formed the official opposition, were harshly critical of the lack of definition of the phrase 'cultural institutions' and viewed this as a foundation for duality throughout all aspects of New Brunswick governmental institutions. See, e.g., the remarks by COR MLA Ed Allen, who described the proposal as 'the most serious, divisive and ultimately destructive proposal that has ever come to the floor of this House,' in ibid., 4721–2.

38 Premier Frank McKenna, New Brunswick, *Journal of Debates (Hansard)*, Session of 1992, vol. 11, (4 Dec. 1992), 4710–13. One challenge to this claim was voiced by COR MLA Ed Allen, 4727–8.

39 The research methods were explained in Poirier-Bastarache, *Report*, 57–61. The study of community leaders encountered the problem that many anglophones refused to participate in the study (92). The results of one of the studies in support of their work appears in René-Jean Ravault, *Perceptions de Deux Solitudes: Étude sur les relations entre les deux communautés de langues officielles du Nouveau-Brunswick* (Québec: Centre internationale de recherche sur le bilinguisme, 1983), no. B-125.

40 Poirier-Bastarache, 61.

41 Ibid., 63.

42 Ibid., 115.

43 Alan Gilmore Buchanan, 'Anglophone Attitudes towards the French and Bilingualism in New Brunswick,' Master's thesis, Queen's University (1983), 33.

44 Ibid., 34. The quotation is taken from George C. Perlin, 'Public Opinion Constraints Governing Responses by the Atlantic Provinces to Constitutional Change Sought by Quebec,' in J.R. Winter, ed., *The Atlantic Provinces in Canada: Where Do We Go from Here?* (Wolfville: Acadia University, 1980), 116.

45 The survey of 4,000 Canadians is reported in *Language and Society* 19 (April 1987). See Tables 2 and 3 for the responses on services in both official languages.

46 Stacy Churchill, and Anthony H. Smith, 'The Time Has Come,' *Language and Society* 19 (April 1987), 8.

47 George Perlin, 'Anglophone Attitudes towards Bilingualism: A Summary of Some Findings from Survey Research,' in Daniel Bonin, ed., *Towards Reconciliation? The Language Issue in Canada in the 1990s* (Kingston: Institute of Intergovernmental Relations, Queen's University, 1992), 109–10.

48 See Steele, *Can Bilingualism Work?*, 47. She explained this in part as stemming from the fact that francophone schools typically contain libraries and theatres to serve the local francophone community which English schools do not. Obviously, these expenditures become in part cultural support subsidies

49 The instance is noted in Emery M. Fanjoy, 'Language and Politics in New Brunswick,' *Canadian Parliamentary Review* 13(2) (Summer 1990): 5.

50 Motion 70 was introduced by Mr Hargrove, whose introductory statement in support appears in the *Journal of Debates (Hansard)*, Session of 1994, vol. 4, 1594–99. The motion was eventually defeated.

51 Sue Calhoun, 'The Poirier-Bastarache Bombshell,' *New Maritimes* (4 May 1985), 7. This article provides both useful background material and a

balanced treatment of the unfolding political controversy. The tenor of these meetings is also captured in the appropriately titled 'Anger, Bitterness Shown over Language Question,' *Daily Gleaner* (Fredericton) (6 April 1985), A1, A3. The hostile behaviour in some instances involved throwing eggs at people, and, in another, smashing television lights.

52 Advisory Committee, *Report*. It should be emphasized that the figures cited in the ensuing summary concern the distribution of briefs, with no account taken of the fact that some briefs are presented by individuals, while others are from organizations. Thus, there is no presumed correspondence between these distributions and those of the public at large.

53 Ibid., 9. Incidentally, these New Brunswick experiences contradict the findings of the Charter Project (discussed earlier) that commitments to equality undergird support for language rights. In this case, equality is conspicuously rejected despite acceptance, albeit grudging, of certain entitlements.

54 Ibid., 26.

55 Ibid., 38–46.

56 Ibid., 35.

57 'New Brunswick's Francophones Brace for Attack on Linguistic Rights,' *Globe and Mail* (6 Sept. 1989), A9. The comments were selected from a survey of its members conducted by the union. The ad appeared in the *Saint John Telegraph-Journal* on 25 Aug. and was distributed throughout the province. In response, the hospital administration, while denying that the views expressed reflected the majority view among hospital employees, gave the union a greater role on its bilingualism committee.

6

Equality of Languages:
Theoretical Considerations

Our fascination with equality lies not in mere theory or established practice, but in the repeated moment of transition from theory into practice.[1]

Perhaps the most neglected aspect of public debate over language rights in Canada concerns the claim to linguistic equality. As the debate intensifies, one of the contentious underlying issues is the implication of equal status of the languages. One recent commentary asserted "The corollary of the equal status principle is the recognition of a constitutional right to work in either official language' and, furthermore, 'equality between the two languages necessarily implies equality between the two language groups.'[2] Such conclusions offer a prescriptive interpretation of language equality, since its proponent admit that this is a recommendation on how the policy *ought* to be interpreted, rather than how it in fact *is* interpreted.

The previous chapter focused on one instance of that debate – specifically the attempt to recognize and implement a commitment to language equality in the province of New Brunswick. This chapter situates discussions of language equality in the context of the literature in political philosophy on the meaning of equality and its application to specific cases. The conception of language equality has varied contents, and some versions of language equality are not readily supported by principles of equality. Perhaps equality of service is the most defensible version of language equality.

'Equality,' 'language equality,' and the principles they involve, and not ancillary policy goals such as the promotion of national unity are the issues here. Second, consideration is exclusively of the dimension of equality, despite the significance of the arguments for 'language rights' that are important foundations for this debate. This decision has two rationales. First, since the New Brunswick approach to language rights is closely modelled on the federal policy, such a discussion would be highly repetitive. Second, the concept of equality has figured significantly in the language debate throughout Canada. As we have seen, the B and B Commission sought to justify national language policy on a notion of 'equal partnership' between the two major language groups. In addition, the authors of the Charter Project study (discussed in Chapter 2) reported that egalitarian attitudes tend to increase support for Charter language rights.[3] On the other hand, they also concluded that 'equality as a value ... occupies a more equivocal, more problematic place in contemporary liberal democratic culture than is usually recognized.'[4] Finally, some analysts have suggested that the kinds of claims regarding language that are the focus of discussion here are in fact to be justified on the requirements of equality rather than on the requirements of the content of language rights.[5] This suggests the importance of a separate exploration of the issue of equality. I shall begin with a brief survey of the meanings of equality and its variations in the philosophy literature.

The Meanings of Equality

Equality has been a prominent topic of discussion throughout the entire history of Western political thought. Its prominence has not produced notable progress in the resolution of the problems that it entails. One commentator concluded that the problem is still where Aristotle left it two thousand years ago.[6] Its longevity, alas, is surpassed only by its ambiguity. 'Equality,' said one analyst of the history of the term, 'is a word with both a venerable ancestry and a prodigious burden of inherited meanings.'[7] Profound disagreements persist over the meaning of the term, the status of the claims that it advances, and the content of such claims. The difficulties begin with its definition.

The meaning of equality is significantly shaped by its contexts. This is illustrated in a brief summary of the definitions of the word 'equality' appearing in the *Oxford English Dictionary*. Therein, equality is defined as

1 The condition of being equal in quantity, amount, value, intensity, etc.
2 The condition of having equal dignity, rank, or privileges with others; the fact of being on an equal footing.
3 In persons: Fairness, impartiality, equity. In things: Due proportion, proportionateness.

At least three different dimensions of equality are suggested here. The simplest is that of *quantity*. Equality exists where individuals possess equal amounts of some thing. 'One person, one vote' is an easy illustration of the point.

A second sense is that of *equal respect*. All individuals are to be considered as possessing equal dignity, and considered on an equal footing. This does not imply quantitative equality, either as its basis, or as part of its execution. One can support a principle of equality before the law without being committed to economic equality regarding possessions. Second, there can be considerable variation in the presumed basis on which the equal respect is grounded. In regard to individuals, this has been based on their common capacity for rational thought, or capacity for moral action, or possession of souls. The absence of consensus on the common traits that justify a commitment to equality has done nothing to undermine such commitment.

Typically, the subject of equality has been individuals. Where the subject is another entity, the importance of establishing the basis of the equality becomes more pressing.

The third sense is that of *fairness or proportionality*. This is the broadest meaning of equality, both in the sense that it overlaps with the concept of justice, and in the sense that it introduces extraneous and undefined standards of judgment by which the equality is to be assessed. Put another way, it implies that there can be degrees of inequality that are consistent with the basic principle of equality. Proportionality, after all, means differential distribution on the basis of some standard of measurement. This is aptly illustrated in the traditional liberal formulation of *equality of opportunity*, whereby the equality in question is the opportunity, rather than the results or benefits. Here the proportionality in question is based on presumed effort and therefore dessert, rather than on any inherent features of the individuals. These various senses of equality are also reflected in different formulations of principles of equality.

Principles of Equality

One version of an equality principle is sometimes referred to as the *weak principle of equality*. It states, 'All persons should be treated equally (in the same way) save when there are reasons for treating them differently.'[8] However, such reasons would be required to pass certain tests of acceptability – impartiality, rational benevolence, and liberty. Impartiality requires that the same action would be assessed the same way no matter who was performing it (save for special extenuating circumstances). Rational benevolence requires that all relevant interests be taken into account in making judgments about actions. Liberty requires respect for the freedom of choice of individuals.[9] In this formulation, the emphasis would obviously not be on the principle itself, but rather on the tests for its exceptions. These tests would necessarily be specific to the instance of equality in dispute. In application, the exceptions would undoubtedly outnumber the rule of identical treatment. As pointed out by Stanley Benn, 'Equality very rarely means treating everyone alike; usually it means getting rid of one system of distinctions and replacing it with another.'[10]

A second version of the principle of equality would be *equal consideration of interests*, so that all individuals would have their interests considered in the determination of appropriate policies. As an operating principle, this one encounters the difficulty that equal *consideration* need not entail equal, or rather identical, *benefit*. For this reason, one observer emphasized that such a formulation is not a genuine principle of equality but rather a version of utilitarianism.[11] However, equal consideration presupposes that benefits must be tailored to individual needs, with the result that there is a necessary diversity of treatment and benefits to meet various needs. This point was underscored by R.H. Tawney, who stated, 'The more anxiously a society endeavours to secure equality of consideration for all its members, the greater will be the differentiation of treatment which, when once the common needs have been met, it accords to the special needs of different groups and individuals among them.'[12] In such circumstances, identifying the equality underlying the diversity of treatment becomes elusive indeed.

An alternative formulation of a principle of equality focuses on the *equality of benefits* themselves. One version of such a principle would state that if there are n As each is entitled to $1/n$ of all the Y. This version ensures a strictly equal division of a good or service (Y) among the pool of eligible recipients (A). It assumes both the availability and divisibility of Y. Another version of the same approach could be stated as follows: All Bs who do not have Y have a right to Y if some As have Y. In this version, the emphasis is on the equality of distribution itself rather than on an entitlement to the good or service (Y) in question.[13] This means that if no As have Y, then no Bs have any right to y either. The fact of the possession of Y by some creates the entitlement for others. Such a principle, of course, will not stand alone. It requires a substantive list of the class of entities that constitute the category Y, as a rather limited set of things would be judged sufficiently important to warrant equal distribution.[14] In addition, a justificatory argument would still be required to the effect that there are entitlements to the list of things that constitute the *Y*.

This version of an equality principle is open to criticism along the lines that its arithmetic transparency is achieved at the expense of substantive equality. It is insensitive to differences in circumstances among cases. For example, it would not normally be considered a violation of equality if only those suffering from particular diseases were to receive certain drugs or medical treatments. Here, need is an intervening consideration overriding quantitative equality of distribution. The equality emerges not in the distribution, but rather in the comparable treatment where different individuals occupy the same circumstances. Accordingly, this principle of equality is not appropriate for all cases of equality either.

These formulations offer diverse approaches to the pursuit of equality. They each have particular strengths and weaknesses as guidelines with which to address issues of equality. In fact, it would appear that each would be the appropriate principle for different cases of equality, so that there is no particular virtue in opting for one version as the fundamental principle of equality. Moreover, to this point, they lack some essential features for their application to particular political issues. For one thing, the *subjects* of such equality must be specified.

Strictly speaking, languages are not properly subjects for purposes of equality. Subjects for equality must be able to receive benefits or else have identifiable interests that can be weighed in making judgments about equality. Languages fail on both counts, since they can neither receive benefits nor possess interests. The individual is an obvious candidate as the proper subject of language equality, however, this individuality must be rooted in community life. In this regard, the designation of the status of languages is a direct reflection of the significance of different language communities in a society.

Although subjects have typically been individuals, it is entirely possible that the relevant units of comparison might be groups, as they are in matters concerning employment equity. In these cases, some of the complexities of equality are encountered, in that certain kinds of inequality at the individual level – preferential hiring for members of minority groups – are justified as serving the purpose of an overall equality. This graphically illustrates the difficulties of both defining and achieving equality in any given society. The difficulties are magnified when applied to the question of language equality.

Forms of Language Equality

As noted earlier, the meaning of equality depends on the substantive context. This is equally true of language equality. Various legislative initiatives reflect different conceptions of language equality and its policy consequences. Both the federal and New Brunswick Official Languages Acts (1969) assert the principle of equality of status for English and French. The important question is what the content of that equality is. Does it refer to the distribution of benefits to the relevant language groups or is it primarily a declaration of the respect with which each is to be treated, or both? Finally, what is the basis for the claim to linguistic equality?

The rationale for federal language policy reflects what might be labelled a *Hobbesian principle of language equality*. Hobbes had asserted that humans were all equal in one fundamental respect – their ability to destroy each other. Any natural differences in strength and fighting ability could be overcome by stealth and weapons. Thus, individuals were confronted with an inescapable balance of mutual terror, in light of which it was only rational to treat each other as political equals, at least insofar as in requiring consent for a social contract.[15] Prime Minister Pierre Trudeau implicitly invoked a similar rationale for existing language policy when he stated,

Why do we have two official languages in Canada? In my opinion, not primarily because of any historical founding rights, though they are important to many people ... We are dealing with straightforward political and social realities ... If only because of sheer force of numbers, either group has the power to destroy the unity of this country. Those are the facts ... These facts leave Canada with only one choice, only one realistic policy: to guarantee the language rights of both linguistic communities.[16]

In regard to languages, the capacity of the English and French linguistic communities to destroy the country is the basis for their mutual recognition – thus a Hobbesian basis for equality. This offers a fragile basis for equality, because it turns on the disruptive capacity of the two languages. Were this capacity lost, then so too would disappear official recognition. This justification for language equality, however, is merely pragmatic and not principled. In face of demands for linguistic equality that appeal to principles of justice, it is mute.

Linguistic equality was thus the underlying principle justifying a regime of language rights. Although central to the policy, the meaning of linguistic equality is strikingly elusive. The vagaries of the concept are neatly captured in one attempt by the government to define it: 'Equality of status of the French and English languages does not mean that they are equal only up to a certain point. Nor, on the other hand, does it mean that they are equal in their practical, everyday application everywhere, all the time, regardless of actual needs and conditions. When the government speaks of 'equality of status' it means an equality that takes into account these apparently contradictory statements.'[17] Although evading tidy definition, equality was interpreted to involve commitments to (roughly) proportional representation of the two languages in the public service, public services in both official languages, and internal use of both languages, within the public service. For purposes of convenience, the forms of linguistic equality might be categorized as follows: equality of legal status, equality of service, and equality of use. Each will be examined in turn.

Equality of Legal Status

Equal status in law as languages of government and its institutions is equality of legal status. In the Canadian federal context, this has conventionally meant that both English and French languages may (or shall) be used in the legislative and judicial processes, and they are of equal validity. If one dispenses with Trudeau's rationale for recognizing equal status, the question arises, is there an alternative basis for this commitment to language equality? Anglophone public opinion in New Brunswick, for example, rejected equality of legal status insofar as it implies equality between the language groups. Further, the inequality in size of the language groups (two-thirds anglophone to one-third francophone) is ground for dismissal of claims to equality between the languages themselves. In this respect, anglophone opinion mirrors in reverse image the logic of the francophone advocate of linguistic equality quoted in the opening paragraph. André Braën had said that language equality requires equality between the language groups. Anglophone opponents are saying, 'That's right, and as we're not equal, the languages can't be equal either!' This logic focuses on the quantitative dimension, whereas the focus should more properly be on the dignity and status dimension. The question would not be whether or not there are an equal number of bodies in each language community. Rather, the question can be asked, are the characteristics of one language community sufficiently similar to those of the majority community to warrant equal status? Does the particular language community, for example, constitute a prominent and established linguistic community within the society which functions in that language? If so, the argument would be made that this is grounds for such recognition. The concern is then more with the symbolic assertion of the place of specific languages in society overall than with the distribution of benefits between communities within it.

Equality of Service

Another sense of language equality is equality of service. It requires that the same degree and quality of government services be available to all citizens in both official languages. This is not as transparently obvious a proposition as it might sound. Although accepting that certain services ought to be provided in the French language, the anglophone public in New Brunswick did not accept the notion that such services should be as readily available as services in English. The result could be summarized as 'French services, yes; equality of service, not necessarily.' This position cannot readily be squared with a rationale based on principles of equality. Equality of benefit would consist only of equality in its availability rather than in its quality. However, quality is an essential ingredient of service.

Consider a call to the tax department for advice on completion of tax returns. One person *A* has her inquiries carefully answered, her options outlined, and the consequences of those options explained. A second caller *B* is treated to peremptory replies of 'yes' or 'no,' and nothing is explained. Although both have been served in some sense, the benefit of the service is vastly different. Obviously, the difference resides in the quality of the service itself – the care and attention to the interests and concerns of the client.

Suppose someone were to establish the rule that all blue-eyed people would receive *A*'s treatment, whereas all brown-eyed people would receive *B*'s treatment. Such a pattern would no doubt be roundly condemned as a violation of basic notions of equal treatment. Yet anglophone opponents appear to blithely contemplate the potential for just such a distinction. The weak principle of equality (treating people in the same circumstances in the same way) would support a demand for equal quality of service. Such a principle, incidentally, does not require recourse to the features of language groups, but merely to their common status as citizens. The conclusion follows that, once an entitlement to service is admitted, one must also accept the implicit adjective 'equal' in front of 'service.' If this is accepted, then there is a fundamental flaw in the rationale operant in anglophone opinion.

Once admitted, the issue then becomes how this is to be met. The argument is occasionally raised that, since most francophones in New Brunswick are in fact bilingual, it is possible to provide them equally good government services *in English*.[18] Accordingly, equality of service does not require bilingual services. However, such an argument is insufficiently appreciative of the importance of differing degrees of fluency in a second language. Many francophones are bilingual, but many of those would demur from describing themselves as *fluently* bilingual. This difference in degree is important for the quality of government services. When someone phones the Goods and Services information line to inquire why plain peanuts are untaxed while salted ones are taxed, his ability to comprehend the answer is immeasurably enhanced when the information is presented in the language in which he is most comfortable and most able to grasp subtle distinctions and fine detail. The same point applies to virtually all the services available from government. For this reason, government services must have a bilingual capacity. Although services can be provided via translation, the delays this necessitates most assuredly result in inferior quality. The individual equal entitlement to services in one's language entails an effective government commitment to at least institutional bilingualism.

There is one important qualification in this formulation of equality of service. It involves a commitment to equal provision of services in comparable circumstances. This is reflected in the ubiquitous phrase, 'where numbers warrant,' as a qualifier to the language rights contained in the Charter of Rights and Freedoms, for example. It is a recognition that governments cannot provide services in their own language to every member of both official language groups, but only to those living in linguistic communities sufficiently concentrated to warrant the commitment. There is a necessary variation in the actual provision of service, depending on circumstances. Thus, the equality consists not in the benefits received by each individual, but in the equal access to services under similar conditions.

From Language Equality to Proportional Representation

The emphasis on service addresses the concerns of francophones as clients of government, but does not deal with their concerns as workers in government services. To address this dimension, a final sense of language equality is noteworthy.

Equality of Use

In government equality of use means that the two languages are used to an equal extent there. Such equality would be proportionate, based on the demographic distribution of language groups. As outlined in the Poirier-Bastarache report, it would require a group of policies embracing proportionate representation in the public service, a recognized right to work in one's mother tongue, and a commitment to duality, a dual linguistic structure as the basis of bureaucratic organization.[19] For example, the New Brunswick Department of Fisheries would have both a francophone and an anglophone division, providing services throughout the province in the language that local demand required.

Duality constitutes the most comprehensive commitment to equality of use, in that it combines the external service commitments of administration with the internal commitments to the use of both languages. However, this option has been so overwhelmingly rejected by the anglophone majority that it is not a viable option. As an aside, it is noteworthy that in one case where it is practised successfully, Belgium, the two language communities are more nearly equally in size than is the case in Canada.[20] This leaves proportional representation as a potentially more acceptable expression of this option.

Proportional representation in public service jobs is an officially accepted practice in New Brunswick whose theoretical justification has remained remarkably sketchy. The Poirier-Bastarache report, for example, simply asserted, 'The two people that live together must, bilingualism apart, be present in the civil service in an equal proportion to that of their people in the Province.'[21] The annual report on the linguistic profile of the New Brunswick public service indicates a relatively close correspondence between the francophone share of the provincial population and its share of the public service jobs.[22]

Language equality has not been understood to consist solely in access to jobs. The Poirier-Bastarache report insisted that 'cultural identity of these groups is at the heart of the concept of equality.'[23] It further maintained 'Equality of status for the groups is impossible to achieve if one of the linguistic groups is relegated to the status of second class citizenship or if they perceive themselves as such.'[24] Similarly, the Bilingualism and Biculturalism Commission argued in its report, 'The equality to which we refer requires that a person who engages in some activity or associates with some institution need not renounce his own culture, but can offer his services, act, show his presence, develop, and be accepted with all his cultural traits.'[25] The B and B Commission viewed this as an expression of 'real equality of opportunity – an equality ensuring that the fact of speaking English or French would be neither a help nor a handicap to a person seeking entry into the institutions affecting our individual and collective life.'[26] Taken in this sense, language equality requires equal capacity to participate in public institutions in either official language. Unlike a policy of non-discrimination regarding race, such a principle requires not that institutions be blind to differences among individuals and cultures, but that they develop a capacity to incorporate those differences. This is the basis for an insistence on proportional representation in the public service above and beyond these other policy proposals. A commitment to using both French and English as languages of work at once displays equal respect for both language groups and permits equitable access to employment in those public institutions. These dimensions of language equality are viewed as jointly necessary for the development of the two language groups rather than simply as instances of language equality itself. Thus, the rationale embraces a promotion-oriented language policy that seeks equality of condition between the language groups.

These justifications are highly controversial since proportional representation is a practice that offends anglophone sensibilities about equal treatment. As noted earlier, anglophones in New Brunswick rejected the notion that groups are entitled to any share of positions in the public service. Similarly, the 1985 Charter Project study reported selective acceptance of affirmative action principles for staffing the public service in Canadian public opinion. Although a majority of both anglophones and francophones endorsed the notion that a proportionate share of top government jobs should be reserved for women, only a francophone majority endorsed the same practice applied to francophones.[27] One can only speculate on the basis of this selective endorsement of the principle by anglophones.

How does equality of opportunity relate to proportional representation? Equality of opportunity focuses on the requirements for equal consideration of individuals. It is concerned to eliminate biases and disabilities, rather than to impose a specific result. The principle of equal opportunity demands that all Canadians receive fair consideration for appointment to the public service. However, this is implicitly limited to those properly qualified for the specific positions that are open. Thus, only those with appropriate skills and credentials may be considered.

The problem with proportional representation is that what may be balanced treatment for both language groups on the whole can be highly arbitrary in isolated decisions. A particular position is to be filled in a particular department and particular individuals are considered for it. If maintaining a quota of language group members is a primary consideration, then individuals will not be given equal consideration on their own merits. This violates a more basic notion of equality – equal consideration – and perhaps the commitment to the merit principle itself.

An anecdote illustrates the problem. An acquaintance once was among those on the short list for a prestigious scholarship in New Brunswick. He related how, prior to the individual interviews that were part of the selection process, the sole francophone candidate was openly bragging that he was going to get a scholarship because he was the only francophone in the group. He was in fact selected as a scholarship recipient. Although he was presumably every bit as qualified as the other candidates, his emphasis on his ethnicity as a guarantee of his success could only prove intensely galling to his competitors. Furthermore, they might be tempted to conclude that performance was in his case at least a secondary consideration. This of course offends against equal treatment of individuals and raises charges of reverse discrimination.[28]

If the operating assumption is that public service positions are a benefit that ought to be equitably distributed, then there are some obvious defects in this view. Obviously, the positions are not equally distributed, but awarded to the individuals best qualified to perform specific responsibilities. Thus, the distribution must be subordinate to the functional requirements. Moreover, the *raison d'être* of public service positions is the provision of service, and the primary consideration must surely be the recruitment of individuals best able to provide those services. Thus, if a fluently bilingual anglophone was in a particular instance the best available person for a position designated 'French essential,' would it not be desirable to choose such a person over a francophone? To answer in the affirmative suggests that proportional representation should not be viewed as a goal in itself, but as a means to other goals in the public service.

Language skills may be considered as one significant qualification for certain jobs, but generally the major determinant of which language skills are significant will be determined by the language of service required for a position or its work environment. If, to take an extreme case, English language fluency was considered an essential qualification for all positions, and anglophones comprised the entire group of fluent English speakers, it would not violate the requirements of the standard principle of equality of opportunity if anglophones made up the entire public service.

On the surface, the effects vary depending on assumptions about the linguistic characteristics of the francophone and anglophone populations, and about the language requirements for public service positions. If we assume that all francophones are fluently bilingual, and that all positions in the public service require English language fluency, then francophones would be eligible to fill all positions. A policy of proportional representation, in the New Brunswick context, would mean that one-third of the civil service would be staffed by francophones; two-thirds, by anglophones. Consequently, on the negative side, a francophone would compete for a smaller number of jobs, but, on the positive side, the competitive field would be commensurately smaller. Viewed solely in mathematical terms, this policy would have only modest effects on the opportunities for employment of francophones in the public service.

If, on the other hand, we assume that all francophones are 'French unilingual,' and that all positions still require English language proficiency, then they are ineligible for any. By the same token, to designate a position as requiring bilingual proficiency is to largely restrict the pool of applicants to francophones – given the prevailing distribution of bilingual capacity in New Brunswick and Canada. The impact of the proposal thus depends upon the designated language(s) of work and the language skills of individual citizens.

This is a reminder that the designation of positions significantly tilts the 'level playing field' between francophones and anglophones in the matter of access to jobs. Put more strongly, the choice of language of work and the requisite language skills constitutes a mechanism of systemic discrimination for the two language groups. Systemic discrimination in this case would constitute a set of otherwise neutral rules that would disadvantage one language group or the other in the pursuit of job opportunities. It is of course an unavoidable issue, since even choosing not to create a policy on the issue is to inherit one form or another of the problem.

Can equality of service and equality of opportunity be sufficient goals without a commitment to proportional representation? Although this might be possible in theory, the New Brunswick experience of the past twenty years casts doubt on its practicality. The Poirier-Bastarache report stated that French is rarely a language of work in the New Brunswick public service, even in departments with predominantly bilingual personnel.[29] It further concluded that prospects for service in the French language were uncertain at best outside predominantly francophone regions. These findings suggest that the primary goals of New Brunswick language policy are decidedly elusive. The same point is advanced in the federal context, when one analyst insisted that 'equitable representation is necessary to ensure a practical application of the right to work in either of the official languages and the provision of services of equal quality in both official languages.'[30]

These observations offer the most persuasive rationale for a commitment to proportional representation. Although not a component of linguistic equality itself, it is nevertheless a mechanism by which the basic goals of linguistic equality can be pursued. It provides a target that can be readily monitored and is highly visible. It therefore lends itself to more ready achievement. Furthermore, it offers a means of ensuring a substantial francophone presence in the public service, and a precondition for the development of French as a language of service and work. It accordingly serves as a symbol of commitment to language equality that may not be complemented by success on the primary goals. Accordingly, proportional representation is defensible as the most effective indirect means towards equality of opportunity and the policy goals of equality of service and the promotion of both official languages within the public service.

Delimiting Language Equality

As the quotations from government spokespersons and policy documents amply attest, language rights have generally been justified on the grounds of a commitment to equality. For all the frequency of its invocation, the working concept of equality has been amorphous at best. Equal treatment under equal circumstances is a broad approximation of its policy content. As few if any circumstances are similar in language matters, much is left open to dispute. This is particularly unfortunate since the very concept of equality itself remains strongly contested.

These reflections suggest a more readily defensible version of language equality. Equality of legal status is consistent with the principle of equal respect and, therefore, is an acceptable version of language equality in those contexts where both language communities constitute relatively complete societies. It would be unacceptable as the only version of language equality, however, primarily because its benefits are largely symbolic. It is important as a sign of status for the designated languages, and it assures that the laws and practices of the governmental institutions reflect the existence of those languages. Nonetheless, this version of language equality can be largely invisible to the vast majority of the public.

If we focus on equal consideration of interests as the central element of language equality, equality of service has important attractions. It offers a relatively unambiguous content to language equality – the availability and quality of service available to each individual from government. This presents an intuitively obvious benefit that all would perceive an essential interest in enjoying equally. Moreover, equality of service suggests itself as an interpretation that distributes benefits equally among citizens of different linguistic communities and is therefore more defensible to both. However, this does not satisfactorily resolve the matter of equitable access to public service positions for both language groups, and thus a commitment to proportional representation is a necessary means to ensure equality of opportunity.

What appears defensible in principle, however, is intensely contested in practice. Anglophones and francophones disagree sharply over the meaning and implications of language equality. Although entitlements to government services in both official languages is endorsed, the notion of equality on which it rests is decidedly frail.

Notes

1 Douglas Rae, *Equalities* (Cambridge: Harvard University Press, 1981), 4.
2 André Braën, 'Language Rights,' in Michel Bastarache, ed., *Language Rights in Canada*, trans. Translation Devinat et Associés (Montreal: Les Éditions Yvon Blais, 1987), 48, 54–5.
3 See Paul M. Sniderman, Joseph F. Fletcher, Peter H. Russell, and Philip E. Tetlock, 'Political Culture and the Problem of Double Standards: Mass and Elite Attitudes toward Language Rights in the Canadian Charter of Rights and Freedoms,' *Canadian Journal of Political Science* 22 (June 1989): 272–4.
4 See Paul M. Sniderman, Joseph F. Fletcher, Peter H. Russell, and Philip E. Tetlock, *The Clash of Rights: Liberty, Equality, and Legitimacy in Pluralist Democracy* (New Haven: Yale University Press, 1996), 119.
5 Pierre Foucher, 'The Right to Receive Public Services in Both Official Languages,' in Bastarache, *Language Rights*, 198.
6 See John Rees, *Equality* (London: Macmillan, 1971), Chap. 7.
7 Sanford A. Lakoff, *Equality in Political Philosophy* (Cambridge: Harvard University Press, 1964), 12.
8 Its weakness, incidentally, stems from its silence concerning acceptable reasons.
9 Rees, *Equality*, 108, 116–17. My presentation here briefly summarizes Rees's treatment of the issues.
10 Stanley I. Benn, 'Equality, Moral and Social' in Paul Edwards, ed.-in-chief, *The Encyclopedia of Philosophy*, vols. 3 and 4 (New York: Macmillan, 1967), 41.
11 Richard Norman, *Free and Equal: A Philosophical Examination of Political Values*

(Oxford: Oxford University Press, 1987), 62. In the ensuing pages, Norman challenged two variations of a utilitarian argument for equality, both of which are oriented to issues of economic equality, and hence of limited utility regarding issues such as language.

12 R.H. Tawney, *Equality* (rev. ed.) (London: Allen and Unwin, 1952), 39. This quote is from Benn, 'Equality,' 41.

13 These formulations are two of a set developed in Joseph Raz, *The Morality of Freedom* (London: Oxford, 1986), 225. Raz regarded the latter type of formulation as 'the paradigmatic (strictly) egalitarian principles.' Ibid., 226.

14 Douglas Rae hypothesized a Society E in which all goods would be divided in strictly equal fashion once, and then suggested that no historical society could possibly meet the conditions of its existence. See Rae, *Equalities*, 5–7.

15 Hobbes, *Leviathan*, Part I, Chap. 13, C.B. MacPherson, ed. (Harmondsworth: Penguin 1968).

16 Canada, House of Commons, *Debates* (31 May 1973), 4303.

17 Government of Canada, *A National Understanding* (Ottawa: Minister of Supply and Services, 1977), 46.

18 A leader of the COR party in New Brunswick argued,'It's unnecessary to produce (things) in both languages for 30 per cent of the population. Eight-five per cent of them (francophones) can speak both languages. They can read English.' (Quoted in 'Activists Denounce French-language Plan in N.B.,' *Globe and Mail* (28 Feb. 1990), A9.

19 Task Force on Official Languages, *Towards Equality of the Official Languages in New Brunswick: Report* (Fredericton, 1982), 413. (Hereafter cited as Poirier-Bastarache).

20 The distribution of Dutch and French speakers is approx. 55% to 45% in Belgium, a pattern of rough quantitative equality that may sustain a system of duality. See Kenneth D. McRae, *Conflict and Compromise in Multilingual Societies* vol. 2, *Belgium* (Waterloo: Wilfrid Laurier University Press, 1986), Ch. 4.

21 Poirier-Bastarache, 126. It noted that this is not the case in New Brunswick where francophones are underrepresented, constituting 33% of the population, but only 27.8% of the public service as of 1980.

22 As of the 1981 census, francophones represented 33.6% of the N.B. population. In 1986, francophones constituted 31.6% of the N.B. public service. See Government of New Brunswick, Official Languages Branch, *Linguistic Profile of Employees in the Public Service* (Sep. 1986), Table 1, 19.

23 Poirier-Bastarache, 413.

24 Ibid.

25 Royal Commission on Bilingualism and Biculturalism, *Report* vol. 1, *The Official Languages*, xl. (Ottawa: Queen's Printer, 1969).

26 Ibid., xlii.

27 See Sniderman *et al.*, *Clash of Rights*, 152–4. The reported figures (in Figure 5.6, at 153) were as follows: 26% of the anglophone public endorsed a proportional share of top jobs for francophones, while 52% supported this practice for women; 65% of the francophone public supported the practice for francophones, while 63% endorsed it for women. As with language rights, francophones are more inclined to support the same principles applied to others as they are for their own group. The political elites, on the other hand, strongly supported this affirmative action plan for francophones.

28 Obviously, this issue would arise where gender requirements were the determining factor as well.

29 Poirier-Bastarache, 161.

30 Braën, 'Language Rights,' 48.

7

The Status of Third Languages

The more anxiously a society endeavours to secure equality of consideration for all its members, the greater will be the differentiation of treatment which, when once the common needs have been met, it accords to the special needs of different groups and individuals among them.[1]

R.H. Tawney

In recent years the issue of language equality has been complicated by demands from a new quarter. Some Aboriginal spokespersons now seek equal status with English and French for their languages.[2] Such claims are not entirely novel. When the idea of official languages was first proposed in Canada, representatives of some allophone language groups argued unsuccessfully for some recognition of their languages. If language policy is to be based on concepts such as rights and equality, these proposals need to be seriously assessed and therefore invite more detailed examination of the basis for claims to equal status in general.

This chapter discusses allophone and Aboriginal claims as particular cases of an argument for linguistic equality. Both the specific arguments of Aboriginal groups and a broad justificatory argument for linguistic equality developed within a liberal political framework are advanced. The emphasis is conceptual and analytic, rather than historical, constitutional, or legal. In the process, the criteria relevant to defensible claims to linguistic equality are emphasized. What follows presents the argument for linguistic equality for Aboriginal languages.

Linguistic Equality for Aboriginal Languages

The argument for linguistic equality for Aboriginal languages has two themes. First, because of the precarious state of many Aboriginal languages, with several bordering on extinction, substantial government support is required to revitalize them. The prospect of linguistic extinction is particularly significant and literal, as these languages are unique to Canada. Second, the revitalization of Aboriginal languages is an important component of reducing the social inequalities experienced by Aboriginal peoples. This link stems from the importance of language to the vitality of Aboriginal cultures. One Native leader spoke for many when he avowed:

Our native language embodies a value system about how we ought to live and relate to each other ... it gives a name to relations among our kin, to roles and responsibilities among family members, to ties with the broader clan group ... There are no English words for these relationships because your social and family life is different from ours. Now if you destroy our languages, you not only break down these relationships, but you also destroy other aspects of our Indian way of life and culture, especially those that describe man's connection with nature, the Great Spirit, and the order of things. Without our language, we will cease to exist as a separate people.[3]

The destruction of their languages is linked to the social disintegration of Aboriginal communities in a way that undermines efforts to improve the lot of Aboriginal peoples. Thus, linguistic promotion is a prerequisite for social promotion of Aboriginal peoples. In particular, the need for language promotion efforts through educational institutions, and government financial support for related activities by Native communities is emphasized.

Aboriginal peoples insist that their languages be accorded equal treatment with the two official languages. They emphasize that 'only by viewing Aboriginal language rights within the context of the constitutional protections offered to the two official languages in Canada, can the problem be seen as an equality rights issue.'[4] The Assembly of First Nations has developed a set of demands for linguistic equality with the two official languages. The Assembly demands:

- That Aboriginal languages be accorded equality of status and equal rights and privileges as to their use as in the English and French languages;

- That legislative or other instruments directed at Aboriginal peoples be prepared either in print or for broadcast in the several Aboriginal languages;
- That government services be provided in an Aboriginal language in those areas where numbers warrant such special measures;
- That the ability of an Aboriginal employee to speak in his or her language be given due account with respect to the concept of bilingualism as it relates to the appointment and advancement of personnel.[5]

These claims present a direct challenge to the exclusive primacy of English and French as official languages in Canada. Some of them are on first examination insufficiently developed. Does, for example, the call for 'equal status' with English and French include the use of Aboriginal languages as languages of Parliament and government publications; or as languages of work within the public service? If so, do these claims extend to all fifty-three Aboriginal languages in Canada? These issues are far from clear. These demands do not so much present a sustained argument for equality with English and French as they suggest strands of various arguments for government support for the Aboriginal languages. In addition, their main thrust is tailored to the particular circumstances of the Aboriginal languages, and are therefore not readily applicable to other languages.

Nevertheless, elaborating the manner in which these demands can be advanced in the context of arguments for equality is instructive. Part of this examination requires a closer scrutiny of the dimensions of equality. Another part requires development of a general rationale for linguistic equality per se.

On what basis can language groups claim status equal to other language groups? As we have noted earlier, the simplest principle of equality is *equality of treatment*. Language groups in similar circumstances should be treated in much the same way. That principle granted, what are the relevant circumstances that are similar? Some would insist that languages should have a roughly equal number of speakers in a society to enjoy equal treatment. Thus, the fact that only one-quarter of Canadians speak French, while two-thirds speak English is often taken to be decisive evidence that the French language does not deserve equal status with English.

This view makes the quantitative aspect of equality a precondition of the other components of equality. However, this is inconsistent with our established expectations regarding equality. Although there is probably no sense in which any two individuals are quantitatively equal, for purposes of political life they are nonetheless treated as such. This is because the inequalities in question are subordinate to the broader purposes of the individual within the political community. The same point applies to linguistic equality. The number of speakers of a language, although important, is only one dimension of the substantive issues.

Assessing the Claim

The Aboriginal claim to linguistic equality is seriously challenged by a comparison of the relative sizes of these linguistic communities. According to the 1981 census of Canada, the Aboriginal languages *collectively* constituted approximately one-half of 1 per cent of the population, with 108,620 individuals speaking these languages as a home language. The largest single Aboriginal language, Cree, with 51,325 home language speakers, constituted 0.2 per cent of the Canadian population.[6] The 1991 census data revealed a similar pattern with only modest variations. The total number of Aboriginal home language users increased absolutely to 116,000, but declined relatively to 0.42 per cent of the Canadian population. At the same time, the number of Cree home language speakers declined marginally to 50,650, or 0.18 per cent of the Canadian total.[7]

This one-hundredfold difference in size (between French and the largest Aboriginal language) indicates a reasonable basis for an important distinction in the relative status of these languages. This is not to suggest that there should be no recognition of Aboriginal languages. For example, Switzerland has granted some status to one of its tiny minority languages, Romansh.[8] It is a language of service within its territorial domain, but not an official language. Similar distinctions may be in order for some Aboriginal languages in Canada.

Two other aspects of equality are more important than numerical equality in the argument for linguistic equality. As Kymlicka has argued, 'People are owed respect as citizens and as members of cultural communities.'[9] For the individual members of these linguistic communities, a commitment to linguistic equality would symbolize an *equality of respect* for these languages and their communities.

Second, where languages are central to the daily life of established communities in a country, it is readily arguable that a concern for the *equal consideration of interests* requires state recognition of certain languages. Where languages are used in the daily lives of people, they reflect their essential interests. Language is the medium through which individuals are able both to imbibe their group history, culture, and norms, and to pass it on to the next generation. It is, more immediately, the context within which they earn their daily bread and encounter the social, economic, and political issues that engage their attention as citizens. Kymlicka underscored this relationship to culture and to individual capacity for choice of life goals in observing that 'whether or not a course of action has any significance for us depends on whether, or how, our language renders vivid to us the point of that activity. And the way in which language renders vivid these activities is a matter of our cultural heritage.'[10] A more important basis for linguistic equality, then, is the significance of the language for the communities, rather than the specific size of the various communities.

Are all languages equally important to their cultural communities? Although it can be readily argued that English and French are equally important to the life of their respective cultural communities, the same cannot be so readily asserted of Aboriginal languages. The situation within most of the fifty-three Aboriginal language communities is one of varying degrees of linguistic assimilation. Overall, about three-quarters of the Aboriginal peoples use English or French as their home language. Use of Aboriginal languages tends to be more heavily concentrated among older age groups. A recent publication reported the average age of Aboriginal language speakers as over forty, a clear indication of its declining presence in the younger generation.[11] Only three of these fifty-three Aboriginal languages (Cree, Ojibwa, and Inuktitut) are judged to have good long-term survival prospects.

More tellingly, Phillips reported that 'many children have little opportunity to come in contact with the spoken language of their heritage outside native language instruction programs in the schools.'[12] In light of these circumstances, one must question the centrality of these languages in the daily lives of their cultural communities and their importance to their cultures. More pointedly, what necessity is there for governments to address Aboriginal peoples in languages they, the Aboriginal peoples themselves, do not use? In this respect also there is a fundamental difference between the two official languages and Aboriginal languages.

The response to such challenges is twofold. On the one hand, the socioeconomic plight of Aboriginal peoples is perverse evidence of the importance of the traditional languages. It is the loss of these languages that has partly induced an erosion of traditional values and norms that offered continuity and self-respect to Aboriginal peoples. Accordingly, the revitalization of these languages is viewed as an essential precondition to 'restore pride of ancestry to Canada's native peoples.'[13] Second, the loss of Aboriginal languages was not a product of Aboriginal indifference to their languages, but the result of systematic efforts by governments to discourage their use.[14] The present state of affairs is bleak testimony to the efficacy of those policies. This reality generates special duties on governments to help undo what they have done.

Cultural Membership as a Primary Good

One line of argument is suggested by Kymlicka, in emphasizing the principle of equality of choice for cultural minorities with regard to what John Rawls has called 'primary goods.' Kymlicka's argument was framed to address a rather different set of problems, to wit, the justification of special constitutional status for certain minority cultural groups. It is somewhat surprising, in fact, how *little* attention is devoted to the question of language and culture. In what follows, I shall recast Kymlicka's argument in a more narrowly focused vein, to provide a rationale for linguistic equality.

Kymlicka began with the proposition that 'cultural membership is a primary good'[15] that must be equally respected for all individuals. Primary goods, as defined by Rawls, are 'things that every rational man is presumed to want.' The principal social elements of such primary goods are 'rights and liberties, powers and opportunities, income and wealth.'[16] These goods are the essential prerequisites for the pursuit of a good life. By including cultural membership in this group, Kymlicka emphasized that 'cultural membership is not a means used in the pursuit of one's ends. It is rather the context within which we choose our ends, and come to see their value, and this is a precondition of self-respect, of the sense that one's ends are worth pursuing. And it affects our very sense of personal identity and capacity.'[17] Retention of the traditional language of a community is frequently an important component of cultural membership. According to Kymlicka, cultural minorities are often at an important disadvantage in this regard especially where they do not share the language of the majority community. Consequently, the majority naturally enjoys a resource that minorities can only obtain through special public provision, or legislation, aimed to subsidize access to such resources.

Compensatory measures are justifiable on the grounds that these differences of linguistic opportunity arise largely from the differences in socioeconomic and cultural circumstances that are *not* a result of choices made by members of linguistic minorities. As Kymlicka pointed out,

Aboriginal fears about the fate of their cultural structure, however, are not para-noia – there are real threats. The English and French in Canada rarely have to worry about the fate of their cultural structure. They get for free what Aboriginal people have to pay for: secure cultural membership. This is an important inequal-ity, and if it is ignored, it becomes an important injustice ... special political rights are needed to remove inequalities in the context of choice which arise before people even make their choices.[18]

This difference in circumstance means that Aboriginal communities expend important resources just to secure their cultural context, thereby reducing that which is available to pursue their own life plans, resulting in an inequality of opportunity with the non-Aboriginal majority. Lan-guage rights for Aboriginal cultural communities are thus justifiable as an important contribution to the creation of an egalitarian environment for Aboriginal peoples.

Although Kymlicka offered an important argument for recognition of linguistic equality, some of his pronouncements on language education may undercut his argument. When discussing minority language educa-tion, Kymlicka maintained that, although one cannot prevent members of cultural communities from pursuing education in other languages, there is no obvious grounds for public subsidy for it:

People should have, as part of the respect owed them as members of a cultural community, the opportunity to have a publicly funded education in the language of their community; but whether they have the opportunity to have a publicly funded education in another language is perhaps a matter of policy (just as subsi-dizing cultural exchanges is) with people neither having a right to it nor a right to prevent it.[19]

An important qualification to this general point is the role a language plays in the life of a cultural community. Where a language is integral to community life, the state should support a full array of educational opportunities in this language both to promote the language and to ensure that individuals have opportunities available within their linguistic community. This would flow from both a commitment to equality of respect and equality of opportunity.

Where this is not the case, a conflict arises between the requirements of respect and those of opportunity. One study reported that some Native parents are demanding French as a second language rather than their Native language for their children, on the grounds that this offers them a significantly expanded range of economic options for the future.[20] In effect, these parents are making judgments about what best serves the essential interests of their children, about the best education for them. In such cases, they would be opting out of an education in the minority culture's community language. It seems inappropriate to conclude that they would not thereby be entitled to publicly funded education. Presumably, they would be equally entitled to a publicly subsidized education on the grounds that it would be consistent with the broad purpose of the education system in general, the benefits to which they are equally entitled.

This example raises a broader question about Kymlicka's line of argument, concerning the issue of choice. One critic has challenged this argument on two counts. First, he argued against the justifying rationale, inequality of circumstances, by emphasizing that 'there is no good reason to think that only minorities can face inequalities which are not the product of their choices.'[21] Physically challenged and poor people are two examples. Since we do not argue for special rights for these individuals, 'lack of control over circumstances' is not an appropriate foundation for special entitlements. Second, 'the idea that *all* minority members face the *same* inequality of circumstances seems absurd.'[22] Rather, different individuals in the minority cultural community may be more or less privileged than non-members. This suggests that the special consideration should extend to all the relatively underprivileged rather than to a whole class such as a minority group.

In reply, Kymlicka insisted that such criticisms are irrelevant to the case at hand. In the first place, 'We match the rights to the kind of disadvantage being compensated for.'[23] Thus, different sources of disadvantaged circumstances call for different remedies. To borrow from earlier examples, different physical ailments are treated by various means, because they are the necessary remedies to the specific problems. This is so despite that one case might require two aspirin and another, heart surgery, that is, considerable differences in the expenditure of social resources to solve the problems. There is no inconsistency involved in the differences between the two cases. Second, Kymlicka insisted that it is not that a cultural minority is being granted 'special rights'; rather, they are being accorded the same rights as the majority culture – to wit, the opportunity 'to live and work in their own language and culture.'[24] Kymlicka's reply has particular force in the context of language equality, as what is proposed is a granting of privileges to the Aboriginal population, without suppressing the rights and opportunities of the majority population.

By the same token, this opportunity must not suppress the rights and opportunities available to the members of the minority language group either. In a subsequent work, Kymlicka distinguished between rights that offer external protections from the dominant society versus those that impose internal restrictions on the group members and argued that the latter are unjustifiable.[25] An example would arise where members of Aboriginal communities were required to be educated in their traditional language, that is, did not have the option of choosing an education in the dominant language of the society. In the context where the language is marginal to the community itself, this would constitute discrimination even where imposed by the community's own leadership, because it would significantly disadvantage the individual members in the pursuit of their life plans. On the other hand, where the language is an important element of everyday life, it would not qualify as an internal restriction in the first place – Quebec's language policy preventing francophones from enrolling in the publicly funded English language school system being the most prominent Canadian example.

A more encompassing criticism of Kymlicka's argument emerges in John Danley's claim that 'one's culture is not ultimately a circumstance for which one has no responsibility'[26] It is suggested that cultural membership is not analogous to physical handicaps in that everyone would happily be relieved of the burdens of physical handicaps, given the opportunity. If they were not so willing, societal obligation to compensate for such handicaps is removed. Cultural membership, this argument continues, should be viewed in a similar vein, as a dispensable burden that is subject to choice. Danley insisted,

One cannot choose not to be born into an Inuit or a Pueblo tribe. One can be responsible only for one's response to that given ... Nonetheless, individuals must still take responsibility for their culture. One can be raised a strict German Lutheran or Serbian Greek Orthodox, but there comes a point in life at which one must choose whether to be a strict German Lutheran or Serbian Greek Orthodox.[27]

In the North American context, Aboriginal peoples have the option of assimilation available to them. Therefore, they have some measure of control over their cultural circumstances, that is, choice.

Kymlicka is further taken to task for his insistence that individuals may choose to reject particular practices within a culture without thereby abandoning the culture. This, it is suggested, implicitly acknowledges the important role of choice involved in cultural membership. If individuals are free to choose which elements of a culture they will embrace, they are also free to choose acceptance or rejection of the particular culture as a whole. Although acknowledging that cultural membership may be crucial to personal identity, it is emphasized that

This does not demonstrate that gradual voluntary assimilation into another culture constitutes a wrongful harm to specific persons or to society. It does not demonstrate that gradual voluntary assimilation threatens personal identity, agency, or development. It does not suggest that assimilation into another culture undermines self-respect. Assimilation into another culture is not necessarily identical to stripping an individual of her culture.[28]

Citing the examples of various waves of immigrants to the United States from diverse cultures, all of whom have voluntarily assimilated to American language and culture, this critic argued that no harm has been proven to have been done to anyone in these processes, and therefore no special entitlements arise for these cultural groups.

This criticism is particularly striking in the context of language entitlements and the arguments presented in Canada by Aboriginal peoples. It patently dismisses the significance of the content of specific cultures, to assert that any cultural context provides an adequate foundation for personal identity and self-respect. Danley's use of the immigrant experience in the United States is illuminating and particularly convenient for his argument. Immigrants present a case where individuals have moved from one cultural context to another where their traditional cultural institutions and practices are non-existent. In these circumstances, the notion of voluntary choice is often an adequate characterization of the situation. Furthermore, it would seem insupportable to claim that such individuals were entitled to a re-creation of their cultural environment because it was important to their self-identity and personal development. The question would invariably arise, if it was that important why did they leave?

The Aboriginal experience, however, is different from the immigrant in important ways. The most obvious is that it is indigenous to the larger political community, and therefore does not represent a departure from the culture merely by being there. For that reason, the Aboriginal peoples have, initially at least, as strong a claim to cultural support as the larger community. One must as well appreciate that the historical context of this linguistic assimilation is far from a matter of choice. Residential schools, the absence of government services in Aboriginal languages, and concerted efforts to suppress Aboriginal culture are all part of a sorry tale of cultural oppression. Finally, the widespread discrimination against

Aboriginal peoples is telling evidence that the choice of cultural assimilation to the dominant North American culture is largely closed. In short, the particular case of Aboriginal cultures makes a mockery of this critique.

This dismissal of cultural attachment as a mere product of choice involves an inversion of Kymlicka's value priorities. Rather than treating attachment to traditional culture as a peculiar choice that people may make, it is more in keeping with a respect for choice to emphasize it as an assertion of value priorities that ought to be respected and supported in some ways.

The issue of harm is also treated in a somewhat cavalier fashion. The dimensions of harm are not identified, though Kymlicka's *presumed* definition that it is 'an invasion of certain core interests' is noted. Beyond that, Danley is content to assert that the 'disquieting loss' associated with the disappearance of traditional culture does not constitute harm.[29] This assessment does not square with the reports of many of those subjected to these losses. Speaking of the significance of loss of the capacity to function in one's language, Pierre Trudeau once compared it to being choked.[30] Aboriginal groups have described the loss of their languages as a fundamental alteration of their lives. In one evocative case, an educated Norwegian discovered he was no longer able to communicate in adult language with his own father in their native tongue.[31]

If these reports are at all indicative, one must ask what more would be necessary for harm to occur? The transition process for those linguistically assimilated often occurs over two or three generations. Those most prone to harm are the first generation; subsequent generations gradually accommodate, to the point where, typically, they know only a few expressions in their traditional language. If we focus on the harm involved in loss of language, it is apparently a diminishing experience for subsequent generations. But for the first generation, it is quite traumatic. Furthermore, the Aboriginal argument emphasizes that the loss of the traditional languages continues to undermine the vitality of contemporary Aboriginal communities, so that the loss afflicts the community as a whole above and beyond personal disquietude. The issue of harm, however, is not primary in Kymlicka's analysis, but quite subordinate to the principle of respecting cultural communities in due measure.

Special Grounds for Linguistic Promotion

The rationale developed here for linguistic equality emphasizes the status of language as a 'primary good' for the members of a linguistic community, essential for the development and pursuit of their life plans. In the final analysis, the fact that the Aboriginal languages are not widely used in their respective communities undercuts the force of a claim that language attains such status in Aboriginal communities. In general, these languages cannot be said to frame the context of choice for many of the members of these communities, since they are quite often not the languages of daily living. Thus, their recognition cannot reasonably be said to be a precondition for the effective pursuit of the life's plan Aboriginal community members.

This is buttressed by the observation that 'neither the Métis nor the Indian national political organizations have given much emphasis to the issue of language survival in constitutional talks with the federal and provincial governments.'[32] A general claim to equal status with English and French is also indefensible in light of the different roles the languages play in the lives of their respective communities. In addition, the very modest size of the Aboriginal language group militates against making it a language of government operations. Thus, it would be difficult to justify making these Aboriginal languages of equal legislative or constitutional status with the two official languages.

What cannot be justified at the national level may be accommodated at a provincial or regional level. In 1988 federal insistence on official status for English and French, but not any of the Aboriginal languages, in the territorial legislature, was challenged by local politicians who insisted that French, the language of only 5 per cent of the population, did not deserve a higher status than that of the more numerous Aboriginal languages. Two years later, the Northwest Territories Official Languages Act was amended to grant six Aboriginal languages, Chipewyan, Cree, Dogrib, Gwich'in, Inuktitut, and Slavey, equal status with English and French.[33] In this case, the Aboriginal languages were the languages of everyday life for the major components of the regional political unit, and thus they had a strong claim to recognition as languages of government. This is a circumstance not duplicated in the provinces.

A more general model is that offered by Quebec's legislative treatment of its Aboriginal language minorities. Bill 101 exempted Cree, Inuktitut, and Naskapi from its application on reserves, and recognizes the right of individuals and corporate bodies to use Cree and Inuktitut in the territories governed by the James Bay Agreement. In regard to education, Cree and Inuktitut are to be the languages of education for schools governed by Aboriginal school boards. Bill 101 simultaneously imposed an obligation on these schools to pursue the goal of instituting French as a language of instruction to ensure access for their students to higher education in Quebec. By the same token, it required administrative bodies to develop a capacity to communicate in French with both clients and other bodies in the province. Thus, Quebec legislation, despite not granting official status to Aboriginal languages, respects their status within those areas where Aboriginal authority is recognized.[34]

Although they may not be entitled to constitutional recognition of their language rights, the particular experience of Aboriginal languages as the objects of government repression offers a ready justification for some compensatory measures aimed at revitalizing these languages.[35] The most important area for initiative must be education in the Native language, either as a medium or subject of instruction. The importance of such efforts has long been recognized, however, the commitments by both federal and provincial governments have been strikingly modest. A 1985 review of the situation reported that 52 per cent of status Indian students received no instruction in their Native language, while only 24 per cent were exposed to it as a medium of instruction.

These figures disguised rather dramatic variations among the provinces. At one extreme is Atlantic Canada, where 70 per cent of these students receive no Native language instruction; on the other, the province of Quebec, where 83 per cent of students are taught their Native language either as a medium or subject of instruction or both.[36] Quebec is also remarkable as a province where Algonkian languages thrive as home languages, and where Algonkian language retention is strong in all age groups. These results are partly a consequence of certain natural advantages – the geographic isolation of these tribes, for instance; but the relatively extensive commitment of the provincial government is also an important factor. Since the 1960s Quebec governments have signed agreements with the Cree and Inuit to administer their own school systems, committed resources to develop pedagogical materials for teaching Native languages, and, in Bill 101, recognized the right of Native people to instruction in their Native languages. This extensive provincial commitment is echoed in the relatively strong federal commitment of educational resources to these groups in Quebec.[37] Such resources are important in reinforcing language retention among Aboriginal groups.

These prospects are contingent on the interest the Aboriginal people themselves have in such endeavours. There has been rather cautious support in the past, but the past fifteen years have witnessed a renewed interest in Aboriginal language education among the Aboriginal peoples. One Native leader reported in 1984 that 'in Southern Ontario there has been a resurgence of Indian culture and the people have identified language as a top priority in education. Parents are saying – even if I cannot speak the language, I want to give my children the opportunity to learn the language and perpetuate the culture.'[38] In response to these demands, the Ontario government announced that it planned to provide funding for programs in Aboriginal languages as part of the regular elementary and secondary school curriculum upon request from fifteen students interested in such instruction.[39] Such initiatives, repeated by various provinces throughout Canada, would offer the most important resource for the preservation of Aboriginal languages. To that end, it would be defensible for Aboriginal groups to demand that their provincial governments recognize their right to education in their own languages, comparable to the Quebec arrangements.

The demand for government services in Aboriginal languages is a difficult matter. In general, these languages are too small and too little used to justify such commitments by governments. Even if governments were to attempt such policies there would be a serious problem of lack of supply of appropriately qualified people to offer such services. In the Northwest Territories, the Inuit discovered that a conventional government bureaucracy would have to be staffed with non-Aboriginal peoples – who would not speak their language – in the new territorial government of Nunavut. Instead, they chose to radically decentralize government programs and services to the community level to ensure that Native peoples would control their operation.[40] Presumably, this would also enable local communities to decide the language of government service for themselves. This suggests that the question of the language of government services is best addressed in the context of Aboriginal self-government. Nevertheless, certain linguistic accommodations can readily be incorporated. Provision of Aboriginal interpreters in trials is one significant commitment that is consistent with the general principle that individuals have a right to fully understand the legal proceedings to which they are party.[41] Similarly, where essential health and social services cannot be provided in the language of the recipient, governments ought to take steps to ensure their effective provision. At a minimum, this might simply mean using a community member as an interpreter or aide in the provision of the service. Finally, support for radio broadcasting in Aboriginal languages, as is done in the Northwest Territories, would offer an important alternative to the mainstream mass media.

One commentator on the issue of support for Aboriginal languages emphasized,

What is important, fundamentally, is that the community decides on the uses and purposes for which the language is to be retained. Some communities may simply wish to preserve the language, to maintain it perhaps in ritual contexts (Ojibwa is already a ritual language in some communities). Others may desire to use the native language as the working language of the community. Still others may want to keep it as a portable symbol of their Aboriginal identity; the young people may not speak it, but they want to know something about it, they want to identify themselves with it. In short, government has no right to prejudge the form the language retention efforts should take in any particular community. The best it can do is to understand a 'typology' of language retention approaches and to ensure that its investment meets particular needs as defined by particular communities at a certain moment in time.[42]

This comment is a reminder that these initiatives regarding Aboriginal languages are particularistic and not subject to the same rationale as language rights in general. In the earlier discussion, language entitlements were founded on the demonstrated persistence of the language for groups with deep roots in the community. Obviously, few Aboriginal languages meet this standard. Furthermore, for most of the Aboriginal groups, there is no immediate prospect of a revival of their languages in daily life. The diversity of their linguistic circumstances requires that each assess the appropriate goals for their communities and act accordingly.

After extended experience with these educational and cultural opportunities, the Aboriginal peoples will presumably have a greater opportunity for choice of languages for their community lives, at which point the argument for enhanced status can be joined anew. In the interim, there is a ready argument for *special recognition* for Aboriginal languages, to heritage language education, and cultural support based on their history of discriminatory treatment. A more general claim to broader linguistic equality must await the fruits of these initial efforts.

The Claims of Heritage Languages

Canada has long celebrated its self-image as a multicultural mosaic, wherein different groups are free to maintain their distinct traditions. The formal commitment to the principle is reflected in the policy of multiculturalism, which extends financial support to many groups for cultural activities. The rationale for these initiatives has developed in the context of a commitment to multiculturalism rather than from an extension of the concept of language rights. Given the prominence accorded language for English and French cultures in discussions of language policy, this lack of emphasis is, at least at first look, rather surprising. However, the omission was entirely intentional, as the government sought to accommodate allophone opposition to their exclusion from official language policy through this means. Furthermore, it could hardly be otherwise, because it was simply presumed that all other language groups must assimilate to one of the two principal languages of Canadian society. In fact, the official language policy of bilingualism has been a periodic source of grievance to some of these larger allophone language communities. When the B and B Commission considered the question, it urged privileges for such groups rather than rights. Regrettably, the commission did not respond directly to a minority report urging recognition of group rights for certain regional languages (German, Ukrainian, Italian, and Eskimo–Indian).[43] In regard to non-official languages, the B and B report revealed some sensitivity to criticisms of the government's treatment of other languages. The government denied that official bilingualism involves only special groups, on the grounds that virtually all Canadians speak one of the two official languages. However, it apparently granted legitimacy to these allophone criticisms in its acceptance of the notion 'that initiatives designed to assist people from diverse ethnic origins to retain their mother tongue are entirely consistent with the official language policy and, indeed, can make an important contribution to its success.'[44] The success in question concerns the acceptance of English and French as the official languages of the country – a clear signal of its subordinate character to official langauge policy.

The government did, however, suggest some standards for judging when recognition of other languages is in order, which could conceivably have resulted in some recognition for Ukrainian. The recommended standards included a significant number of Canadians who ordinarily use a particular language and who demonstrate a resolve to maintain it. Nevertheless, the opportunity for an in-depth examination of the allophone claim to language rights was largely by-passed. One of the few Canadian discussions to broach the subject of language rights for other language groups in Canada was careful to extend toleration rights rather than promotion-oriented rights. It proposed a constitutional amendment asserting that third languages 'may not be restrained or restricted in their natural development' without making commitments to accommodate them except in the courts. Even here, the extent of such accommodation was unspecified. It might consist simply of a right to an interpreter. Significantly, the rationale was framed more in terms of national unity and national identity than in terms of due recognition of language entitle-ments.[45]

Allophone groups, however, have not petitioned for equal status with English. They have noted that, outside Quebec, they meet the criteria for some official recognition as well as French does. For the most part, this has rendered the conclusion that French does *not* deserve recognition, rather than the claim that other languages must also be recognized. In addition, since allophone groups are often composed of relatively recent immigrant groups, it is conventionally maintained that they are not entitled to claim language rights in any event. Thus, Kymlicka, in posing the question of why French Canadians have language rights but Greek speakers do not, simply noted that Greeks, unlike French Canadians, are not a national minority and considered that a sufficient answer to the question.[46]

However, a policy that recognizes a concept of language rights as a fun-damental entitlement, as many Canadians do, must in principle consider the claims of all relevant language communities. Furthermore, when Aboriginal languages are considered, the status of heritage languages of comparable size readily arises. The Aboriginal language with the largest population base, Cree, is only the sixteenth most common non-official language in Canada, ranking just below Hungarian and Vietnamese.[47] Thus, there are numerous candidates for claims to comparable treatment with Aboriginal languages. This was pointedly illustrated by the response of a federal cabinet minister to proposals for constitutional entrench-ment of Inuktitut in the new territory of Nunavut. He rejected the con-cept on the grounds that 'if we do that, we'll have to protect the language rights of Italian-speaking immigrants in Toronto.'[48] Although the minis-ter was ignoring the differences in political context – Nunavut would be a self-governing territory wherein Inuktitut is spoken by a plurality of the population – it was also true that there are nine times as many individuals in Toronto alone whose mother tongue is Italian than there are Inuktitut speakers in the whole country. Thus, the question of the status of heri-tage languages inevitably arises when new candidates for recognition are proposed. What follows suggests some guidelines for assessing claims to such recognition.

Criteria for Assessment of Allophone Languages

The most prominent allophone languages cannot claim the important advantage of indigenous status as can Aboriginal languages, English, and French. Accordingly, to merit consideration, their claims to promotion-oriented language rights must be formulated in relation to a set of general criteria. The initial criteria would be the same as those for any language group. In general, the criteria would consist of (a) the size of the group, (b) the importance of its language to its community life, and (c) the persistence of the language.

The size of the language group in absolute and relative terms is an important consideration especially in the practicality of provision of government services. Obviously, a language group must be sufficiently large to constitute a viable community or locus of daily life for the group members. Although there are wide variations internationally in what constitutes a minimum population percentage, in Canadian discussions, the figure of 10 per cent occurs with striking regularity. There is nothing absolute or necessarily consistent in this figure, because in some cases a much smaller percentage would offer a significant population concentration; in others cases – many rural areas – a much higher percentage would be justified for practical reasons.

The legitimacy of the claim is more immediately linked to the importance of the language to the community life of the cultural group. It should not be assumed that ethnic identity is critically important to those identified as ethnic.[49] This needs to be determined through an analysis of the behaviour of members of minority linguistic groups. Do its members use their ancestral language throughout the spheres of private life, in the home, with neighbours, and in private social and cultural institutions? To the extent that they maximize the use of the language in the spheres available to them, they demonstrate their commitment to the importance of their language. This of course assumes the absence of any official measures designed to repress the use of other languages. One of the best indicators of this commitment is the use of the language in the home. This is why the preferred definition of language group members concerns which language they use in their homes.

The third criterion is closely related to the second, and is more pertinent in the allophone case than the Aboriginal for reasons previously noted. The persistence of the language is an important consideration when dealing with groups defined as immigrant. Where the members of a language group consist largely of first-generation immigrants, the issue remains to be determined. As well, the extent of interest a group has in maintaining its language is also unclear. Finally, the claim of the language group becomes more credible as it increasingly acquires the status of a native language. The distinction is reflected in the *European Charter for Regional or Minority Languages*, which recognizes as minority languages only those 'traditionally used within a given territory of a State by nationals of that State who form a group numerically smaller than the rest of the State's population.'[50] The definition explicitly excludes those of immigrants, and stresses both the historical linkages of a language with an area, and its concentration within specific areas. A widely scattered linguistic minority would not possess the claims that a regionally concentrated but less numerous linguistic minority would. Such a diffuse minority would also possess only the barest prospect of retaining their language in any event. The rationale is succinctly stated in Heinz Kloss's observation, 'Only after the group has managed to keep the language and a feeling for the language alive among the grandchildren of the immigrants, only after the language can be held to have taken root, can the state be requested to promote the language.'[51] Based on this approach, promotion-oriented language rights become arguable only for 'natives of native parentage.'

These criteria are reasonably linked to the standards applicable for the recognition of language rights in general. Granted their reasonableness, how closely do allophone languages in Canada meet them? Approximately 8 per cent of Canadians reported a non-official language as their home language in the 1991 census.[52] When broken into individual languages, the numbers become rather modest. In 1986 only two allophone languages were spoken at home by approximately 1 per cent of Canadians – Italian and Chinese. Neither language constitutes a sufficient share of the national population, to warrant national recognition. At the provincial level, only Chinese, at 2.5 per cent of the British Columbia population, constitutes a significant, albeit modest share of a provincial home language population.[53] The surprising prominence of Chinese is related to substantial immigration. From the 1971 census to the 1991 census, the population whose mother tongue is Chinese has increased from 94,900 to 516,900, making it the second most numerous non-official language group.[54] The number of Chinese home language speakers increased by 27 per cent (from 181,485 to 230,480) between 1981 and 1986, clearly an immigration-inspired growth.[55] At present, many of these people speak a language in which they were raised and educated. What will the pattern of language retention be in two generations?

The Italian experience may be instructive here. The Italian community has been continuously reinforced by a steady influx of immigrants to Canada which has helped sustain cultural vitality and the Italian language. However, the Italian community experienced a 21 per cent decline in its home language population (from 344,480 to 271,835) between 1981 and 1986,[56] despite maintaining a mother tongue population almost unchanged since 1971 (1971, 538,400; 1991, 538,700).[57] This indicates the power of the forces of linguistic assimilation.

Both these language groups tend to be concentrated in major urban areas – over two-thirds of the Italian community is in Toronto and Montreal; over two-thirds of the Chinese community is in Toronto and Vancouver – which generally tends to increase linguistic assimilation. The exception occurs when these communities are residentially concentrated and thus able to maintain linguistic islands where their languages can be used in many aspects of private life. Given their geographic contexts, one would expect a gradual process of linguistic assimilation to occur. However, if that is not the case, the three-generation yardstick becomes a useful barometer to assess any language claims that might arise from these groups.

Notably absent from this group is Ukrainian. Its experience is highly indicative of the long-term trends for third languages in Canada. As previously reported, the B and B Commission Minority report argued that the Ukrainian language community possessed justifiable claims to official recognition in some regions of Canada, primarily in the Prairies. It had long-established roots in communities in Ontario and western Canada, and strong patterns of language transmission. Bolstered by a large influx of immigrants in the 1920s, the Ukrainian language community grew rapidly in the ensuing decades. In 1951 Ukrainian was the largest non-official language group in Canada, with 352,300 individuals claiming it as their mother tongue. The 1971 census reported 580,660 Canadians whose ethnic origin was Ukrainian, and 309,890 who claimed it as their mother tongue, dropping it to third place among non-official languages. By the 1991 census, it had dropped to fifth place, with 201,300 claiming it as mother tongue, a decline of over 100,000 since 1971.

These figures if anything understated the decline of the Ukrainian language. In the 1981 census, 81,475 claimed it as their home language, only 28 per cent of the mother tongue population. In the 1986 minicensus, this number declined still further to 46,150, and Ukranian dropped off the list of top ten home languages in Canada.[58] This reflected the linguistic assimilation of the third generation of Ukrainian Canadians. Of those presently in the twenty-five to twenty-nine-year-old age group, only 10 per cent of those claiming Ukrainian ethnic origin still use that language in the home.[59] The trend of a continuing decline appears fairly pronounced. Of course, the case for recognition of Ukrainian had focused on a regional level rather than national. At present, the case would not hold even at the provincial level. As of 1986 the largest concentration of Ukrainian home language individuals is in Ontario, with 20,790 or two-tenths of one percent of the province's population. The next largest is Alberta with 8,440, which is only a fractionally larger share of Alberta's population.[60] The case for some recognition of Ukrainian, whatever legitimacy it might have had, is clearly past. This is just as the language has reached its fourth generation when it would normally, using the third-generation rule of thumb, become a candidate for official support. The same fate very possibly awaits the other languages that are presently more numerous.

It would appear that none of the allophone languages at present meet the criteria for official recognition, either because of insufficient numbers or insufficient elapsed time for the languages to have visibly taken root in Canadian society. However, this forecloses only the promotion-oriented complex of entitlements that apply to English and French. It remains the case that a commitment can be made to toleration rights for these languages. As well, a modest commitment in education would reflect a respectful attitude towards these languages and cultures, marginally improving their prospects for survival.

In fact, over the past twenty years governments in Canada have extended a variety of commitments to heritage language education. As of 1989 there were 129,000 students studying sixty languages in supplementary schools across Canada.[61] In 1971 Alberta became the first province in Canada to legalize languages other than English or French as media of instruction in the public school system. The Prairie provinces permit bilingual instruction in, for example, Ukrainian–English, German–English, and Chinese–English. In most provinces, language classes are supplementary to or part of the regular schoolday, but are not languages of instruction. Since 1988 Ontario has adopted a policy that heritage language instruction will occur whenever parents of twenty-five students in one school board request it. In Atlantic Canada, heritage language education is not generally supported in the public school system. Overall, the extent of commitment by various provincial governments reflects the strength and vitality of the allophone language groups in different parts of the country. In this regard, the political realm is more sensitive to the diversity of circumstances of linguistic minorities than perhaps a constitution or national policy could be. However, it is an appropriately modest promotion of languages as a prelude to their future consideration.

It is worth noting that the rationale for these initiatives has developed in the context of a commitment to multiculturalism rather than from an extension of the concept of language rights. Somewhat ironically, multiculturalism policy has been strikingly inattentive to language promotion efforts as an integral component of cultural preservation, focusing instead on festivals and cultural performances, sometimes criticized as 'song and dance' multiculturalism.[62]

As it turns out, this orientation corresponds to the limits of public support for such policies. In Ontario, a proposal to permit heritage languages as languages of instruction was quietly dropped in the face of substantial opposition from the anglophone majority. The controversy in Ontario clearly indicated that the public did not perceive 'ethnic communities' to have rights to minority language education. Although they were willing to accept public funds being used to subsidize these educational programs, they did not support their inclusion as languages of instruction.[63] In general, the federal government has been reluctant to develop its policies regarding commitments to multilingualism, apparently fearing its implications for French–English relations.[64] This ambivalence has been encouraged by the reticence of ethnic minority communities to lobby for such programs. Consequently, the role of heritage language programs serves primarily to provide exposure to the languages rather than act as a foundation for their preservation.

Language services in heritage languages may well emerge in response to the need to provide services to those without the capacity to function in English. In September 1995 *Maclean's* and *Toronto Life* magazines announced plans to produce Chinese language editions of their publications to serve the rapidly growing Chinese community in Canada. This initiative is viewed as a means 'to help integrate the Chinese reader into Canadian mainstream society.'[65] Initially offered on a trial basis, they may become a permanent feature of the Canadian publishing scene. On another front, AT&T, the American telecommunications giant, has extended its Language Line Services throughout Canada, thereby offering language interpreter services for most major languages on an immediate basis. Some Toronto area hospitals have committed to this service as a means of providing health care to immigrants who don't speak English or French.[66]

These initiatives are important mechanisms for the provision of services, education, and information to those who cannot communicate in the dominant languages. Their very existence is a telling indication of the growing importance of third languages in the coming century, and of the likelihood that the issue of their status in Canadian society will be the subject of more extensive debate.

Conclusion

This analysis has suggested that the claims of Aboriginal and heritage language groups to language rights are tenuous. Neither possesses the characteristics to warrant comparable treatment with English or French. Aboriginal languages either are spoken by too few individuals or else are not the main languages of those cultural communities themselves. However, because of a history of the active repression of their languages, a case can be made that Aboriginal peoples ought to enjoy special privileges to education in their languages as part of a societal effort to support the rekindling of these languages. Heritage languages, despite in some cases being used by substantial numbers of individuals, still need to demonstrate that these communities are able to sustain the languages across several generations. The one language that might have met this condition, Ukrainian, has become an instructive demonstration of the compelling force of linguistic assimilation.

Although a case for official recognition of language rights per se for either category of groups is not supported by this analysis, it is heartening to note the degree to which a more informal recognition has been extended through a variety of education programs. Those provinces with significant long-standing linguistic minorities have tended to offer educational opportunities that roughly parallel those available to official language minorities. Other provinces have subsidized heritage language classes for interested citizens. These are important gestures of support for the minority language communities.

Notes

1 R.H. Tawney, *Equality* (rev. ed.) (London: Allen and Unwin, 1952), 39. This quote is from Stanley I. Benn, 'Equality, Moral and Social,' in Paul Edwards, ed.-in-chief, *The Encyclopedia of Philosophy*, vols. 3 and 4 (New York: Macmillan, 1967), 41.

2 See Carol Karakwas Stacey-Diabo, 'Aboriginal Language Rights in the 1990s,' in Ryszard I. Cholewinski, ed., *Human Rights in Canada: Into the 1990s and Beyond* (Ottawa: Human Rights Research and Education Centre, University of Ottawa, 1990), 139–64. See also Assembly of First Nations, *The Aboriginal Language Policy Study* (Ottawa, 1988) which pointedly notes the extent of government support for the French language in Canada and also suggests that language rights form part of traditional 'Aboriginal rights.' The study assumed

that Aboriginal languages should have the same rights and resource entitlements as the French language.

3 Eli Taylor, of the Sioux Valley Reserve in Manitoba, as quoted in Stacey-Diabo,
'Aboriginal Language Rights,' 141.

4 Ibid., 140.

5 Ibid., 162. This is a partial list of the demands, specifically those making claims
about linguistic equality.

6 These figures are from the 1981 Canadian census data on home language used
by individuals. This measure of language populations is generally considered
the most reliable indicator of the persistence of languages in Canada. It is also
the most conservative estimate, since it excludes those who are linguistically
assimilated. This is particularly salient for Aboriginal peoples, three-quarters
of whom use either English or French as their home language. The linguistic
demography of Aboriginal languages was usefully summarized by Gordon E.
Priest in, 'Aboriginal Languages in Canada, ' *Language and Society* 15 (Winter,
1985): 13–19. Similar patterns were reported in Sondra B. Phillips, *Aboriginal
Languages in Canada: A Research Report* (Ottawa: Government of Canada,
Department of Indian and Northern Affairs: 1985), Table 2.

7 These figures are from Statistics Canada, *Profile of Canada's Aboriginal Population* (cat. no. 94-325, 1995), Table 1. Census reports on Aboriginal populations
are particularly subject to estimation errors, so that small percentage changes
in the figures may simply reflect the error margins. They may also reflect the
fact that Statistics Canada separated single responses from multiple responses
for home language use. The latter, numbering 26,525, are not distributed
among the various Aboriginal languages, so that the former figures reflect
single responses to the question. .

8 The Swiss arrangements were analysed in K.D. McRae, *Conflict and Compromise
in Multilingual Societies*, Vol. 1, *Switzerland* (Waterloo: Wilfrid Laurier University
Press, 1983).

9 Will Kymlicka, *Liberalism, Community and Culture* (Oxford: Oxford University
Press, 1989), 151.

10 Ibid., 165.

11 See James Frideres, *Native Peoples in Canada: Contemporary Conflicts* (3rd ed.)
(Scarborough: Prentice-Hall, 1988), 156–9. Frideres cites research estimating
that nine Native languages have long-term viability, though this group consists
of languages with 1,000 or more Native speakers, groups far too small to
sustain claims to official recognition as discussed here.

12 Phillips, *Aboriginal Languages*, 7.

13 Ibid., 1.

14 This is briefly noted by Peter Christmas in, 'How Can We Preserve Our Native
Language?' *Canadian Issues* 9 (1989): 172. The widespread adoption of such
goals in various nations is documented in Tove Skutnabb-Kangas and Robert
Phillipson, *Wanted! Linguistic Human Rights* (Roskilde, Denmark: Roskilde
Universitetcenter, Lingvistgruppen, ROLIG-papir 44, 1989).

15 Kymlicka, *Liberalism*, 183.

16 John Rawls, *A Theory of Justice* (Cambridge: Harvard University Press, 1971), 62.

17 Kymlicka, *Liberalism*, 192.

18 Ibid., 190.

19 Ibid., 195.

20 Phillips, *Aboriginal Languages*, 21. Some go so far as to suggest that language
education is a matter for the Native families and religious institutions; that
public education should be concerned with improving economic prospects
for Aboriginal youth. See p. 20.

21 Chandran Kukathas, 'Are There Any Cultural Rights?' *Political Theory* 20(1)
(1992): 123.

22 Ibid., 122.

23 Will Kymlicka, 'The Rights of Minority Cultures: A Reply to Kukathas,' *Political
Theory* 20(1) (1992): 141.

24 Ibid., 141.

25 'We need to distinguish two kinds of claims that an ethnic or national group
might make. The first involves the claim of a group against its own members;
the second involves the claim of a group against the larger society. The first
kind is intended to protect the group from the destabilizing impact of *internal
dissent* (e.g., the decision of individual members not to follow traditional practices or customs), whereas the second is intended to protect the group from
the impact of *external decisions* (e.g., the economic or political decisions of the
larger society). To distinguish these two kinds of claims, I call the first 'internal restrictions' and the second 'external protections.' Will Kymlicka, *Multicultural Citizenship* (Oxford: Oxford University Press, 1995), 35. Kymlicka
defined internal restrictions as applying primarily to basic civil and political
liberties (36); my example broadens his definition beyond Kymlicka's
intended scope, though it is consistent with the thrust of his argument.

26 John R. Danley, 'Liberalism, Aboriginal Rights, and Cultural Minorities,'
Philosophy and Public Affairs 20 (2) (1991): 176.

27 Ibid., 177.

28 Ibid., 179.

29 Ibid., 181.

30 Pierre Trudeau remarked, 'That is exactly why limiting a person's use of his
language can cause in him such a trauma, because you are interfering with

something almost as basic as breathing.' See Canada, House of Commons, *Debates* (31 May 1973), 4303.

31 The man's experience was discussed in Skutnabb-Kangas and Phillipson, *Wanted!*, 34–7.

32 Anastasia Shkilnyk, '*A Proposal for an Aboriginal Languages Policy,*' unpublished Discussion Paper, March 1985, as quoted in National Indian Brotherhood, *The Aboriginal Languages Policy Study* (1988), 83.

33 Bill 27 was passed by the Canadian Parliament on 29 Oct. 1990. The amendments to the Official Languages Act for the NWT received assent in the NWT Assembly 6 April 1990. See An Act to Amend the Official Languages Act, Statutes of the NorthWest Territories 1990, Ch. 7. See also, 'French–English Battle Creeps into NWT,' *Globe and Mail* (10 Feb. 1990), A1. On the subject of language use in the NWT, see Donald M. Taylor and Stephen C. Wright, 'Language Attitudes in a Multilingual Northern Community,' *Canadian Journal of Native Studies* 9(1) (1989): 85–119.

34 See Government of Quebec, *Charter of the French Language, Revised Statutes of Québec*, c.11, Secs. 87–9 and 95–7. The education provisions protect other languages of instruction, such as English, where already established in these schools.

35 For an overview of the evolution of government policy on native languages, see Linda Tschanz, *Native Languages and Government Policy: An Historical Examination*, (London, Ont: Centre for Research and Teaching of Canadian Native Languages, University of Western Ontario, 1980).

36 These figures are drawn from Table 8 in Phillips, *Aboriginal Languages*, 22. The figures are reported for the 1982–83 academic year and are adapted from the Nominal Roll data (1983) prepared by the Education Directorate, Indian and Inuit Affairs Program, Department of Indian Affairs and Northern Development.

37 See Phillips, *Aboriginal Languages*, 34–8.

38 Joe Miskokoman, president of the Union of Ontario Indians, is quoted in 'Extinction Feared if Native Tongues Not Used in Schools,' *Globe and Mail* (14 July 1984), 14.

39 'Ontario to Offer Native Language Courses,' *Globe and Mail* (13 July 1984), 3.

40 'Tough Sledding for Inuit Government,' *Globe and Mail* (26 Nov. 1992), A19. The plan would combine the 375 government programs and replace the elaborate network of government bodies with a much simpler form. A product of Inuit and Dene leaders working with senior managers in government, it is described as a 'unique made-in-the-North model of government administration.'

41 A useful model is that proposed in Nova Scotia for MicMac interpreters in trials at the request of Micmac witnesses or accused. At present, interpreters

are used when a Micmac defendant is perceived to face cultural or linguistic barriers to a fair trial. See Attorney-General, Government of Nova Scotia, 'Marshall Update / Justice Reform Review,' mimeo. 20 May 1992), 19.

42 From Shkilnyk, *Proposal*, 35, quoted in National Indian Brotherhood, *Aboriginal Language Policy Study*, 99.

43 'Separate Statement by Commissioner J.B. Rudnyckyj,' Royal Commission on Bilingualism and Biculturalism, *Report*, vol. 1, *The Official Languages* (Ottawa: Queen's Printer, 1969), 157–9.

44 Ibid., 137.

45 See Marcel Faribault and Robert M. Fowler, *Ten to One: The Confederation Wager* (Toronto: McClelland and Stewart, 1965), 126, see also 44–5.

46 Kymlicka, *Multicultural Citizenship*, 46. Subsequently, he raised other considerations pertinent to the issue, e.g., that voluntary immigration entails waiving rights to cultural preservation and that immigrant groups are less likely to maintain a 'societal culture' which offers its members significant options. Ibid., 95–101. However, the implications of the case where such a societal culture is maintained by such groups was not addressed.

47 See Table 3.9 in Brian Harrison and Louise Marmen, *Languages in Canada*, (Ottawa: Statistics Canada, 1994), 33.

48 The statement was made by William McKnight, Minister of Indian Affairs and Northern Development, and quoted in 'Inuit, Ottawa Row on Language Rights Slows Land Accord,' *Globe and Mail* (26 Sept. 1988), A5.

49 See the articles by Norman Buchignani and Paul Letkemann and Morton Wienfeld in J.W. Berry and J.A. Laponce, eds., *Ethnicity and Culture in Canada* (Toronto: University of Toronto Press, 1994) for a more elaborate statement of this theme.

50 Council of Europe, *European Charter for Regional or Minority Languages: Explanatory Report* (Strasbourg: Council of Europe, 1993), 42.

51 Heinz Kloss, 'Language Rights of Immigrant Groups,' *International Migration Review* 5(2) (1971): 260.

52 Harrison and Marmen, *Languages in Canada*, 30.

53 These figures are drawn from Statistics Canada, *Census Canada 1986: Languages Part 2* (Ottawa: Statistics Canada, 1989), (Cat. No. 93-103), Table 1.

54 Harrison and Marmen, *Languages in Canada*, 26.

55 Statistics Canada, Census 1986 *Canada: A Linguistic Profile*, Table 6, 27. (Cat. 98-131).

56 Ibid.

57 Harrison and Marmen, *Languages in Canada*, 26.

58 Statistics Canada, Census 1986 *Canada: A Linguistic Profile*, Table 6, 27. (Cat. 98-131).

59 See John de Vries, *Explorations in the Demography of Language and Ethnicity: The Case of Ukrainians in Canada* (Ottawa: Center for Research on Ethnic Minorities Etc., 1983). The census data are from Harrison and Marmen, *Languages in Canada*, Table 3.4, 26.

60 The 1986 figures are from Statistics Canada, *Census Canada: Languages Part 2* (Cat. No. 93-103), Table 1.

61 These figures are from Jim Cummins and Marcel Danesi, *Heritage Languages: The Development and Denial of Canada's Linguistic Resources* (Toronto: Garamond, 1990), 26.

62 The policy was sharply criticized from one immigrant's perspective in Neil Bissoondath, *Selling Illusions: The Cult of Multiculturalism in Canada* (Toronto: Penguin, 1994).

63 Ibid., 33–43.

64 Manoly Lupul remarked that 'multilingualism' was a 'dirty word' for federal officials, discussion of which was quietly discouraged in the advisory committee on multiculturalism. See his 'Comments,' in David Schneiderman, ed., *Language and the State: The Law and Politics of Identity* (Cowansville: Les Éditions Yvon Blais, 1989), 305.

65 'Magazines Launch Chinese Editions,' *Globe and Mail* (28 Sept. 1995), A6. The statement was made by Peter Li, manager of the *Ming Pao Daily News*, a partner with *Toronto Life* in its venture.

66 Apparently, over 60 organizations in Canada have already signed contracts for this service. See 'Translators on Call to Span Language Gaps,' *Globe and Mail* (15 May 1996), A6.

8

Contemporary Challenges to National Language Policy

If the political development of language rights continues without any attempt at rationalizing and without raising new ideas or new principles capable of guiding this development, there is a strong possibility that current rights will be diminished.[1]

Recently, the general thrust of national language policy has been criticized on grounds of both principle and practice. Several scholars have argued that national language policy is seriously misguided and is actually sabotaging its intended purpose. According to Kenneth McRoberts, 'In many parts of Canada official bilingualism has become a discourse which has little relationship to social reality.'[2] He cited the case of Saskatchewan, where the opponents of the suppression of French as an official language in the legislature blithely ignored the demographic reality of the marginal presence of francophones in the province and, more particularly, in the legislature. McRoberts suggested that, rather than serving to increase national unity, the federal effort to extend official bilingualism to the provinces inspires resentment and generates additional political tensions.[3] He concluded that 'a strong argument can be made for freeing the provinces from constitutional obligations with respect to language.'[4]

Another critic, John Richards insisted that 'Canadian language policies in aggregate, however, are so manifestly incompatible and ambiguous that they have engendered cynicism, confusion, and anger.'[5] Voicing many of the same arguments as McRoberts, he nevertheless suggested an explicit division of authority over language issues between the federal and provincial governments, coupled with constitutional entrenchment of three basic language rights for official language minorities from their provincial governments. These would be, where numbers warrant, the rights to education, government services including health and social services, and, finally, major criminal court proceedings in the minority language. He also proposed the entrenchment of a right to reasonable support for preservation of linguistic heritage for allophone groups.[6]

Scott Reid, in a third line of criticism, suggested that federal policy has deviated seriously from any principles of linguistic justice that it might have originally embraced, to the point where it effectively endorses 'asymmetrical bilingualism,' a system of 'full rights to speakers of French, second class status to speakers of English.'[7] This asymmetry derives primarily, though not exclusively, from a comparison of federal government policy and Quebec provincial policy. Reid proposed that federal bilingualism policies be restricted to the major areas of official minority language demographic concentration (roughly from Ottawa to Moncton, New Brunswick) and that numerous policies be revised to reduce the overextended commitment, in personnel and financial resources, to bilingualism programs.

Taken as a group, these criticisms are strikingly incompatible. Although all share some important criticisms of existing language policy, in each case, two of the three would presumably reject the proposed solution of the third. One might well ask, as does one francophone defender of existing national policy, what does English Canada want? In various forms, these proposals embrace the territorial option to language policy. However, it is not at all clear that these solutions effectively address the problems that they identify or offer the basis for linguistic peace. A similar position is also advocated by some francophone voices with a different set of concerns. Focusing on the needs of the francophone community, Laponce and Castonguay criticized federal policy as both ineffective outside Quebec and counterproductive within it. They propose the territorial solution as the option most likely to preserve the French language at least within its stronghold of Quebec.

These criticisms, which raise several different sets of concerns with federal policy, are apparently in tune with recent turns in policy leanings within Ottawa. Some Ottawa journalists reported that the previous Conservative government, in the wake of its tribulations with the extension of official language policy, was inclined to assign control over language policy to the provinces.[8] These developments indicate the need for an examination of the territorial option as a more viable alternative to the status quo. In what follows, I shall suggest that the critique is less compelling than it first appears and that existing policy is closer to the basic territorial position than is admitted. Furthermore, to the extent that existing policy deviates towards the personality principle, it is more attuned with public opinion than is the proposed alternative.

Two aspects of the question will be examined. First, what variations of territorialism are being advocated? Second, what are the implications of these options for national unity? The answers to these questions will offer the basis for assessing whether these alternatives are in fact improvements to the status quo.

Provincial Control over Language Policy

One approach to a territorial policy is to remove all constitutional limits upon provinces in their choice of language policy. This would free them to develop policies deemed most appropriate to their particular circumstances. This would involve amending Section 133 of the Constitution Act, 1867 by deleting those clauses applying to Quebec, and Section 23 of the Charter of Rights and Freedoms (minority language educational rights) plus references to New Brunswick in the languages rights clauses of the Charter (subsection (2) of Clauses 16–20). Beyond this, it would presumably involve removal of the clauses from provincial constitutions that parallel the Section 133 provisions.

This proposal is broadly consistent with the direction suggested, but ignored, by the Pépin-Robarts Task Force, that is, towards federal bilingualism with provincial freedom to set language policies within the provinces. It should be noted, however, that the Pépin-Robarts proposals included a recommendation that provinces enact legislation guaranteeing minority official language education, the right to receive provincial health and social services in either official language where numbers warrant, and the right to a criminal trial in one's principal language, either French or English. This combination of proposals was politically astute, and anticipated the course of development at the provincial level.

Nevertheless, an assessment of each component of these recent reform proposals is valuable in identifying the core problems that need to be addressed and the advantages and limitations of these proposals.

Down with Section 133?

Technically, Section 133 applies only to the federal government and the province of Quebec. More broadly, its equivalent text was embodied in the constitutions of the Prairie provinces when they first achieved self-governing status – Section 23 of the Manitoba Act and Section 110 of the Northwest Territories Act, which applied to Alberta and Saskatchewan. The proposal to remove Section 133 obligations has considerably greater validity regarding these parallel provisions in the Prairie province constitutions than for Section 133 as such. It is certainly the case that, in regard to their present demographic presence on the Prairies, there is no substantial case for recognition of the French language as officially equal to English in any of the legislatures of the Prairie provinces. In each case, these provisions were entrenched at a time when francophones constituted a much larger share of the provincial populations.

In recent decades, the demographic basis has been largely eliminated. In each case, the provinces had taken actions to override these provisions. The forerunners to Alberta and Saskatchewan had repealed the relevant provision, but subsequently (much later) were judged to have made technical errors in the process which invalidated the effort. Manitoba passed legislation in 1890 proclaiming English as the only official language, only to be overruled by the Supreme Court ninety years later. Furthermore, there is no consensus in those provinces that the French language has a legitimate claim to official recognition. Thus, a constitutional entitlement has persisted long past the point where its sociopolitical base or a political consensus sustained it.

In the past fifteen years, bitter conflicts have arisen in each of these provinces over attempts to claim entitlements under these provisions. However, the subsequent resolution of these same conflicts has had the effect of eliminating the grounds for their re-occurrence. In the wake of the 1988 Mercure decision, wherein the Supreme Court ruled its legislation invalid because it was passed only in English, the Saskatchewan government replaced Section 110 with legislation reducing the status of French.[9] In response to *l'affaire Piquette*, the controversy ignited by an MLA addressing the legislature in French, the Alberta Legislature passed the *Alberta Languages Act*, under which the province explicitly removed Section 110 of the Northwest Territories Act from its constitution.[10]

Manitoba has experienced a wrenching political controversy over Section 23 of the Manitoba Act. With the judicial overturning of the 1890s legislation making English its only official language, many millions of dollars have been expended to translate Manitoba statutes into French and to conform to the legislative and judicial requirements of Section 23. The attempt by the NDP government of Manitoba in 1983 to expand the constitutional status of French within government met with an overwhelming negative reaction which ultimately defeated the initiative.[11]

In each of these cases, the political controversies arose from efforts to enforce pre-existing elements of the provincial constitutions that were locally viewed as anachronistic. Ultimately, the constitutional position of French was in each case considerably reduced. These examples confirm one element of the critics' position. The attempt to enhance the position of the French language by constitutional means where the French minority constitutes a marginal social group cannot be other than counterproductive. At the same time, the Manitoba example suggests the utility of legislative and administrative means. Somewhat ironically, the subsequent Conservative government largely adopted by administrative means what it adamantly opposed as legislation.[12]

This is instructive regarding avenues to acceptable language policy expansion in the Prairie context. The government plan to expand French language services has been grudgingly accepted by both anglophones and francophones alike. Since francophones constitute only 2.3 per cent of the provincial population, the current case for official bilingualism within the province is modest at best.[13] However, it is noteworthy that some measure of responsiveness to minority language groups was deemed necessary by even the harshest critics of official bilingualism. This suggests that territorial solutions are not a necessary prerequisite to linguistic peace in the Prairies.

While the critics' position is endorsed by the Prairie experiences, it is questionable regarding the Quebec case. Only Quebec is governed by Section 133 guarantees. However, the specific provisions of Section 133 have been minor elements of the language disputes that developed there. For anglophones, the major controversies have focused on access to the English language school system, the availability of health and social services, and commercial signs. For francophones, these issues plus the language of the workplace have been prominent. In all these matters, Section 133 provisions have been either irrelevant or incidental to the conflicts. Granted, at 11 per cent of the provincial population, the current anglophone case for an officially bilingual Quebec is increasingly tenuous. However, rescinding Section 133 regarding Quebec would neither eliminate Quebec's concerns about reinforcing French nor undermine the position of Quebec anglophones.

It would be apparently evenhanded to assert that neither Manitoba francophones nor Quebec anglophones deserve the constitutional protection for their respective languages they currently enjoy. Accordingly, Section 133 as it applies to Quebec and Section 23 of the Manitoba constitution could be repealed. As an amendment to the Canadian Constitution affecting only one province, deletion of Section 133 would require a federal Parliament and the Quebec Assemblée Nationale to pass resolutions to that effect. Thus, a federal Parliament composed of representatives predominantly from anglophone areas would be requested to deprive Quebec anglophones of traditional language rights. Somehow this does not sound like a recipe for linguistic peace. Rather, it is likely to ignite the language issue nationally even more dramatically than these aforementioned cases have.

The ill-fated Meech Lake constitutional reform package is similarly instructive. It proposed to institutionalize a dualist conception of Canada as English–French and to recognize the distinct character of Quebec society. Both components were contentious. The dual character of Canada was rejected as insensitive to the multicultural reality of Canada and as creating benefits for francophone minorities to which they were not otherwise entitled. Like the constitutional provisions discussed above, it appeared to impose obligations that were not justifiable on the basis of local conditions in Western Canada. On the other hand, the 'distinct society' clause was viewed in English Canada as potentially exempting the Quebec government from recognizing the linguistic rights of anglophones. It only underscores the lesson here that what was deemed seriously threatening to anglophones was rejected as inadequate window-dressing by many francophones.[14] The subsequent Charlottetown proposal on constitutional reform also failed, in part because of intense opposition to proposals viewed as granting Quebec special treatment – the revised 'distinct society clause' and the guarantee of 25 per cent of the seats in the House of Commons.[15] The lesson here is that any attempt to alter constitutional arrangements on language regarding Quebec, especially where they are perceived as special treatment, are likely to provoke sufficient political controversy as to negate the purpose of the endeavour.

Down with the Charter Section 23?

The other constitutional limitation regarding language from which provinces could be freed is the official language minority education requirements imposed by Section 23 of the *Charter*. Each province would then be free to determine whether or not to offer such services within its borders. Provinces would not be forced into providing such services by court decisions initiated by determined minorities, as in Nova Scotia.[16] In consequence, francophones outside the 'bilingual belt' would lose the only effective resource available to demand services which they generally do not have or have only recently acquired. In addition, Quebec anglophones would lose the Charter Section 23 extensions which overrode Bill 101's limits on access to English language instruction. The 'Canada clause' grants English-speaking citizens educated anywhere in Canada in English moving to Quebec the right to access to the English language education system. The 1993 amendments to Bill 101 contained in Bill 86 effectively incorporated the provisions of the 'Canada clause' into Quebec's language law. In one sense, the Charter provisions are thus redundant. However, it is of some significance that Quebec acceptance only occurred after the courts had ruled Quebec's regulations unconstitutional. In the absence of the Charter Section 23, many Quebec anglophones would legitimately fear the potential loss of a right to education service which they currently enjoy.

The intent of such a proposal is to eliminate political conflicts which otherwise would not happen, thereby reducing threats to national unity. However, this option confronts the core of the language issue in Canada. As one francophone analyst has trenchantly observed, 'There will be no lasting accommodation between French and English Canadians until just settlement of the education question extinguishes the last smouldering ember of fear about schools.'[17] Whereas the availability of government laws in both languages is largely secondary for most people, access to education in one's mother tongue is generally viewed as vital to the survival of one's language. If it is not an essential precondition to linguistic survival, it is nevertheless an important facilitating condition. That being the case, the removal of Section 23 would be viewed as a complete abandonment of both official language minorities. If provincial governments outside the bilingual belt were to close minority language schools or refuse to create them, it would increase pressure on Quebec governments to reduce their commitments to English language schooling – and a bitter spiral of declining commitments could easily ensue. It is difficult to see how such a change would reduce language strife in Canada. It would more likely exacerbate it.

An additional question is whether the Charter education provisions are the contentious domain in any event. The research on public opinion reported earlier makes emphatically clear that minority language education enjoys broad national support. Moreover, the minority language education clauses emerged from a provincial consensus developed in earlier federal-provincial meetings, wherein the provinces endorsed such commitments in principle. The process parallels that advocated in the Pépin-Robarts report. Thus, to put it in different terms, there is a broad moral consensus on the legitimacy of minority language education. The problem here is primarily one of establishing the minimum criteria for entitlement to the service. At a time of significant financial contraction in the educational sector, carving another slice out of the shrinking pie is bound to create turmoil. However, once clear administrative rules are developed, one might expect these constitutional obligations to assuage linguistic anxieties.

Proposals to assign full control over language to the provinces as a means of resolving national unity problems ignores the important reality that language is effectively already in provincial hands.[18] The relative silence of the constitution on language matters has meant that jurisdiction over language is incidental to authority allocated in the Constitution. Thus, provinces already control many important areas for language policy. The success of Quebec's Bill 101 is the best indicator of this fact. The judicial restraints on Quebec's Bill 101, for all the controversy they have generated, have left its major components intact. The legislation has dramatically altered the relative positions of the two languages in the province in favour of French. Further powers over language are unnecessary. As one Québécois commentator noted, 'It's difficult to imagine what more could be done on the language front, since Quebec's language law is a wall-to-wall security blanket. It's as much a guarantee as one can have in a democratic society.'[19] While Quebec governments might seek, largely for symbolic reasons, greater control over language matters, other areas, for example exclusive control of immigration, offer more important opportunities to address factors that impinge on linguistic security.

In any event, regarding proposals for freeing the provinces from constitutional impositions on language policy, it would be fair to say that, were we to begin anew on the matter of language protection in Canada, it is quite possible that New Brunswick would be the only province which would include official language minority protection. However, in the present context, the costs of such innovations would be comparable to the political controversies they seek to avoid. By the same token, it must be admitted that experience to date suggests that any attempt to extend such constitutional impositions more broadly is equally likely to induce political controversy. In this area, the status quo is the least controversial political option.

Unlike the above-noted proposals, John Richards advocated a set of constitutionally entrenched language rights. But like these proposals, the thrust of his treatment was to encourage provincial discretion concerning their recognition. On the face of it, there is a considerable expansion of language duties for the provinces, especially regarding the provision of provincial government services to official language minorities. However, since Richards expected, quite reasonably, that the francophone minority would fail to meet the 'where numbers warrant' qualification in most provinces, his proposal is less innovative than it first appears. While not explicitly stated, it would replace those provisions in provincial constitutions which require the official equality of both languages. This impact is suggested in his observations that English would experience a reduced status in Quebec, while Western provinces would cease to translate statutes into French.[20]

On the other hand, the wording of Richards's clause on language education raises the possibility of expanded access to the English language education system in Quebec. Whereas the present Charter applies the 'Canada clause' to define entitlement, Richards referred to 'official language minorities.' The accompanying footnote acknowledges the different operational definitions the term might be given, observing in passing that it might be defined as those receiving an education in English anywhere in the world.[21] Obviously, such an approach would intrude once again on a highly sensitive aspect of Quebec language policy, and exacerbate rather than reduce linguistic tensions.

Beyond that, Richards supported entrenchment of a commitment to 'reasonable' provincial government funding for allophone groups to preserve their linguistic heritage. The boundaries of this commitment are unclear. Presumably it would imitate federal policy on multiculturalism, which emphasizes cultural supports rather than language services. However, Richards implied a broader commitment when, in illustrating the impact of his proposals, he included 'better services in Cantonese and Punjabi in British Columbia.'[22] If this means government services in allophone minority languages, it invites entire new dimensions of language demands for provincial governments to address. Of course, the provision of such language services may not involve constitutional recognition of such entitlements. If it does, the rationale for such entitlements would also require elaboration and acceptance. These measures would address a pronounced criticism of official bilingualism from Western Canadians in particular. However, as emphasized earlier, the complaint in Western Canada has focused on the proposition that francophones are not entitled to such services, rather than that allophones should also receive them. This possibility invites new combatants into the fray for linguistic status – not a prospect to induce linguistic peace.

Although Richards's call for an explicit division of powers over language would reduce the federal role, he nevertheless accepted federal initiatives on language within areas of federal jurisdiction. Even here, Richards's emphasis is on restricting commitments to those areas with significant francophone populations. For example, he emphasized the fact that viable francophone communities only exist within the bilingual belt. Furthermore, while embracing most of the Pépin-Robarts proposals, he did not specifically include the Pépin-Robarts advocacy of a right to access to radio and television services in either official language. As one francophone critic noted of Richards' proposals, 'It does not allow for the preservation and development of the French language and culture in this country.'[23] In reply, Richards would argue that federal expenditures to such ends outside Quebec are currently excessive and would probably be reduced were his proposal to be implemented. However, if that is true, then the case for entrenching language rights to provincial government services is correspondingly weakened. Under these circumstances, the Pépin-Robarts proposal for provincial statutes rather than constitutional entrenchment appears more in keeping with the expected conditions to prevail under Richards's schema.

Finally, it is difficult to square Richards' critique of current language policies with his proposals for reform. Although he described current policies as 'manifestly incompatible and ambiguous,' for the most part, his reforms modestly amended existing policies. For example, while the contradiction in policies is most starkly illustrated by the Quebec restrictions on English versus the federal promotion of French, Richards called for constitutional protection for Quebec's right to restrict English on commercial signs in Quebec, and acknowledged that Quebec's English-speaking linguistic minorities must simply accept that English will not be treated as equal to French in Quebec.[24] At the same time, he advocated a continued though reduced commitment to promotion of the two official languages in Canada. If that is the case, then some of the central contradictions in Canadian language policies are admitted to be inescapable. That reality must inform assessments of these current policies.

Restricting Federal Bilingualism

The territorial option also proposes a different regime of language rights recognized by the federal government. It proposes that the federal government divide the country into specific zones wherein services would be provided in the majority language of that zone. Within Quebec, for example, the federal government might designate the Montreal Metropolitan Area as a bilingual region, but designate the remainder of the province unilingual French for purposes of federal government services. The corollary of this approach would be that the federal government would not maintain commitments to promote French outside these bilingual or French majority areas or English in Quebec outside the Montreal area. Linguistic minorities would be left to sink or swim on their own. The advocates of territorial bilingualism view this as a harsh but pragmatic necessity, which will reduce ineffective expenditures and reduce political tensions over the preferential access to cultural supports enjoyed by francophone groups, especially in areas where they are outnumbered by allophone groups, for example, the West.

This issue goes to the core of the criticisms voiced about federal official language policy. Francophone critics of territorialism, as illustrated above, reject this policy option on the grounds that it means almost certain demise for the remaining francophone communities outside the 'bilingual belt.' Furthermore, it involves a rejection of the notion of Canada as a bi-national community. In effect, it adopts the image of Canada advocated by the Parti Québécois, of a French Quebec and an (almost) entirely English rest of Canada (ROC). Francophone critics of this option view it as undermining national unity. Its supporters insist that this proposal simply brings language policy into step with the inexorable demographic realities and, furthermore, that these inconsistencies in turn fuel opposition to existing language policy. Therefore, a policy more attuned to the language demography of the country would be more broadly acceptable – and therefore supportive of national unity.

Asymmetrical Bilingualism?

The charge of 'asymmetrical bilingualism' may be relevant to this point. Scott Reid contrasted national government language policies with those of the provincial government of Quebec. He asserted that 'as conceived by its advocates, asymmetrical bilingualism extends full and extensive rights to Canada's francophone minority – which is widely dispersed across nine provinces – and imposes strict limits on Quebec's English speakers, who are mostly located in a single city.'[25] On the face of it, this is fundamentally misguided and out of step with the assumptions of the territorial proposals. If the federal and Quebec comparison is the essential one, then that effectively subverts the notion of provincial independence itself in favour of the principle of one consistent language policy for the whole country. The general assumption among advocates of the territorial option has been that the federal and provincial spheres are two separate domains within which different approaches could be pursued. Québécois might as easily note the contradiction between federal promotion of English within Quebec and Alberta's rejection of French language rights.

For equity comparisons, it would be more appropriate to compare policies among provinces with comparable minorities. Thus, it would make sense to compare Quebec policies with those of Ontario or possibly New Brunswick, the only provinces with significant francophone minorities. Although both provinces have adopted policies extending government services and educational opportunities to their francophone minorities, Quebec has made a commensurately greater commitment to its anglophone minority. Most anglophones have access to English language education systems for their children; most have access to government services and to health and social services in their language. The same cannot be said within Ontario or New Brunswick, wherein administrative implementation struggles to achieve fulfilment of the legislative principles.[26] On this basis, any asymmetry in bilingualism policy at the provincial level favours anglophones, not francophones.

For federal legislation, the relevant comparison would be between the treatment accorded the different official language minorities across the country. Federal policy itself is alleged to be asymmetrical since it 'clearly favours the French language and French-speakers over the English language and anglophones.'[27] The evidence for this is rather vague, but one example given is the 'Canada clause' in the Charter, which permits greater restrictions on access to English language educational institutions in Quebec than it does on French language institutions in the rest of Canada. This is a rather curious example since it offers as much to rebut the claim as it does to support it.

Section 23 of the Charter is asymmetrical in that it permits the Quebec government alone exemption from the provisions of Section 23 (1) (a). This section will apply to Quebec only when its government officially accepts it. This is highly unlikely, so the asymmetry will remain in place. The effect is to allow French mother tongue naturalized immigrants access to French language minority schools outside Quebec, while not permitting their English mother tongue counterparts access to English language schools in Quebec. This feature affects a relatively small proportion of the Quebec population. According to the 1991 census reports by Statistics Canada, immigrants (of all mother tongues) constitute only 8.7

per cent of the Quebec population.[28] A study by Quebec's Conseil de la langue française reported that 19.1 per cent of English mother tongue students in 1989 were enrolled in the French language primary/secondary school system.[29] Even ignoring that some of these students would be there through parental choice still means that 80 per cent of English mother tongue students have access to the English language school system. Thus, the remainder of Section 23 covers the vast majority of Quebec citizens and is fully symmetrical in its entitlements across Canada.

This asymmetry notwithstanding, it is hard to square this clause with the claim that federal policy is biased towards French. It was, after all, entrenched despite considerable opposition from the Quebec government about this intrusion on its constitutional turf. In fact, one francophone advocate of territorial solutions, sharply criticized Section 23 because, unlike Section 15, the equality rights clause, it 'excludes language from the right to enjoy unequal rights in the form of affirmative action,' which, he believed, ultimately reinforces the position of English to the detriment of French.[30] Although I would not embrace such a stance, this critique is a reminder that the two languages face very different challenges. In Quebec immigrants flock to the English language school system, potentially threatening the position of French. As emphasized earlier in the assessment of Quebec language policy, a case can be made that immigrants to Quebec whose mother tongue is English can be granted access to English language schools without threatening the dominance of French. However the continuing perception among Québécois that French is imperilled makes any such reforms improbable. In English Canada, with the exception of French immersion programs for a small number of anglophones, only the diminishing francophone minority seeks education in French. The dominant status of English is not remotely challenged. The design of Section 23 must be weighed in this context.

Ironically, the argument could be made that federal language policy reflects the territorial principle already. Federal administrative policy guidelines on the language of work within federal institutions clearly specify that French is an option for employees only in designated areas with substantial francophone populations – Northern and Eastern Ontario, Quebec, New Brunswick, and the National Capital Region.[31] The 1988 reforms of the Official Languages Act have added the requirement of 'comparable treatment' for francophone minorities in relation to the language of work practices for the anglophone minority in Quebec, in Section 35 (1) (b). In this area, federal policy is consistent with a territorial approach and basically symmetrical in design.

The same is not true of language of service to the public. The federal initiative has progressively expanded to offer bilingual services in all regions of the country, at least in major urban centres. This has led to various charges. Some anglophone critics contend it is a waste of money and resources and only inflames anglophone opposition to the policy. On the other hand, numerous francophones complain that the commitment fails in practice and amounts to only lip-service. Mordecai Richler's anecdote about a francophone's frustrations in obtaining French language services at the Toronto airport is a telling illustration of this problem.[32] These mutually contradictory complaints invite the question – would a territorial approach better serve the intended purpose of national language policy?

Promoting Minority Languages?

A final concern about federal policy is its effectiveness. Federal language policy clearly seeks to foster the vitality of official language minorities, and, in that respect, some suggest it is at odds with the territorial option and ineffective as well. Jean Laponce argued that language rights are territorially rooted in the institutions and social networks of a particular geographic space.[33] In addition, he maintained that a language policy of territoriality, which locates decision-making powers regarding language in the group, is the only policy consistent with the long-term survival of minority languages. On this basis, he criticized the language provisions of the Canadian Charter of Rights and Freedoms as a mistaken policy which undermines a territorial approach to language policy in Quebec and thereby threatens the survival of the French language. As an illustration of the correct approach, Laponce cited favourably the Swiss policy of establishing fixed boundaries within particular cantons to determine the official language of all government services. His position stems in part from his conviction that 'a language is threatened as soon as it is no longer spoken universally at home, at work, at play, at market, with kin, with friends and fellow workers.'[34] For this reason, a language must be given an exclusive territorial domain in which to operate.

In response to this argument, one might begin with the empirical question of whether the language rights in the Charter threaten the French language in Quebec. There is good reason to doubt that they do. The census data, for instance, indicate extremely high rates of language retention among Quebec francophones, to the extent that language loss is negligible.[35] The major threat to the dominance of French has come from immigrant assimilation to the English language via the English language education system. The education provisions of Quebec's Bill 101 have effectively eliminated this problem, with the result that the 'Canada clause' of the Charter has virtually no effect on increasing the strength of the English language in Quebec. Consequently, it is very doubtful that the individual language rights for the anglophone minority pose a threat to the vitality of the French language in Quebec.

Laponce's view is shared by another francophone critic of federal policy, who bases his critique on demographic patterns. Charles Castonguay reported a growing phenomenon of francophone linguistic assimilation to English throughout English Canada and to a modest degree within Quebec as well. He claimed that a net 6,000 Québécois, all under age twenty-five, assimilated to English during the 1970s, despite the facts that two Quebec governments passed major laws to reinforce the French language and that the Quebec English minority actually shrank in size. He concluded from this that the main factor in the appeal of English is 'the economic and cultural pervasiveness of English in North America.'[36] He criticized federal bilingualism policy as, on the one hand, being inadequate to overcome the forces of assimilation for non-Quebec francophones, and on the other, interfering with Quebec's efforts to reinforce the French language within Quebec through Section 23 of the Charter. Castonguay concluded that a territorial language policy is necessary to encourage linguistic assimilation to French in Quebec, coupled with policies promoting the Quebec economy and granting Quebec more substantial powers. Notably, these latter are viewed as perhaps more important than the former.[37]

Castonguay's recommendations on language reform are based only tangentially on his evidence. In fact, his evidence offers significant data to challenge both his and Laponce's position. If anything, it is clear that federal language policy within Quebec is largely irrelevant to the position of the French language. According to Castonguay's figures, despite federal bilingualism policy, the anglophone population decreased in Quebec by over 79,000 from 1971 to 1981. The Charter protections for minority language education that came into force in 1982 were similarly ineffective. From 1981 to 1991 the anglophone population declined a further 45,000.[38] The main reason for these declines is the continuing exodus of anglophones from Quebec. One could argue that the exodus would be greater in the absence of the Charter protection and federal bilingualism, but it cannot be maintained that these figures are consistent with a strong anglophone language community in Quebec that threatens the francization of Quebec.

These findings are also relevant to challenging Laponce's stance. Laponce maintained that 'a fixed linguistic boundary enclosing a unilingual territory remains the best and probably the only effective way to protect a linguistic minority in the long run.'[39] That it is the best way is almost certainly true. It does not mean, however, that it is necessary for language survival. A recent study of language minorities around the world offered several cases where language minorities manage to survive without this territorial advantage. The same study emphasized the fundamental importance of use of the language in the home, community, and private life as critical foundations to language survival.[40] Quebec francophones enjoy both sets of linguistic advantages. The Quebec language legislation offers ample testimony that the Quebec government already possesses Laponce's main factor in language survival, namely, political control over language within its territorial space. In conjunction with its other strengths, the French language experiences widespread use throughout family, community, educational institutions, and economic life. A 1986 Statistics Canada survey on use of one's mother tongue reported that over 95 per cent of Québécois used their language at home, work, with friends, and even watching television.[41] Thus, the French language possesses all the major components in the survival of a language within its territory. In such circumstances, the federal language policy may reinforce the anglophone minority somewhat, without threatening the position of French.

Francophones outside Quebec enjoy none of these advantages. In addition to constituting small, dispersed minorities outside New Brunswick, they are engulfed in an English-speaking environment. For example, even though 64 per cent of francophones outside Quebec report that they use French at work, only 34 per cent use it more often than English.[42] The rate of anglicization increases with each census. Whereas Castonguay reported the rate at 28 per cent as of the 1981 census, it has risen to over 33 per cent for the 1991 census.[43] As Castonguay emphasized, a major factor in this process is marriage outside the language community, which accounts for roughly half of all francophone marriages outside Quebec and New Brunswick. These personal factors strongly influence linguistic assimilation and are of course beyond the capacity of legislation to affect.

On the other hand, these francophone minorities have proved surprisingly resilient. Whereas there were 676,000 individuals whose home language was French outside Quebec in 1971, there were still 636,600 as of the 1991 census. The population whose mother tongue is French continues to rise, from 926,000 in 1971 to 976,000 in 1991.[44] These figures cover a period in which minority language education rights were not generally available. One scholar expects the Section 23 provisions to significantly improve the prospects for francophones outside Quebec.[45] Admittedly, this will not overcome the force of other factors in linguistic assimilation, but it may well mitigate them. In any event, this francophone minority will persist for a significant time.

Despite such modest prospects, it is useful to remember that the rationale for federal policy was not based on its ability to stem linguistic assimilation, but rather to provide institutional support to improve their prospects. In that respect, the policy is undoubtedly significant. The important impact of federal efforts is strongly endorsed in Richard Joy's observation that 'with present federal support withdrawn, the linguistic minorities would eventually disappear through assimilation or out-migration.'[46]

One important line of criticism stems from anglophones who emphasize its futility in light of the small size of francophone communities in many areas and criticize it as both economically inefficient and as an unreasonable burden on anglophones in those regions. Scott Reid cited the requirement for bilingual postal services in Vawn, Saskatchewan, where three bilingual employees are required to service the twenty francophones who constitute 30 per cent of the population of sixty-five.[47] He also criticized the provision of bilingual services in twelve of the 600 post offices in Toronto since the city has only a small proportion of its population who are francophone (1.7 per cent).[48]

On the other hand, various critics have noted the often large gap between policy commitment and implementation in the provision of such service.[49] Similarly, Reid reported that the attempt to identify the twelve locations for bilingual postal services in Toronto took seventy days – a sad commentary on the effectiveness of the policy.

The two sets of examples are useful bases for commentary about federal policy and the advantages and disadvantages of the territorial option in relation to anglophone opinion. Contrary to the assumptions of several advocates of territoriality, anglophone opinion is generally supportive of official bilingualism in relation to federal government services across the country and to a surprising extent for provincial government services as well. National polls conducted in 1990 and 1991 reported that anglophone majorities everywhere except the Prairies supported federal government services in both languages, and majorities everywhere supported provincial government services where numbers warrant.[50] However, this support is not unconditional. The appearance of several political parties across the country whose *raison d'etre* is in large part opposition to official bilingualism is a sobering reminder of the sensitivity of the issue. As in New Brunswick, anglophone support for language policy is highly sensitive to its anticipated impact on local career opportunities. While extensive designation of bilingual positions may be tolerable in far-off Ottawa, it becomes a matter of concern when it appears locally. It inspires intense opposition when it is seen to conflict with common sense – such as creating bilingual positions where they are not apparently required or seem an extravagance. In this regard, French language postal services in Vawn would seem likely to stimulate opposition, whereas it is difficult to believe that anglophones would object to the extremely modest commitment to such services in Toronto.

Whither National Unity

An assumption underlying the territorial option is the expectation that the incidence of language conflict will be reduced, or at least kept to the local level, thereby removing it from the national stage and reducing its impact on national unity. A francophone critic of this option, Donald Savoie, insisted that such an innovation would unavoidably threaten national unity: 'The point is that English Canada cannot have it both ways – it cannot have a united Canada while leaving the promotion of the French fact to Quebec alone.'[51] Pointing to the relatively modest progress of minority language programs even in New Brunswick and Ontario, the provinces with the most substantial French language minorities, he insisted that transferring authority over language to the provinces 'would be tantamount to gutting efforts at promoting French outside Quebec.'[52] In reply, one might emphasize that it would still be possible for the federal government to maintain its commitment to bilingualism programs nationwide. However, this has more credibility regarding Section 133 changes than it does for Section 23 of the Charter. If Savoie's point is valid, it would appear that Canada remains between the proverbial rock and hard place on this subject.

Furthermore, the history of Canadian language controversies suggests that they tend to become national issues despite the absence of a constitutional basis for particular claims. John Turner's political gaffes on the Manitoba and Quebec language issues is instructive in this regard. As Liberal leader in the 1984 election campaign, Turner attempted to avoid the

Manitoba controversy regarding French language services by dismissing it as a 'provincial matter.' He adopted a similar stance in relation to Bill 101. This was roundly condemned as a flawed understanding of the fundamental elements of Canadian political life.[53] Conservative leader Brian Mulroney was strongly supported in his ringing defence of minority language rights in Manitoba. This was a telling reminder that the language issue in Canada is a national issue, despite what the Constitution might say or political commentators might wish.

Federal language policy has always been designed with one eye firmly fixed on its impact on Québécois opinion about the Canadian federation. In addition, the B and B Commission acknowledged that this policy must be implemented in the face of considerable anglophone opposition to its principles. Thus, it was recognized as an unpopular but necessary national policy. Although some critics of national language policy mistakenly assume that Québécois supporters of independence are affronted by national language policy, in fact the current policy has been well received in Quebec. A CTV poll from the Meech Lake era reported that 90 per cent of Quebeckers favoured a bilingual national government, and 61 per cent wanted their provincial government to be officially bilingual as well.[54] More pointedly, the Official Languages Act is one of the few federal policies to escape Bloc Québécois criticism, for the very good reason that it would contradict public opinion in Quebec.[55] A recent analysis of Québécois support for the sovereignty option reported that perceptions of the French language as threatened, coupled with positive expectations about its prospects under sovereignty, significantly increases support for sovereignty. The authors suggested that the best way to increase support for sovereignty is by heightening perceptions of its threatened state.[56]

The corollary of this finding is that the capacity of the federal government to demonstrate its commitment to promoting the French language can reduce the perceived benefits of independence. Consequently, the proposed reforms to federal language policy far from assuaging Québécois anxieties, would only exacerbate them. To take the most extreme example, what effect would the elimination of bilingual labelling of consumer products have other than to heighten francophone concerns about the status of their language?[57] The changes would presumably be happily received only by those anglophones opposed to existing language policy. Although this might reduce Western alienation, it would be largely irrelevant regarding Quebec's political concerns and counterproductive in reinforcing Québécois attachment to Canada. The road to greater national unity does not travel the avenue of linguistic devolution.

One advocate of reform advanced much the same assessment of Quebec reaction, only to draw more subtle conclusions in support of the territorial option. Kenneth McRoberts acknowledged that the federal government must adopt a French face in Quebec, that it must incorporate French as a working language and employ Québécois in significant numbers. That, however, is the limit of the necessary response to Quebec separatism. The additional efforts, comprising a national commitment to French language services and encouraging similar initiatives by provincial governments, was judged to be misguided and counterproductive.[58]

This assessment may be politically astute regarding what would be a *tolerable* minimum national policy for Quebec. It does underestimate the degree of concern Québécois have about the status of French across Canada. In the spring, 1990, in the wake of controversies over several Ontario municipalities declaring English to be the only language of municipal services, Decima posed questions to Canadians about language policy in a national poll. Specifically, it asked Canadians if they would support English-only laws for their community. A parallel question was asked about French within Quebec. The poll discovered that Québécois rejected French-only language policy for their communities by a margin of two to one (66.2 per cent opposed; 33.8 per cent in favour). On the other hand, non-Quebec anglophones were evenly divided on the question (50.2 per cent opposed; 49.8 per cent in favour). Clearly, Québécois were unambiguously opposed to such a policy approach.[59]

On the issue of which level of government should protect linguistic minorities, poll results from 1988 indicated consistent, but variable, patterns of opinion among both Québécois and anglophones. Two-thirds of Québécois believed that their provincial government should have primary responsibility for protecting the rights of its anglophone minority, but they were evenly divided on which level of government should protect the francophone minorities in other provinces. On the other hand, 61.6 per cent of anglophones outside Quebec thought the federal government should have primary responsibility to protect the rights of the Quebec anglophone minority, whereas a small majority (53.2 per cent) thought the federal government should assume a similar role regarding francophone minorities outside Quebec.[60] These figures indicate that Québécois are somewhat more likely to support a territorial option than are anglophones, but that in both cases there is no clear consensus in either direction. It also suggests that options palatable to Quebec might well incite negative reactions in the rest of the country.

In assessing the reactions to the territorial option it is useful to recall the findings reported earlier on the public consensus on language rights. The data from various polls discussed in connection with the practice of language rights reveal a broad national consensus regarding a short list of language rights. These include minority language education as the most broadly supported, and federal government services in both official languages. The public opinion polls are remarkable for the consistency with which this pattern of support has been maintained despite the various language disputes which have arisen since the passage of the federal Official Languages Act.

In terms of political viability, it would appear that the present array of language policy commitments, consisting of a short list of constitutionally entrenched language rights applicable to only the federal government and New Brunswick, national commitments to minority language education, the modest requirements of Section 133 for Quebec and freedom for the remaining provinces is closely attuned to the public predispositions in these matters; in fact, more closely attuned than is the territorial option itself. Coupled with the provincial legislation in Ontario extending government services in designated areas, one could suggest that the expectations of the Pépin-Robarts task force have been brought to fruition.

Conclusion

The advocates of the territorial option have more accurately identified the shortcomings of specific aspects of the prevailing language policy than made a case for its abandonment. They have correctly emphasized that a wholesale commitment to a language policy based on the personality principle for both the federal and provincial governments will more likely undermine national unity than reinforce it. However, the case for a territorial approach by the federal government itself is not persuasive. It ignores the extent to which both anglophones and francophones recognize rights to language services for their respective minorities and support a federal role in their protection. In light of this support, the present policy conforms to public sentiment more closely than either expansion or retrenchment. At the same time, it appears that federal attempts to expand its commitment to bilingual services runs afoul of this support when it is perceived as a violation of common sense or a threat to the economic interests of the majority group. Thus, the status quo, although not entirely satisfactory to anyone, nevertheless may well be the best option under the circumstances – a typically Canadian solution.

Notes

1 Pierre Foucher, 'Language Rights Legislation and Case Law: Current Situation and Assessment of Twenty Years of Legislative and Judicial Activity,' in
   Daniel Bonin, ed., *Towards Reconciliation? The Language Issue in Canada in the
   1990s* (Kingston: Institute of Intergovernmental Relations, Queen's University
   1992), 119.

2 Kenneth McRoberts, *English Canada and Quebec: Avoiding the Issue* (North York,
   Ont.: Robarts Centre for Canadian Studies York University 1991), 20. Other
   contributors to this view include Robert Young, 'How to Head Off the Crisis,'
   Globe and Mail (10 Jan. 1991), A2?; William Thorsell, 'Deep Fault Lines Are
   Driving This Country Apart,' *Globe and Mail* (30 March 1991), D1, D5; Kenneth
   Whyte, 'Official Bilingualism Has Failed to Achieve Its True Purpose' [The
   West], *Globe and Mail*, (8 May 1993), D2.

3 Ibid., 91.

4 Ibid., 43.

5 John Richards, 'The Case for an Explicit Division of Powers over Language,' in
   John Richards, François Vaillancourt, and William G. Watson, *Survival: Official
   Language Rights in Canada* (Toronto: C.D. Howe Institute, 1992), 18. Richards
   position is also stated in somewhat modified form in his *Language Matters:
   Ensuring that the Sugar Not Dissolve in the Coffee* (Toronto: C.D. Howe Institute
   Commentary 84 (Oct. 1996).

6 Ibid., 34–5.

7 Scott Reid, *Lament for a Notion: The Life and Death of Canada's Bilingual Dream*
   (Vancouver: Arsenal Pulp Press, 1993), 17.

8 See 'Cranky and Confused over Language,' *Globe and Mail* (20 April 1991), D1.
   The lack of subsequent action on this front suggests that all the options are
   difficult in this area.

9 On the Saskatchewan legislation see Saskatchewan, An Act respecting the Use
   of the English and French Languages in Saskatchewan, Statutes of
   Saskatchewan 1988–89, c.L-6.1. It received assent 26 April 1988. It repealed
   Sec. 110, but made the status of French subject to Cabinet regulation. For a
   commentary on the development of the Saskatchewan controversy, see Kent
   McNeil, 'Threatening Minority Rights,' *Globe and Mail* (18 April 1988), A7.
   The Mercure case, which arose from a speeding ticket issued only in English,
   is reported as *Regina* v *Mercure*, [1988] 1 Supreme Court Reports 234

10 For the Alberta controversy, see Alberta, Languages Act, Statutes of Alberta
   (consolidated to 1997) vol. 9, c.L-7.5. It received assent 6 July 1988. The
   Alberta controversy was discussed by Timothy Christian in, 'L'affaire Piquette,'
   in David Schneiderman, ed., *Language and the State: The Law and Politics of*

Identity (Cowansville: Les Éditions Yvon Blais, 1989), 107–21. Christian was careful to emphasize that while there was some local support for Piquette's constitutional claims, there was none for the *moral* claims for the status of French.

11 The legislation to amend the Manitoba constitution was presented to the legislature on 4 July 1983. See Manitoba, *Hansard*, (4 July 1983), 4056–7.

12 See 'Manitoba Tories Follow NDP Language Policy,' *Globe and Mail* (3 Feb. 1989), A4. For a critical analysis of the entire controversy, and a sceptical view of the importance of these constitutionally entrenched language rights, see Nelson Wiseman, 'The Questionable Relevance of the Constitution in Advancing Minority Cultural Rights in Manitoba,' *Canadian Journal of Political Science* 25(4) (1992): 697–721.

13 This figure consists of those people who claim French as a home language in the 1991 census. The francophone population defined by mother tongue is slightly higher, at 4.7%. These figures are drawn from the 1991 census data reported in Brian Harrison and Louise Marmen, *Languages in Canada* (Scarborough: Statistics Canada / Prentice-Hall, 1994), Tables 2.3 and 2.2 respectively, 17, 15.

14 For a presentation of and a response to these issues see the articles by Evelyn Kallen, 'The Meech Lake Accord: Entrenching a Pecking Order of Minority Rights,' and José Woerling, 'A Critique of the Distinct Society Clause's Critics,' 349–69 and 171–207 respectively, in Michael Behiels, ed., *The Meech Lake Primer* (Ottawa: University of Ottawa Press, 1989).

15 The 25% guarantee was opposed by 63% of Canadians, the highest score obtained among individual items, whereas the distinct society clause was opposed by 43%. These results are based on a national survey of 1,115 respondents, conducted in the last week of the referendum campaign. For an analysis of the findings, see Lawrence Leduc and Jon H. Pammett, 'Referendum Voting: Attitudes and Behaviour in the 1992 Constitutional Referendum,' *Canadian Journal of Political Science* 28(1) (1995): 3–34.

16 See Wayne MacKay, 'Minority Language Educational Rights Vindicated,' in Schneiderman, *Language and the State*, 123–40. Based on his involvement in the *Lavoie* case in Nova Scotia, MacKay concluded that 'the spur of legal action is often necessary to prod the government into recognizing and acting upon its constitutional obligations,' 140. In British Columbia, francophone groups have renewed their 1989 lawsuit against the provincial government to force it to create an autonomous francophone school board. See 'Parents Pursue Education Lawsuit,' *Globe and Mail* (8 Jan. 1995), A3.

17 Joseph Eliot Magnet, 'Minority-Language Educational Rights,' *Supreme Court Law Review* 4 (special issue) (1982), 195.

18 As suggested in Young, 'How to Head Off the Crisis.' Young acknowledged that the federal government 'would continue to function in two languages, its public voice might be French in Quebec and English in other provinces.' Richards proposed a constitutional amendment granting the provinces (or Quebec alone) control over the public use of language within the province, as a means of ensuring that Quebec has a 'robust' authority over language. However, it is clear that a 'distinct society' clause is more immediately pertinent to the problems Richards sought to redress. See his *Language Matters*, 26–30.

19 Lysiane Gagnon, 'Language Is No Longer the Issue; Control over Immigration Is,' [inside Quebec], *Globe and Mail* (7 Jan. 1995), D3.

20 Richards, *Survival*, 35–6.

21 Ibid., 34. See n34 on the same page.

22 Ibid., 36.

23 Yvon Fontaine, 'A Comment,' in Richards, *Survival*, 62.

24 Richards, *Survival*, 35–6.

25 Reid, *Lament for a Notion*, 16–7.

26 The provincial overviews presented by the Commissioner of Official Languages offers useful insight into the relative accomplishments of the various provinces in these areas. See, e.g., his *Annual Report 1994* (Ottawa: Minister of Supply and Services, 1995), 88–95.

27 Reid, *Lament for a Notion*, 63.

28 This figure was reported in 'Canada's Ethnic Patterns Changing,' *Globe and Mail* (9 Dec. 1992), A8.

29 See Table A-1 in Richards, *Survival*, 83. The original source was Conseil de la langue française, *Indicateurs de la situation linguistique au Québec* (Québec: CLF, 1991), Tables 3.1.1 and 3.2.1, 29,37.

30 Jean A. Laponce, *Languages and Their Territories*, trans. Anthony Martin-Sperry (Toronto: University of Toronto Press, 1987), 163–4.

31 See Treasury Board, *Revised Official Language Policies in the Public Service of Canada* (Ottawa: Minister of Supply and Services, 1977), 13.

32 Mordecai Richler, 'Language Problems,' *Atlantic* (June 1983), 16. According to Richler, a Dutch immigrant porter had to be conscripted to provide French language services otherwise unavailable at the Air Canada desk.

33 Laponce, *Languages and Their Territories*, 156.

34 Ibid., 16.

35 See, e.g., Jacques Henripin, 'Two Solitudes in 2,001?,' *Language and Society* 4 (1981): 15–19.

36 Charles Castonguay, 'The Anglicization of Canada, 1971–1981,' *Language Problems and Language Planning* 11 (Spring 1987): 29. These figures address only anglo-francophone net linguistic assimilation for the 1981 census.

Overall, Castonguay reported that the French language group increased by 8,000 through net linguistic assimilation. Ibid., Table 7, 28. More generally, the relative demographic weight of the French language in Quebec increased as well to 82.5%. This latter pattern has been extended in the 1991 census as well, which reports the French home language population as 83% of the Quebec population. See Harrison and Marmen, *Languages in Canada*, Table 2.3, 17.

37 Castonguay, 'Anglicization,' 30–3.

38 Ibid., Table 8, 29. The latter figures are from Harrison and Marmen, *Languages*, Table 1.3, 10.

39 Laponce, *Languages and Their Territories*, 187.

40 See Joshua A. Fishman, *Reversing Language Shift: Theoretical and Empirical Foundations of Assistance to Threatened Languages* (Clevedon: Multilingual Matters, 1991). The most striking example is the case of Ultra-Orthodox Yiddish in the United States. Laponce also recognized the importance of these other factors. See his *Languages and Their Territories*, 159.

41 Reported in Harrison and Marmen, *Languages*, Chart 4.3, 46. This is not to say that they used French exclusively.

42 Statistics drawn from 1986 Statistics Canada data reported in Harrison and Marmen, *Languages in Canada*, 45.

43 Castonguay, 'Anglicization,' 27; Harrison and Marmen, 60.

44 These statistics are compiled from Harrison and Marmen, *Languages*, Tables 2.1, 2.4 and A.3, at 14, 16, and 79 respectively.

45 See Edmund Aunger, 'The Decline of a French-Speaking Enclave: A Case Study of Social Contact and Language Shift in Alberta,' *Canadian Ethnic Studies* 25(2) (1993): 65–83. Aunger emphasized that the English language education system has had a significant role in linguistic assimilation. He anticipated that the new French school established in 1990 could have a significant impact on rates of linguistic assimilation.

46 Richard J. Joy, *Canada's Official Languages: The Progress of Bilingualism* (Toronto: University of Toronto Press, 1992), 9. Joy was dubious about the long-term prospects of francophone communities outside the bilingual belt. He later remarked, 'It appears clear that, as francophones move away from the Quebec border, they can have little hope of hearing the French language spoken by their grandchildren.' Ibid., 52.

47 Reid, *Lament for a Notion*, 139–40. He speculated that there may be only a single family of francophones if home Language, rather than mother tongue, is the operating definition of language group.

48 Ibid., 144–6.

49 Richler, 'Language Problems,' 16.

50 Overall, 61% of anglophones supported federal language services and 76% supported provincial services. These results were reported from CBC–*Globe and Mail* National Surveys in June–July 1990 and April 1991. See Tables 10 and 11 in George Perlin, 'Anglophone Attitudes towards Bilingualism: A Summary of Some Findings From Survey Research,' in Bonin, *Towards Reconciliation?* 105–6.

51 Donald J. Savoie, *The Politics of Language* (Kingston: Institute of Intergovernmental Relations, Queen's University, 1991), 19.

52 Ibid., 20.

53 See 'Turner Stumbles in Quebec,' *Maclean's* (23 April 1984), 23; 'The New Politics of Language,' *Maclean's* (2 April 1984), 14–7.

54 Reported in William Hynes, 'Keep Canada Tuned in to Both Languages,' *Globe and Mail* (3 April 1991), A19. The polls were released in the midst of the Meech Lake crisis, when presumably Quebeckers would have been relatively upset over anglophone resistance to the reform package. The poll results are consistent with the findings in Quebec over the past two decades.

55 A point emphasized in Lysiane Gagnon, 'Why Sovereignists Don't Attack the Official Languages Act,' *Globe and Mail* (14 Jan. 1995), D3. Gagnon remarked, 'only die-hard separatists do not care about the state of French throughout Canada. All other Quebeckers do, and the last time I looked at a poll, they were a rather strong majority.'

56 See Richard Nadeau and Christopher J. Fleury, 'Gains linguistiques anticipés et appui à la souveraineté du Québec,' *Canadian Journal of Political Science* 28(1) (1995): 35–50.

57 William Thorsell, e.g., dismissed bilingual labelling as a 'bureaucratic aggravation' in 'To each, our own,' *Globe and Mail* (30 March 1991), D5. These provisions are accused of imposing 'an annual $2 billion burden on Canadian consumers,' in Reid, *Lament for a Notion*, 240.

58 See Kenneth McRoberts, 'Making Canada Bilingual: Illusions and Delusions of Federal Language Policy,' in David P. Shugarman and Reg Whitaker, eds., *Federalism and Political Community: Essays in Honour of Donald Smiley* (Peterborough: Broadview Press, 1989), 163–7.

59 These figures are based upon results reported in *Decima Quarterly*, no. 41 (Spring 1990). As I have indicated previously, these figures were compiled for me based on reported home language and province of residence. It should be noted that the sample of Québécois is relatively small, at 313. Even with a substantial error margin, the results are strongly indicative of majority opinion. The sample of anglophones outside Quebec was 1,005.

60 These figures are based on findings reported in *Decima Quarterly*, no. 34 (Summer 1988). The specific questions were numbers 1720 and 1722.

9

Conclusion

Upon emerging from a suburban Tokyo train station three years ago, I sought vainly to identify a passerby on the street who might speak sufficient English to direct me towards a community festival we wanted to attend. All the Japanese street signs were completely indecipherable. I was totally unable to derive information from my immediate environment. Salvation came from my travelling companion who, noting that there was a dominant direction to the movement of the throngs of pedestrians, suggested that we act on the assumption that they were heading towards the same event that we were.

This experience was a powerful lesson in the importance of language to our capacity to function in society. For many people, the language they speak is like the air they breathe – an essential asset the very abundance of which removes it from conscious reflection. The restriction of either poses serious threats to the capacity of individuals to pursue their lives and thus becomes an object for sustained consideration. While oxygen remains blessedly abundant, languages themselves are increasingly challenged by a linguistically plural environment, leading to demands for their protection and promotion.

This inquiry has examined the normative foundations for such demands upon language policy in Canada. Two elements have provided the major grounds for debate – the notions of language rights and language equality. I have concluded that the former is more defensible in theory and in practice as a normative grounding for language policy.

To designate language entitlements as rights is to call forth a rich intellectual tradition with substantial implications for governments. Two models of rights have been applied to assess the claim of language to such status. Drawing on the conventional philosophical understanding of

rights, I have suggested that language rights share the essential characteristics of established rights and thus are justifiable as human rights – albeit
with some qualification. The qualifications are as important as the basic
assertion. Whereas maintenance of one's language is arguably of paramount importance to individuals and groups, this cannot always be
presumed. It depends on the place of a language in the daily life and
the self-definition of the cultural community. Insofar as a language is a
vital component of a well-established functioning language community,
that community has a legitimate claim upon the larger community to reasonable efforts to recognize and sustain that language.

A more important qualification attends the specific scope of the language right. In their broadest form, language rights fail to meet another
important characteristic of rights, namely, universality. As we have seen,
the *strong promotion* sense, that is, of living one's life in a language, generates an inescapable internal conflict of rights and duties between members of different language communities. Only the *weak promotion* form,
that is, the right to sustain the language, surmounts this fundamental
problem. Thus, I conclude that the weak promotion form of language
rights meets the criteria of a human right in the appropriate contexts.

Using these criteria, my analysis has suggested that anglophones and
francophones are entitled to language rights, but the claims of Aboriginal
and allophone language groups are tenuous. Neither possesses the characteristics sufficient to warrant comparable treatment with English or
French. In many cases, Aboriginal languages either are spoken by too few
individuals or else are not the main languages of those cultural communities themselves. Allophone language communities, although in some
cases representing substantial numbers of individuals, still need to
demonstrate that they are able to sustain their languages across several
generations.

Alternatively, rights may be viewed as a reflection of the established values, attitudes, and practices of a society. When the Canadian experience
is examined in this context, the results are somewhat mixed. In regard to
the substance of language rights, there are two streams of development at
work. The constitutional stream of language rights is limited and is
closely patterned on the public consensus on language rights. The one
exception concerns health care and social services, wherein the constitutional stream in fact lags behind Canadian opinion and could be
expanded in relation to such entitlements. The federal legislative stream
of language rights is consistently expansive, significantly extending entitlements regarding the use of the two official languages in the courts and

as a language of work in government institutions. Somewhat surprisingly, this approach is based on an official rationale that is decidedly modest in its pragmatic justification of language entitlements on the requirements of national unity. This in turn is echoed in judicial interpretation of language rights as a second-order right based on political compromise. In both instances, these views are leavened periodically with judgments that language rights are fundamental to human development. The ambiguity remains as to their ultimate character in national institutions.

At the provincial level, the pattern is decidedly more mixed. The Prairie provinces have tended to curtail their commitments to French in governmental institutions, and Ontario has legislated more extensive government services in the French language. Quebec and New Brunswick offer a study in contrasts in their comprehensive legislation of language rights. The Quebec approach to the nature of language rights is distinctly different from what it appears at first sight. Quebec policy has been excessively intrusive in very specific areas – commercial signs. Nevertheless, it has simultaneously fully respected the array of language rights that are nationally recognized. The exception has concerned minority language education, where Quebec applied a more restrictive set of entitlement criteria – subsequently discarded in Bill 86. With its inclusion of health and social services, Quebec language policy embraces the most extensive set of language rights in Canada – hardly surprising, as Quebec citizens display the strongest commitment to a generous practice of language rights of all Canadians. However, this is worth emphasizing because perceptions concerning Quebec language laws have been excessively influenced by its treatment of commercial signs.

These governmental practices are reflected in Canadian public opinion on language rights. A careful distinction must be drawn between the federal and provincial domains. At the national level, there is a reasonably high level of agreement regarding a limited set of entitlements regarding the official languages. This set includes services from the *federal* government, minority language education, and hospital services. Provincially, there is substantial regional variation, with Quebec and Atlantic Canada accepting a somewhat more expanded list, and British Columbia accepting none, leading to the conclusion that there are at best somewhat selective regional *practices*. In fact, the Manitoba–Ontario border constitutes a dividing line between the broad acceptance of a practice of language rights and its rejection. Nonetheless, Western Canada extends either plurality or majority support for the various elements of the practice accepted in the rest of the country.

Viewed in terms of a national practice, there is a significant disjunction between what a political theory of language rights would endorse versus that which garners significant support in public opinion. A theory that treats language rights as a fundamental human right is inherently expansive, extending progressively through the various domains of individual life. It invites extension into such areas as the language of work, opportunities for cultural expression, and availability of private sector services in one's language. The existing practice embraces a limited set of language rights, covering government services, hospital services, and minority language education. Even in these areas, support is qualified by the requirement that such services not impinge on the economic prospects of the English-speaking majority to any significant degree. The practice of rights is therefore largely immune to expansion, for the practical reason that any expansion would offend the operant qualification. There is then an ongoing tension between what a theory of language rights as human rights would propose and what the prevailing practice of rights will tolerate.

Its limits notwithstanding, what is striking is the broad acceptance from both language groups for the essential supports for languages from governments. The pattern of attitudes depicted here suggests not generosity, but a willingness to grant the entitlements that affect vital interests. This offers a tough-minded, but nonetheless solid foundation for an enduring framework for language rights in Canada.

The second broad theme has concerned the issue of language equality. Both the federal and New Brunswick experiences illustrate the extent to which language equality remains not only essentially contested in principle, but essentially muddled in legislative expression. As discussed earlier, national language policy was originally inspired by notions of language equality between the English and French communities as a core principle in its design. A similar, but more expansive rhetoric animated the later New Brunswick policy initiatives. Neither resonated sympathetically with their respective public opinions and were never fully developed regarding their precise content.

Their debates on language policy demonstrated that anglophones and francophones disagree sharply over the meaning and implications of language equality. Whereas francophones tend to interpret equality as a statement of the status of the two communities, anglophones tend to conceive equality as a statement about treatment accorded individuals. After various flirtations with other forms of equality, the New Brunswick government has ultimately settled upon equality of service as the core meaning of language equality. This is a prudent strategy, since anglophone

public opinion apparently rejects most of the means to the effective realization of the end they allegedly accept.

At the federal level, claims of group equality offend as soon as they
become linked to bases of action. This applies whether it is francophones
advancing claims in national institutions, anglophones in Quebec institutions, or Aboriginal groups in either. Thus, the emphasis has turned to
language *rights* rather than language *equality*. The two are not mutually
exclusive. Language rights embrace one important dimension of equality,
that is, equality of treatment of individual members of official language
minorities. However, one can speak of language rights without indulging
in assertions about the relative status of the language groups under
discussion. Such assertions are an integral component of debate about
language equality more broadly conceived.

Recognizing these potential tensions, some have suggested that federal
language policy should be radically altered to base language rights on the
linguistic characteristics of the territory in which groups reside. However,
the case for a territorial approach by the federal government itself is not
persuasive. It ignores the extent to which both anglophones and francophones recognize rights to language services for their respective minorities and support a federal role in their protection. In light of this support,
the present policy conforms to public sentiment more closely than either
expansion or retrenchment. At the same time, it appears that federal
attempts to expand its commitment to bilingual services run afoul of this
support when it is perceived as a violation of common sense or a threat to
the economic interests of the majority group. The status quo, while not
entirely satisfactory to anyone, nevertheless may well be the best available
option under the circumstances. Language rights, in their various
manifestations, are thus – like debate over federalism and the status of
Quebec – a permanent feature of Canadian political life.

References

Allnut, David. (1982) 'The Quebec Public Service,' in *The English of Québec: From Majority to Minority Status,* ed. Gary Caldwell and Éric Waddell, eds. Quebec: Institut Québécois de Recherche sur la Culture, 225–36.

Assembly of First Nations. (1988) *The Aboriginal Language Policy Study* (mimeo.) Ottawa: Author.

Aunger, Edmund. (1993) 'The Decline of a French-Speaking Enclave: A Case Study of Social Contact and Language Shift in Alberta.' *Canadian Ethnic Studies* 25(2): 64–83.

Barbeau, Raymond. (1965) *Le Québec Bientôt Unilingue?* Montreal: Les Éditions de L'Homme.

Bastarache, Michel. (1986) 'L'interpretation judiciaire des garanties linguistiques: un tour d'horizon.' *Égalité* 17: 137–42.

– (1986) 'Les droits linguistique dans le domaine scolaire: Guide d'interpretation de l'article 23 de la Charte Canadienne des droits et libertés.' *Égalité* 19: 147–69.

– ed. (1987) *Language Rights in Canada.* Montreal: Les Éditions Yvon Blais.

Bastarache, Michel, and Michel Saint-Louis. (1982) 'De l'égalité formelle à l'égalité réelle entre les deux communautés linguistiques du Nouveau-Brunswick.' *Égalité* 7 (autumn): 15–50.

Beaudoin, Gérald A. (1979) 'Linguistic Rights in Canada,' in *The Practice of Freedom: Canadian Essays on Human Rights and Fundamental Freedoms,* R. St. J. MacDonald and John P. Humphrey, eds. Scarborough: Butterworths, 197–207.

Beaujot, Roderic P. (1980) 'A Demographic View on Canadian Language Policy.' *Canadian Public Policy* 6: 16–29.

Beaujot, Roderic, and Barbara Burnaby. (1987) *The Use of Aboriginal Languages in Canada: An Analysis of 1981 Census Data.* Ottawa: Minister of Supply and Services.

Beaujot, Roderic, and Kevin McQuillan. (1982) *Growth and Dualism: The Demographic Development of Canadian Society*. Toronto: Gage.

Beckton, Clare. (1982) 'Freedom of Expression "(S.2{b})," ' in *The Canadian Charter of Rights and Freedoms: Commentary*, Walter S. Tarnopolsky and Gérald A. Beaudoin, eds. Toronto: Carswell, 75–121.

Berger, P. (1979) *Facing Up to Modernity*. Harmondsworth: Penguin.

Berry, J.W., and J.A. Laponce, eds. (1994) *Ethnicity and Culture in Canada*. Toronto: University of Toronto Press.

Bibby, Reginald. (1990) *Mosaic Madness*. Toronto: Stoddard.

– (1987) 'Bilingualism and Multiculturalism: A National Reading,' in *Ethnic Canada: Identities and Inequalities*, Leo Driedger, ed. Toronto: Copp Clark Pitman, 158–69.

Bissoondath, Neil. (1994) *Selling Illusions: The Cult of Multiculturalism in Canada*. Toronto: Penguin.

– (1993) 'A Question of Belonging: Multiculturalism and Citizenship,' in *Belonging: The Meaning and Future of Canadian Citizenship*, William Kaplan, ed. Montreal: McGill-Queen's University Press, 368–87.

Bonin, Daniel, ed. (1992) *Towards Reconciliation? The Language Issue in Canada in the 1990s*. Kingston: Institute of Intergovernmental Relations, Queen's University.

Borins, Sandford F. (1984) 'Language Use in the Federal Public Service: Some Recent Survey Results.' *Canadian Public Administration* 27(2): 262–8.

– (1983) *The Language of the Skies: The Bilingual Air Traffic Control Conflict in Canada*. Montreal: McGill-Queen's University Press.

Bourhis, Richard Y. (1994) 'Ethnic and Language Attitudes in Quebec,' in *Ethnicity and Culture in Canada*, J.W. Berry and J.A. Laponce, eds. Toronto: University of Toronto Press, 322–60.

– (1994) 'Bilingualism and the Language of Work: The Linguistic Work Environment Survey,' in *French-English Language Issues in Canada*, issue ed. Richard Y. Bourhis. *International Journal of the Sociology of Language* 105/106: 217–66.

– (1984) 'The Charter of the French Language and Cross-Cultural Communication in Montreal,' in *Conflict and Language Planning in Quebec*, ed. Richard Y. Bourhis, Clevedon: Multilingual Matters 174–204.

– (1984) ed. *Conflict and Language Planning in Quebec*. Clevedon: Multilingual Matters.

– (1994) issue ed. *French-English Language Issues in Canada: International Journal of the Sociology of Language* (105/106).

Bouthillier, Guy, and Jean Meynaud, eds. (1972) *Le Choc des langues au Québec (1960–1970)*. Montreal: Les Presses de l'Université du Québec.

Braën, André. (1987) 'Language Rights,' in *Language Rights in Canada*, Michel

Bastarache, ed. Trans. Translation Devinat et Associés. Montréal: Les Éditions Yvon Blais, 3–63.

Brazeau, Jacques. (1958) 'Language Differences and Occupational Experience.' *Canadian Journal of Economics and Political Science* 24 (1958): 532–40.

Breton, Albert. (1978) 'Nationalism and Language Policies.' *Canadian Journal of Economics* 11(4): 656–68.

Breton, Raymond. (1986) 'Multiculturalism and Canadian Nation-Building,' in *The Politics of Gender, Ethnicity and Language in Canada*, research coordinators Alan Cairns and Cynthia Williams. Toronto: University of Toronto Press, 27–66.

Brett, Nathan. (1991) 'Language Laws and Collective Rights.' *Canadian Journal of Law and Jurisprudence* 4(2): 347–60.

Brotz, Howard. (1980) 'Multiculturalism in Canada: A Muddle.' *Canadian Public Policy* 6(1): 41–6.

Buchanan, Alan Gilmore. (1983) *Anglophone Attitudes towards the French and Bilingualism in New Brunswick*. Master's thesis, Queen's University.

Buchignani, Norman, and Paul Letkemann. (1994) 'Ethnographic Research,' in *Ethnicity and Culture in Canada*, J.W. Berry and J.A. Laponce, eds. Toronto: University of Toronto Press, 203–37.

Canada. (1977) *A National Understanding of the Official Languages of Canada*. Ottawa: Minister of Supply and Services.

– *Canada Gazette*. (1992) 'Official Languages (Communications with and Services to the Public) Regulations.' Part II, vol. 126, no. 1, 1 Jan.

– Commissioner of Official Languages. *Annual Report* (various years). Ottawa: Minister of Supply and Services.

– (1997) *Language Rights in 1996*. Ottawa: Minister of Supply and Services.

– (1996) *Language Rights in 1995*. Ottawa: Minister of Supply and Services.

– (1995) Office of the Commissioner of Official Languages. *Service to the Public: A Study of Federal Offices Designated to Respond to the Public in Both English and French*. Ottawa: Minister of Supply and Services.

– Parliament. House of Commons. *Debates* (various years).

– (1987) Parliament. House of Commons. Standing Committee on Multiculturalism. *Multiculturalism: Building the Canadian Mosaic*. Ottawa: The Standing Committee on Multiculturalism.

– (1968) Royal Commission on Bilingualism and Biculturalism. *Report*. Ottawa: Queen's Printer.

– (1965) *Preliminary Report*. Ottawa: Queen's Printer.

– (1994) Statistics Canada. *Home Language and Knowledge of Languages*. 1991 Census Technical Reports. Ottawa: Minister of Industry, Science and Technology (cat. 92-336E).

(1995) *Profile of Canada's Aboriginal Population.* Ottawa: Statistics Canada (cat. no. 94-325).

- (1984) *Aboriginal Languages in Canada.* Ottawa: Minister of Supply and Services.
- (1989) *Census Canada 1986: Language Part 2.* Ottawa: Statistics Canada (cat. No. 93-103).
- (1989) *Canada: A Linguistic Profile.* Focus on Canada. Census 1986 Ottawa: Statistics Canada (cat. 98-131).
- (1979) Task Force of Canadian Unity. *A Future Together: Observations and Recommendations.* Ottawa: Minister of Supply and Services.
- (1979) *A Time to Speak: The Views of the Public.* Ottawa: Minister of Supply and Services.
- (1979) *Coming to Terms: The Words of the Debate.* Ottawa: Minister of Supply and Services.
- Treasury Board. (1983) 'Equality of Access to Employment in the Federal Public Service by Members of both official Language Groups: A Clarification.' 10 May. Circular No: 1983-30.
- (1977) *Revised Official Language Policies in the Public Service of Canada.* Ottawa: Minister of Supply and Services.
- (1979) *Language Reform in Federal Institutions.* Mimeo. Ottawa.
Cairns, Alan, and Cynthia Williams, research cordinators. (1986) *The Politics of Gender, Ethnicity and Language in Canada.* Toronto: University of Toronto Press.
Caldwell, Gary, and Waddell, Éric, eds. (1982) *The English of Québec: From Majority to Minority Status.* Quebec: Institut Québécois de Recherche sur la Culture.
Castonguay, Charles. (1987) 'The Anglicization of Canada, 1971–1981.' *Language Problems and Language Planning* 11 (Spring): 22–34.
- (1979) 'Why Hide the Facts?: The Federalist Approach to the Language Crisis in Canada.' *Canadian Public Policy* 5(1): 4–15.
- (1976) 'Pour une politique des districts bilingues au Québec.' *Journal of Canadian Studies* 11(3): 50–9.
Chartrand, Jean-Philippe. *Inuktitut Language Retention among Canadian Inuit: An Analysis of 1971 and 1981 Census Data.* Monograph. Ottawa: Center for Research on Ethnic Minorities, Etc., Carleton University, n.d.
Cholette, Gaston. (1988) 'Les droits linguistiques des Québécois sont-ils vraiment protégés par la Charte de la langue française.' *L'Action Nationale* 78(1–2): 95–101.
Cholewinski, Ryszard I., ed. (1990) *Human Rights in Canada: Into the 1990s and beyond.* Ottawa: Human Rights Research and Education Centre, University of Ottawa.

Christian, Timothy. (1989) 'L'affaire Piquette,' in *Language and the State: The Law and Politics of Identity*, David Schneiderman, ed. Cowansville: Les Éditions Yvon Blais, 107–21.

Christmas, Peter. (1989) 'How Can We Preserve Our Native Language?' *Canadian Issues* 9: 169–74.

Churchill, Stacy, and Anthony H. Smith. (1987) 'The Time Has Come.' *Language and Society* 19: 4–8.

Clark, Lovell, ed. (1968) *The Manitoba School Question: Majority Rule or Minority Rights?* Toronto: Copp Clark Pitman.

Coleman, William D. (1983) 'A Comparative Study of Language Policy in Quebec: A Political Economy Approach,' in *The Politics of Canadian Public Policy*, Michael M. Atkinson and Marsha A. Chandler, eds. Toronto: University of Toronto Press, 21–42.

– (1981) 'From Bill 22 to Bill 101: The Politics of Language under the Parti Québécois.' *Canadian Journal of Political Science* 14 (3): 459–85.

Conklin, William E. (1979) *In Defence of Fundamental Rights*. Alphen aan den Rijn, Netherlands: Sitjhoff and Noordhoff.

Cook, Ramsay C., C. Brown, and C. Berger. (1969) *Minorities, Schools and Politics*. Toronto: University of Toronto Press.

Coons, W.H., Donald M. Taylor, and Marc-Adélard Tremblay, eds. (1977) *The Individual, Language and Society in Canada*. Ottawa: Canada Council.

Coulombe, Pierre A. (1995) *Language Rights in French Canada*. New York: Peter Lang.

Council of Europe. (1993) *European Charter for Regional or Minority Languages: Explanatory Report*. Strasbourg: Council of Europe.

Cranston, Maurice. (1967) 'Human Rights, Real and Supposed,' in *Political Theory and the Rights of Man*, D.D. Raphael, ed. Bloomington: Indiana University Press, 42–53.

– (1962) *What Are Human Rights?* New York: Basic Books.

Cummins, Jim, and Marcel Danesi. (1990) *Heritage Languages: The Development and Denial of Canada's Linguistic Resources*. Toronto: Garamond.

Daigle, Jean, ed. (1980) *Les Acadiens des Maritimes*. Moncton: Centre d'Études Acadiennes.

Danley, John R. (1991) 'Liberalism, Aborginal Rights and Cultural Minorities.' *Philosophy and Public Affairs* 20 (2) (Spring): 168–85.

Danto, Arthur C. (1984) 'Constructing an Epistemology of Human Rights: A Pseudo Problem?' in *Human Rights*, ed. Ellen Frankel Paul, Fred D. Miller, and Jeffrey Paul, eds. Oxford: Basil Blackwell, 24–34.

de Varennes, Fernand. (1994) 'Language and Freedom of Expression in International Law.' *Human Rights Quarterly* 16(1): 163–86.

244 References

de Vries, John. (1986) *Towards a Sociology of Languages in Canada.* Quebec: Centre internationale de recherche sur le bilinguisme.
– (1983) *Explorations in the Demography of Language and Ethnicity: The Case of Ukrainians in Canada.* Ottawa: Center for Research on Ethnic Minorities.
Desserud, Donald A. (1996) 'The Exercise of Community Rights in the Liberal-Federal State: Language Rights and New Brunswick's Bill 88.' *International Journal of Canadian Studies* 14 (Fall): 215–36.
Devine, Patrick. (1977) 'Language Rights in Canada and Quebec's Official Language Act.' *University of Toronto Faculty of Law Review* 35(1): 114–25.
Dinstein, Yoram. (1976) 'Collective Human Rights of Peoples and Minorities.' *International and Comparative Law Quarterly* 25: 102–20.
Dion, Stéphane, and Gaëtane Lamy. (1990) 'La Francisation de la langue de travail au Québec: contraintes et réalizations.' *Language Problems and Language Planning* 14 (2): 119–41.
Dorais, Louis-Jacques. (1978) 'La loi 101 et les Amerindiens.' *Canadian Review of Sociology and Anthropology* 15(2): 133–5.
Doucet, Michel. (1986) 'La Cour suprême et les droits linguistiques du justiciable: une démarche régressive.' *Égalité* 18: 123–40.
– (1986) 'L'affaire Tingley: un recul par rapport au bilinguisme judiciaire.' *Égalité* 17 (Winter): 107–26.
Dunton, Davidson. (1977) 'Recognized, Equitable Duality.' *Journal of Canadian Studies* 12(3): 106–8.
Dworkin, Ronald. (1977) *Taking Rights Seriously.* Cambridge: Harvard University Press.
Edwards, John. (1985) *Language, Society and Identity.* Oxford: Basil Blackwell.
Esman, Milton J. (1982) 'The Politics of Official Bilingualism in Canada.' *Political Science Quarterly* 97(2): 233–53.
European Court of Human Rights. (1968) 'Relating to Certain Aspects of the Laws on the Use of Languages in Education in Belgium (merits).' Series A. *Judgements and Decisions,* 6: 30–6.
Fanjoy, Emery M. (1990) 'Language and Politics in New Brunswick.' *Canadian Parliamentary Review* 13(2): 2–7.
Faribault, Marcel, and Robert M. Fowler. (1965) *Ten to One: The Confederation Wager.* Toronto: McClelland and Stewart.
Fédération des Francophones hors Québec. (1978) *The Heirs of Lord Durham.* Don Mills: Burns and MacEachern.
Feinberg, Joel. (1973) *Social Philosophy.* Englewood Cliffs: Prentice-Hall.
Fishman, Joshua A. (1991) *Reversing Language Shift: Theoretical and Empirical Foundations of assistance to Threatened Languages.* Clevedon: Multilingual Matters.

Flathman, Richard. (1976) *The Practice of Rights.* London: Cambridge University Press.

Fontaine, Yvon. (1989) 'La politique linguistique au Canada: L'impasse?' in *Canada: the State of the Federation 1989,* Ronald L. Watts and Douglas M. Brown, eds. Kingston: Institute of Intergovernmental Relations, Queen's University, 137–49.

– (1992) 'A Comment,' in *Survival: Official Language Rights in Canada,* John Richards, François Vaillancourt, and William G. Watson, eds. Toronto: C.D. Howe Institute, 57–62.

Fortier, D'Iberville. (1985) 'Bilingualism and Canadian Values.' Falconbridge Lecture delivered at Laurentian University in Sudbury, Ontario, Nov.

Foucher, Pierre. (1992) 'Language Rights Legislation and Case Law: Current Situation and Assessment of Twenty Years of Legislative and Judicial Activity,' in *Towards Reconciliation? The Language Issue in Canada in the 1990s,* ed. Daniel Bonin, ed. Kingston: Institute of Intergovernmental Relations, Queen's University, 111–24.

– (1990) 'Language Rights in the 1990s,' in *Human Rights in Canada: Into the 1990s and beyond,* Ryszard I. Cholewinski, ed. Ottawa: Human Rights Research and Education Centre, University of Ottawa, 117–38.

– (1987) 'The Right to Receive Public Services in Both Official Languages,' in *Language Rights in Canada,* Michel Bastarache, ed. Montréal: Les Éditions Yvon Blais, 176–254.

– (1985) *Constitutional Language Rights of Official Language Minorities in Canada.* Ottawa: Minister of Supply and Services (cat. No. S2-162/1985E).

Frideres, James. (1988) *Native Peoples in Canada: Contemporary Conflicts,* 3rd ed. Scarborough: Prentice-Hall.

Gagné, Raymond. (1972) 'French Canada: The Interrelationship between Culture, Language and Personality,' in *Canadian History Since Confederation,* Bruce Hodgins and Robert Page, eds. George Brown: Irwin Dorsey, 521–40.

Gagnon, Alain-G., and Mary Beth Montcalm. (1990) *Quebec: Beyond the Quiet Revolution.* Scarborough: Nelson.

Galipeau, Claude Jean. (1992) 'National Minorities, Rights and Signs: The Supreme Court and Language Legislation in Quebec,' in *Democracy with Justice: Essays in Honour of Khayyam Zev Paltiel,* Alain G. Gagnon and A. Brian Tanguay, eds. Ottawa: Carleton University Press, 66–84.

Gendron, Jean-Denis. (1974) *La Situation du Français comme langue d'usage au Québec.* Quebec: Centre international de recherche sur le bilinguisme (publication B-47).

Gill, Robert M. (1985) 'Language Policy in Saskatchewan, Alberta and British

Columbia and the Future of French in the West.' *American Review of Canadian Studies* 15(1): 16–37.

– (1980) 'Quebec and the Politics of Language: Implications for Canadian Unity,' in *Encounter With Canada: Essays in the Social Sciences.* Occasional Paper Series no. 7. Wayne G. Reilly, ed. Durham, NC: Center for International Studies, Duke University Press, 18–45.

– (1980) 'Bilingualism in New Brunswick and the Future of L'Acadie.' *American Review of Canadian Studies* 10(2): 56–74.

Goldfarb Consultants, Ltd. (1977) *The Searching Nation.* Toronto: Southam.

Goreham, Richard A. (1980) *Group Language Rights in Plurilingual States.* Master of Law thesis, Institut de droit comparé de l'Université McGill.

Green, Leslie. (1991) 'Freedom of Expression and Choice of Language.' *Law and Policy* 13(3): 215–29.

– (1987) 'Are Language Rights Fundamental?' *Osgoode Hall Law Journal* 25(3): 639–69.

Greene, Ian. (1989) *The Charter of Rights.* Toronto: Lorimer.

Haksar, Vinit. (1978) 'The Nature of Rights.' Archiv fur Rechts-und Sozialphilosophie 64(2): 183–203.

Handler, Richard. (1988) *Nationalism and the Politics of Culture in Quebec.* Madison: University of Wisconsin Press.

Hanen, Marsha. (1979) 'Taking Language Rights Seriously,' in *Confederation: Philosophers Look at Canadian Confederation*, Stanley G. French, ed. Montreal: Canadian Philosophical Association, 301–10.

Hargrove, Erwin. (1970) 'Nationality, Values and Change.' *Comparative Politics* 2 (1970): 473–99.

Harrison, Brian, and Louise Marmen. (1994) *Languages in Canada.* Scarborough: Statistics Canada / Prentice-Hall.

Henripin, Jacques. (1981) 'Two Solitudes in 2,001?' *Language and Society* 4: 15–19.

Hobbs, Clement, Ian Lee, and George Haines. (1991) 'Implementing Multicultural Policy: An Analysis of the Heritage Language Program, 1971–1981.' *Canadian Public Administration* 34(4): 664–75.

Hryniuk, Stella. (1992) *20 Years of Multiculturalism: Successes and Failures.* Winnipeg: St John's College Press, University of Manitoba.

Hutchings, David. (1981) 'Language Policy: Ontario, New Brunswick and Manitoba,' in *Provincial Policy Making: Comparative Essays*, Donald C. Rowat, ed. Ottawa: Dept. of Political Science, Carleton University Press, 283–303.

Isaacs, Harold. (1977) *Idols of the Tribe: Group Identity and Political Change.* New York: Harper and Row.

Jackson, John D. (1982) 'The Language Question in Quebec: On Collective and Individual Rights.' in *The English of Québec: From Majority to Minority Status*, Gary

Caldwell and Éric Waddell, eds. Quebec: Institut Québécois de Recherche Sur La Culture, 365–77.

Jacobs, Lesley A. (1991) 'Bridging the Gap Between Individual and Collective Rights with the Idea of Integrity.' *Canadian Journal of Law and Jurisprudence* 4(2): 375–86.

Jeffrey, Brooke. (1983) *Language Policy: The Challenge of the Eighties.* Current Issue Review 83-11E. Ottawa: Library of Parliament.

Jones, Richard. (1987) 'Politics and the Reinforcement of the French Language in the Province of Quebec: 1960–1986,' in *Quebec since 1945*, M.D. Behiels, ed. Toronto: Copp Clark Pitman, 223–40.

Joy, Richard J. (1992) *Canada's Official Languages: The Progress of Bilingualism.* Toronto: University of Toronto Press.

– (1985) 'Canada's Official-Language Populations, as shown by the 1981 census.' *American Review of Canadian Studies* 15(1): 90–6.

Kallen, Evelyn. (1989) 'The Meech Lake Accord: Entrenching a Pecking Order of Minority Rights,' in *The Meech Lake Primer*, Michael Behiels, ed. Ottawa: University of Ottawa Press, 349–69.

– (1982) *Ethnicity and Human Rights in Canada.* Toronto: Gage.

Kamenka, Eugene, and Alice Erh-Soon Tay, eds. (1978) *Human Rights.* London: Edward Arnold.

Kaplan, William, ed. (1993) *Belonging: The Meaning and Future of Canadian Citizenship.* Montreal: McGill-Queen's University Press.

Kerr, Robert. (1980) 'Language and the Law in Canada,' in *Decade of Adjustment: Legal Perspectives on Contemporary Social Issues*, Julio Menezes, ed. Toronto: Butterworths, 20–35.

– (1970) 'The Official Languages of New Brunswick Act.' *University of Toronto Law Journal* 20: 478–85.

Kleinig, John. (1978) 'Human Rights, Legal Rights and Social Change,' in *Human Rights*, Eugene Kamenka and Alice Erh-Soon Tay, eds. London: Edward Arnold, 36–47.

Kloss, Heinz. (1977) *The American Bilingual Tradition.* Rowley, Mass: Newbury House.

– (1971) 'Language Rights of Immigrant Groups.' *International Migration Review* 5(2): 250–68.

Knopff, Rainer. (1989) *Human Rights and Social Technology: The New War on Discrimination.* Ottawa: Carleton University Press.

– (1982) 'Liberal Democracy and the Challenge of Nationalism in Canadian Politics.' *Canadian Review of Studies in Nationalism* 9(1): 23–42.

– (1978–9) 'Democracy vs Liberal Democracy: the Nationalist Conundrum.' *Dalhousie Review* 58(4): 638–46.

- (1979) 'Language and Culture in the Canadian Debate: The Battle of the White Papers.' *Canadian Review of Studies in Nationalism* 6(1): 66–82.

Kralt, John. (1976) *Languages in Canada.* 1971 Census of Canada. Profile Studies: Demographic Bulletin 5.1-7. Ottawa: Information Canada.

Kukathas, Chandran. (1992) 'Are There Any Cultural Rights?' *Political Theory* 20(1): 105–39.

Kuruvilla, P.K. (1989) 'Quebec's Action Was Wrong.' *Policy Options* (May): 7–8.

Kymlicka, Will. (1995) *Multicultural Citizenship: A Liberal Theory of Minority Rights.* Oxford: Clarendon Press.

- (1992) 'The Rights of Minority Cultures: A Reply to Kukathas.' *Political Theory* 20(1): 140–46.

- (1989) *Liberalism, Community and Culture.* Oxford: Oxford University Press.

Lachapelle, Réjean, and Jacques Henripin. (1982) *The Demolinguistic Situation in Canada: Past Trends and Future Prospects,* trans. Deirdre A. Mark. Montreal: Institute for Research on Public Policy.

Lakoff, Sanford A. (1964) *Equality in Political Philosophy.* Cambridge: Harvard University Press.

Laksman, Narasinghe, and Conklin, William E. (1978) 'Constitutional Ideology, Language Rights and Political Disunity in Canada.' *UNB Law Journal* 28: 39–66.

Landry, Rodrigue, and Réal Allard. (1994) 'The Acadians of New Brunswick: Demolinguistic Realities and the Vitality of the French Language,' in *French–English Language Issues in Canada,* issue ed. Richard Y. Bourhis. *International Journal of the Sociology of Language* 105/106: 181–215.

Lapointe, Gérard, and Michel Amyot, eds. (1986) *L'État de la langue française au Québec: Bilan et Prospective,* 2 vols. Quebec: Conseil de la langue française.

Laponce, Jean A. (1987) *Languages and Their Territories,* trans. Anthony Martin-Sperry. Toronto: University of Toronto Press.

- (1985) 'Protecting the French Language in Canada: From Neurophysiology to Geography to Politics: The Regional Imperative.' *Journal of Commonwealth and Comparative Politics* 23(2): 157–70.

- (1982) 'Linguistic Minority Rights in Light of Neurophysical and Geographical Evidence: The Case for Partitions.' Paper presented at the Canadian Political Science Association Meetings, Ottawa.

Laporte, Pierre. (1979) 'Language Planning and the Status of French in Quebec,' in *Two Nations, Many Cultures: Ethnic Groups in Canada,* 2nd ed., Jean L. Elliott, ed. Scarborough: Prentice-Hall, 91–109.

Laqueur, Walter, and Barry Rubin, eds. (1979) *The Human Rights Reader.* New York: New American Library.

Laurin, Camille. (1978) 'Charte de la Langue Française / French Language

Charter.' *Canadian Review of Sociology and Anthropology* 15(2). Special Issue on Quebec, 115–27.

Leblanc, Phyllis. (1995) 'Francophone Minorities: The Fragmentation of the French-Canadian Identity,' in *Beyond Quebec: Taking Stock of Canada*, Kenneth McRoberts, ed. Montreal: McGill-Queen's University Press, 358–68.

Lederman, W.R. (1977) 'Securing Human Rights in a Renewed Confederation,' in *Must Canada Fail?*, Richard Simeon, ed. Montreal: McGill-Queen's University Press, 281–90.

Leduc, Lawrence, and Jon H. Pammett. (1995) 'Referendum Voting: Attitudes and Behaviour in the 1992 Constitutional Referendum.' *Canadian Journal of Political Science* 28 (1): 3–34.

Legault, Josée, and Julius H. Grey. (1993) 'La guerre, yes sir!' *Le Devoir* (26 Jan.), A-8.

Lévesque, René. (1968) *An Option for Quebec* (English transl.). Toronto: McClelland and Stewart.

Levine, Marc V. (1990) *The Reconquest of Montreal: Language Policy and Social Change in a Bilingual City*. Philadelphia: Temple University Press.

MacDonald, Margaret. (1970) 'Natural Rights.' in *Human Rights*, A.I. Melden, ed. Belmont: Wadsworth, 40–60.

MacDonald, Robert J. (1977) 'In Search of a Language Policy: Francophone Reactions to Bill 85 and 63,' in *Quebec's Language Policies: Background and Response*, John R. Mallea, ed. Quebec: Les Presses de L'Université Laval, 219–42.

Macías, Reynaldo F. (1979) 'Language Choice and Human Rights in the United States,' in *Language in Public Life*, James E. Alatis and G. Richard Tucker, eds. Washington, DC: Georgetown University Press, 86–101.

MacKay, Wayne. (1991) 'Minority Language Educational Rights Vindicated,' in *Language and the State: The Law and Politics of Identity*, David Schneiderman, ed. Cowansville: Les Éditions Yvon Blais, 123–40.

MacMillan, C. Michael. (1996) 'Rights in Conflict: Contemporary Disputes Over Language Policy in Quebec.' *International Journal of Canadian Studies* 14 (Fall): 193–214.

– (1990) 'Explaining Support for Language Rights: A Comment on "Political Culture and the Problem of Double Standards."' *Canadian Journal of Political Science* 23(3): 531–6.

– (1983) 'Language Rights, Human Rights and Bill 101.' *Queen's Quarterly* 90(2): 343–61.

– (1980) *Majorities and Minorities: Henri Bourassa and Language Rights in Canada*. Doctoral dissertation, University of Minnesota.

Magnet, Joseph. (1991) 'Comments,' in *Language and the State: The Law and Politics of Identity*, David Schneiderman, ed. Cowansville: Les Éditions Yvon Blais, 141–9.

– (1982) 'Minority-Language Educational Rights.' *Supreme Court Law Review* 4 (special issue): 195–216.

– (1982) 'The Charter's Official Languages Provisions: The Implications of Entrenched Bilingualism.' *Supreme Court Law Review* 4: 163–93.

– (1981) 'Language Rights: Myth and Reality.' *Revue Generale de Droit* 12: 261–70.

Mallea, John R., ed. (1977) *Quebec's Language Policies: Background and Response.* Quebec: Les Presses de L'Université Laval.

Mandel, Michael. (1994) *The Charter of Rights and the Legalization of Politics in Canada* (expanded ed.) Toronto: Thompson.

McDougal, Myres, H. Lasswell, and L. Chen. (1976) 'Freedom from Discrimination in Choice of Language and International Human Rights.' *Southern Illinois University Law Journal* 1: 151–74.

McKee, Brian. *Ethnic Maintenance in the Periphery: The Case of Acadia.* Monograph, Working paper no. 2. Ottawa: Center for Research on Ethnic Minorities, Carleton University, n.d.

McRae, Kenneth D. (1986) *Conflict and Compromise in Multilingual Societies*, vol. 2, Belgium. Waterloo: Wilfrid Laurier University Press.

– (1983) *Conflict and Compromise in Multilingual Societies* vol. 1, Switzerland. Waterloo: Wilfrid Laurier University Press.

– (1978) 'Bilingual Language Districts in Finland and Canada: Adventures in the Transplanting of an Institution.' *Canadian Public Policy* 4(3): 331–51.

– (1975) 'The Principle of Territoriality and the Principle of Personality in Multilingual States.' *International Journal of the Sociology of Language* 4: 33–54.

– (1970) 'The Constitutional Protection of Linguistic Rights in Bilingual and Multilingual States,' in *Human Rights, Federalism and Minorities*, Allan Gotlieb, ed. Toronto: Canadian Institute of International Affairs, 211–27.

McRoberts, Kenneth. (1997) *Misconceiving Canada: The Struggle for National Unity.* Toronto: Oxford University Press.

– (1992) 'Protecting the Rights of Linguistic Minorities,' in *Negotiating with a Sovereign Quebec*, Daniel Drache and Roberto Perrin, eds. Toronto: Lorimer, 173–88.

– (1991) *English Canada and Quebec: Avoiding the Issue.* North York: Robarts Centre for Canadian Studies, York University.

– (1988) 'Making Canada Bilingual: Illusions and Delusions of Federal Language Policy,' in *Federalism and political community: Essays in Honour of Donald Smiley*, David P. Shugarman and Reg Whitaker, eds. Peterborough: Broadview Press, 141–71.

– (1978) 'Comments.' *Canadian Public Policy* 4(3): 325–30.

McWhinney, Edward. (1979) *Quebec and the Constitution, 1960–78.* Toronto: University of Toronto Press.

– (1977) 'Self-Determination for Québec and the French Language Question.' *Jahrbuch des Öffentlichen Rechts der Gegenwart* 26: 513–38.

– (1975–6) 'The French Language and the Consitutional Status of French Canadians,' in *Case Studies on Human Rights and Fundamental Freedoms: A World Survey*, vol. 3, editor-in-chief, Willem A. Veenhoven. The Hague: Marinus Nijhoff, 483–98.

Means, Gordon. (1974) 'Human Rights and the Rights of Ethnic Groups–A Commentary.' *International Studies Notes* 1: 12–18.

Melden, A.I., ed. (1970) *Human Rights*. Belmont: Wadsworth.

Milner, Henry. (1984) 'The Constitution and the Reform of Quebec Education Structure.' *Socialist Studies* 2: 242–54.

Monahan, Patrick. (1987) *Politics and the Constitution: The Charter, Federalism and the Supreme Court of Canada*. Toronto: Carswell.

Monnier, D. (1983) *La question linguistique: l'état de l'opinion publique*. Quebec: Conseil de la langue française.

Morton, F.L. (1985) 'Group Rights versus Individual Rights in the Charter: The Special Cases of Natives and the Quebecois,' in *Minorities and the Canadian State*, Neil Nevitte and Allen Kornberg, eds. Oakville: Mosaic Press, 71–85.

Nadeau, Richard, and Christopher J. Fleury. (1995) 'Gains linguistiques anticipés et appui à la souveraineté du Québec.' *Canadian Journal of Political Science* 28(1): 35–50.

Norman, Richard. (1987) *Free and Equal: A Philosophical Examination of Political Values*. Oxford: Oxford University Press.

New Brunswick, Government of (1968) 'Statement on Language Equality and Opportunity.' Mimeograph. Tabled in the Legislative Assembly by the Hon. Louis J. Robichaud (4 Dec.).

– (1986) Advisory Committee on Official Languages of New Brunswick. *Report.* Fredericton: Government of New Brunswick.

– (1990) Board of Management. *Implementation of the Official Languages Policy: Report.* Mimeograph. (Feb.).

– (1988) *Official Languages Policy.* Mimeograph. (Aug.).

– (1988) *Implementation Guidelines for the Official Languages Policy.* Mimeograph. (Aug.).

– (1982) Cabinet Secretariat. Official Languages Branch. Task Force on Official Languages. (Poirier-Bastarache) *Towards Equality of the Official Languages in New Brunswick: Report.* Fredericton: Government of New Brunswick.

– (1992) Commission on Canadian Federalism. *Report.* Fredericton: Government of New Brunswick.

– Legislative Assembly. *Journal of Debates.* (various years).

– (1986) Official Languages Branch. *Linguistic Profile of Employees in the Public Service.* Mimeograph. (Sept.).

Nova Scotia. Attorney-General. (1992) 'Marshall Update / Justice Reform Review.' Mimeograph. (20 May).

O'Bryan, K.G., J.G. Reitz, and O.M. Kuplowska. (1976) *Non-official Languages: A Study in Canadian Multiculturalism.* Ottawa: Minister of Supply and Services.

Oliver, Michael. (1993) 'The Impact of the Royal Commission on Bilingualism and Biculturalism on Constitutional Thought and Practice in Canada.' *International Journal of Canadian Studies* 7–8 (Spring–Fall): 315–32.

Pal, Leslie A. (1993) *Interests of State: The Politics of Language, Multiculturalism, and Feminism in Canada.* Montreal: McGill-Queen's University Press.

Penton, James M. (1983) 'Collective versus Individual Rights: The Canadian Tradition and the Charter of Rights and Freedoms,' in *The U.S. Bill of Rights and the Canadian Charter of Rights and Freedoms,* William R. McKercher, ed. Toronto: Ontario Economic Council, 174–83.

Perlin, George C. (1992) 'Anglophone Attitudes towards Bilingualism: A Summary of Some Findings from Survey Research,' in *Towards Reconciliation? The Language Issue in Canada in the 1990s,* Daniel Bonin, ed. Kingston: Institute of Intergovernmental Relations, Queen's University, 99–110.

– (1980) 'Public Opinion Constraints Governing Responses by the Atlantic Provinces to Constitutional Change Sought by Quebec,' in *The Atlantic Provinces in Canada: Where Do We Go From Here?* J.R. Winter, ed. Wolfville, NS: Acadia University, 111–22.

Phillips, Sondra B. (1985) *Aboriginal Languages in Canada: A Research Report.* Ottawa: Department of Indian and Northern Affairs.

Phipponeau, Catherine, ed. (1991) *Vers un aménagement linguistique de l'Acadie du Nouveau-Brunswick.* Moncton: Centre de recherche en linguistique appliquée, Université de Moncton.

Plourde, Michel. (1988) *La Politique linguistique du Québec (1977–1987).* Quebec: Institut québécois de recherche sur la culture.

Pool, Jonathan. (1974) 'Mass Opinion on Language Policy: The Case of Canada.' in *Advances in Language Planning,* Joshua A. Fishman, ed. The Hague: Mouton, 481–92.

Priest, Gordon E. (1985) 'Aboriginal Languages in Canada.' *Language and Society* 15 (Winter): 13–19.

Quebec, Government of (1977) *Québec's Policy on the French Language.* Quebec: Éditeur Officiel du Québec.

– (1978) *A Cultural Development Policy for Quebec.* Quebec: Éditeur Officiel du Québec.

– (1972) Commission of Inquiry on the Position of the French Language and on Language Rights in Quebec (Gendron Commission). *Report.* Quebec: Éditeur Officiel du Québec.

– *Journal des Débats de L'Assemblée Nationale.* (various years).

- (1992) Task Force on English Education. *Report to the Minister of Education of Quebec.* (Chambers Report) Quebec: Éditeur Officiel du Québec.

Rae, Douglas. (1981) *Equalities.* Cambridge: Harvard University Press.

Raphael, D.D., ed. (1967) *Political Theory and the Rights of Man.* Bloomington, Ind.: Indiana University Press.

Ravault, René-Jean. (1983) *Perceptions de deux solitudes: Étude sur les relations entre les deux communautés de langues officielles du Nouveau-Brunswick.* Quebec: Centre internationale de recherche sur le bilinguisme.

Rawls, John. (1971) *A Theory of Justice.* Cambridge: Harvard University Press.

Raz, Joseph. (1986) *The Morality of Freedom.* London: Oxford.

Réaume, Denise. (1991) 'The Constitutional Protection of Language: Survival or Security?' in *Language and the State: The Law and Politics of Identity,* D. Schneiderman, ed. Cowansville: Les Éditions Yvon Blais, 37–58.

- (1988) 'Individuals, Groups and Rights to Public Goods.' *University of Toronto Law Journal* 38: 1–27.

- (1988) 'Language Rights, Remedies and the Rule of Law.' *Canadian Journal of Law and Jurisprudence* 1: 35–62.

Rees, John. (1971) *Equality.* London: Macmillan.

Reid, Scott. (1993) *Lament for a Notion: The Life and Death of Canada's Bilingual Dream.* Vancouver: Arsenal Pulp Press.

Richards, John. (1996) *Language Matters: Ensuring that the Sugar Not Dissolve in the Coffee.* C.D. Howe Institute *Commentary* no. 84. Toronto: C.D. Howe Institute (Oct.).

- (1992) 'The Case for an Explicit Division of Powers over Language,' in *Survival: Official Language Rights in Canada,* John Richards, François Vaillancourt and William G. Watson, eds. Toronto: C.D. Howe Institute, 9–56.

Richler, Mordecai. (1991) 'A Reporter at Large.' *New Yorker* (23 Sept.): 40–92.

- (1983) 'Language Problems.' *Atlantic* (June): 10–24.

Sancton, Andrew. (1985) *Governing the Island of Montreal: Language Differences and Metropolitan Politics.* Berkeley: University of California Press.

Sanders, Douglas. (1991) 'Collective Rights.' *Human Rights Quarterly* 13(3): 368–86.

Sapir, Edward. (1949) *Culture, Language and Personality,* ed. D. Mandelbaum. Berkeley: University of California Press.

Savoie, Donald J. (1991) *The Politics of Language.* Kingston: Institute of Intergovernmental Relations, Queen's University.

Savren, Clifford. (1978) 'Language Rights and Quebec Bill 101.' *Case Western Reserve Journal of International Law* 10 (Spring): 543–71.

Schneiderman, David, ed. (1989) *Language and the State: The Law and Politics of Identity.* Cowansville: Les Éditions Yvon Blais.

Scott, Frank R. (1971) 'Language Rights and the Language Policy in Canada.'
    Manitoba Law Journal 4(2): 243–57.
Scowen, Reed. (1991) *A Different Vision: The English in Quebec in the 1990s.* Don
    Mills: Maxwell Macmillan.
Shapiro, Daniel M., and Morton Stelcner. (1982) 'Language Legislation and Male–
    Female Earnings Differentials in Quebec.' *Canadian Public Policy* 8(1): 106–13.
Sheppard, Claude-Armand. (1971) *The Law of Languages in Canada.* Studies of the
    Royal Commission on Bilingualism and Biculturalism, no. 10. Ottawa: Informa-
    tion Canada.
Skelton, O.D. (1917) 'The Language Issue in Canada.' *Queen's Quarterly* 24(4):
    438–77.
Skutnabb-Kangas, Tove, and Robert Phillipson. (1989) *Wanted! Linguistic Human
    Rights.* ROLIG-papir 44. Roskilde, Denmark: Roskilde Universitetcenter,
    Lingvistgruppen.
Sniderman, Paul M., Joseph F. Fletcher, Peter H. Russell, and Philip E. Tetlock.
    (1996) *The Clash of Rights: Liberty, Equality, and Legitimacy in Pluralist Democracy.*
    New Haven: Yale University Press.
– (1990) 'Reply: Strategic Calculation and Political Values – The Dynamics of
    Language Rights.' *Canadian Journal of Political Science*, 23(3): 537–44.
– (1989) 'Political Culture and the Problem of Double Standards: Mass and Elite
    Attitudes toward Language Rights in the Canadian Charter of Rights and Free-
    doms.' *Canadian Journal of Political Science* 22(2): 259–84.
Snow, Gérard. (1981) *Les Droits Linguistiques des Acadiens du Nouveau-Brunswick.*
    Documentation du Conseil de La Langue Française 7. Quebec: Éditeur Officiel
    du Québec.
SORECOM. (1984) 'Sondage auprès des Québécois par SORECOM (mai 1984)
    sur la question nationale et constitutionnelle.' *L'Action Nationale* 74 (4): 425–42.
Stacey-Diabo, Carol Karakwas. (1990) 'Aboriginal Language Rights in the 1990s,'
    in *Human Rights in Canada: Into the 1990s and Beyond,* Ryszard I. Cholewinski, ed.
    Ottawa: Human Rights Research and Education Centre, University of Ottawa,
    139–64.
Stasiulis, Daiva. (1988) 'The Symbolic Mosaic Reaffirmed: Multiculturalism Pol-
    icy,' in *How Ottawa Spends, 1988–89,* K. Graham, ed. Ottawa: Carleton University
    Press, 81–111.
Steele, Catherine. (1990) *Can Bilingualism Work?* Fredericton: New Ireland Press.
Stein, Michael B. (1977) 'Bill 22 and the Non-Francophone Population in
    Québec: A Case Study of Minority Group Attitudes on Language Legislation,'
    in *Quebec's Language Policies: Background and Response,* John R. Mallea, ed.
    Quebec: Les Presses de L'Université Laval, 243–65.
Tawney, R.H. (1952) *Equality* (rev. ed.) London: Allen and Unwin.

Taylor, Charles. (1992) 'The Politics of Recognition,' in *Multiculturalism and 'The Politics of Recognition,'* Amy Gutmann, ed. Princeton: Princeton University Press, 25–73.

– (1991) 'Shared and Divergent Values,' in *Options for a New Canada*, R.L. Watts and D.M. Brown, eds. Toronto: University of Toronto Press, 53–76.

Taylor, Donald, and Ronald J. Sigal. (1985) 'Defining "Québérois": The Role of Ethnic Heritage, Language and Political Orientation,' in *Ethnicity and Ethnic Relations in Canada: A Book of Readings*, 2nd ed., Rita M. Bienvenue and Jay E. Goldstein, eds. Scarborough, Ont.: Butterworths, 125–37.

Taylor, Donald M., and Stephen C. Wright. (1989) 'Language Attitudes in a Multilingual Northern Community.' *Canadian Journal of Native Studies* 9(1): 85–119.

Thibaut, F. and Jean Claude Amboise. (1987) 'L étrange paradoxe d'une liberté devenue obligatoire: la loi 101 sur l'usage exclusif du français dans l'État du Québec.' *Revue du Droit Public* no. 1: 149–72.

Thorburn, H.G. (1971) 'French in the New Brunswick civil service: Ethnic participation and language use.' *Canadian Ethnic Studies* 3: 23–54.

Tremblay, A. (1982) 'Language Rights,' in *Canadian Charter of Rights and Freedoms: Commentary*, Walter S. Tarnopolsky and Gérald A. Beaudoin, eds. Toronto: Carswell, 443–66.

Trofimenkoff, Susan Mann. (1975) *Action Française: French Canadian Nationalism in the Twenties*. Toronto: University of Toronto Press.

Trudeau, Pierre E. (1968) *Federalism and the French Canadians*. Toronto: Macmillan.

Tschanz, Linda. (1980) *Native Languages and Government Policy: An Historical Examination*. Monograph. London, Ont: Centre for Research and Teaching of Canadian Native Languages, University of Western Ontario.

Ullman, Stephen H. (1986) 'The Political Attitudes of New Brunswick's Acadians and Anglophones: Old Wine in Old Bottles.' *American Review of Canadian Studies* 16(2): 161–80.

United Nations, Human Rights Committee. (1993) *Views of the Human Rights Committee under art. 5, par. 4, of the Optional Protocol to the International Covenant on Civil and Political Rights (47th session): concerning Communications Nos. 359/1989 and 386/1989*. (Views adopted 31 March). Mimeograph.

Vaillancourt, François. (1992) 'English and Angophones in Quebec: An Economic Perspective,' in *Survival: Official Language Rights in Canada*, John Richards, François Vaillancourt, and William G. Watson, eds. Toronto: C.D. Howe Institute, 63–94.

– (1992) 'A Comment,' in *Survival: Official Language Rights in Canada*, John Richards, François Vaillancourt, and William G. Watson, eds. Toronto: C.D. Howe Institute, 129–33.

- (1978) 'La Charte de la langue Française du Québec: un essai d'analyse.' *Canadian Public Policy* 4: 284–308.

Van der Meersch, W.J. Ganshof. (1972) 'Les droits linguistiques et culturels des minorités en Europe,' in *The Position of the French Language in Quebec*, vol. 2, *Language Rights*. Gendron Commission. Montreal: Éditeur Officiel du Québec, 136–207.

Van Dyke, Vernon. (1982) 'Collective Entities and Moral Rights: Problems in Liberal-Democratic Thought.' *Journal of Politics* 44(1): 21–40.

- (1980) 'The Cultural Rights of Peoples.' *Universal Human Rights* 2(2) (April–June): 1-21.

- (1977) 'The Individual, the State, and Ethnic Communities in Political Theory.' *World Politics* 29 (3): 343–69.

- (1976) 'Human Rights without Distinction as to Language.' *International Studies Quarterly* 20 (March): 3–38.

- (1974) 'Human Rights and the Rights of Groups.' *American Journal of Political Science* 18(4): 725–41.

- (1973) 'Human Rights without Discrimination.' *American Political Science Review* 67 (Dec.): 1267–74.

- (1973) 'Equality and Discrimination in Education.' *International Studies Quarterly* 17(4): 375–404.

- (1970) *Human Rights, the United States and World Community.* New York: Oxford University Press.

Veltman, Calvin. (1986) 'Assessing the Effects of Quebec's Language Legislation.' *Canadian Public Policy* 12(2): 314–19.

Waldron, Jeremy, ed. (1984) *Theories of Rights.* London: Oxford University Press.

Wardhaugh, Ronald. (1983) *Language and Nationhood: The Canadian Experience.* Vancouver: New Star Books.

Wasserstrom, Richard. (1970) 'Rights, Human Rights and Racial Discrimination,' in *Human Rights*, A.I. Melden, ed. Belmont: Wadsworth, 96–110.

Watson, William G. (1982) 'Separation and the English of Quebec,' in *Survival: Official Language Rights in Canada*, John Richards, François Vaillancourt, and William G. Watson, eds. Toronto: C.D. Howe Institute, 104–28.

- (1992) 'A Comment,' in *Survival: Official Language Rights in Canada*, John Richards, François Vaillancourt, and William G. Watson, eds. Toronto: C.D. Howe Institute, 95–103.

Weir, George. (1934) *The Separate School Question in Canada.* Toronto: Ryerson Press.

Wenner, Manfred W. (1976) 'The Politics of Equality among European Linguistic Minorities,' in *Comparative Human Rights*, Richard Claude, ed. Baltimore: Johns Hopkins University Press, 184–213.

Wienfeld, Morton. (1994) 'Ethnic Assimilation and the Retention of Ethnic Cultures,' in *Ethnicity and Culture in Canada*, J.W. Berry and J.A. Laponce, eds. Toronto: University of Toronto Press, 238–66.

Whitaker, Reg. (1989) 'The Overriding Right.' *Policy Options* (May): 3–6.

Wilson, V. Seymour. (1974) 'Language Policy,' in *Issues in Canadian Public Policy*, G. Bruce Doern and V. Seymour Wilson, eds. Toronto: Macmillan, 253–85.

Wiseman, Nelson. (1992) 'The Questionable Relevance of the Constitution in Advancing Minority Cultural Rights in Manitoba.' *Canadian Journal of Political Science* 25(4): 697–721.

Woerling, José. (1989) 'A Critique of the Distinct Society Clause's Critics,' in *The Meech Lake Primer*, Michael Behiels, ed. Ottawa: University of Ottawa Press, 171–207.

Index